JUVENILE GANGS
IN CONTEXT

Prentice-Hall Sociology Series
HERBERT BLUMER, Editor

PRENTICE-HALL INTERNATIONAL, INC., *London*
PRENTICE-HALL OF AUSTRALIA, PTY. LTD., *Sydney*
PRENTICE-HALL OF CANADA, LTD., *Toronto*
PRENTICE-HALL OF INDIA (PRIVATE) LTD., *New Delhi*
PRENTICE-HALL OF JAPAN, INC., *Tokyo*

JUVENILE GANGS
IN CONTEXT

Theory, Research, and Action

Edited by
MALCOLM W. KLEIN
Youth Studies Center
University of Southern California
Los Angeles, California

In collaboration with
BARBARA G. MYERHOFF
Youth Studies Center
University of Southern California
Los Angeles, California

Prentice-Hall, Inc.
Englewood Cliffs, New Jersey

Current printing (last digit):

10 9 8 7 6 5 4 3 2 1

Library of Congress Catalog No.: 67–10117

Preface

The history of the field of delinquency, both as an area of research and an area in social problem intervention, can be partially reconstructed by reference to a number of outstanding projects and publications. In the area of gang delinquency we might list Thrasher's historic study of gangs in Chicago during the 1920's; the work by Shaw and McKay, which led to the Chicago area project; the work of the New York City Youth Board; David Bordua's summary of delinquency theories published by the Children's Bureau; and finally, the program known as Mobilization for Youth in New York. Further outstanding achievements may come from Walter Miller's study concerning the Roxbury Project in Boston and the work of James F. Short, Jr, and his colleagues in conjunction with the metropolitan YMCA in Chicago. Two projects currently in progress, the Chicago Youth Development Project, and the Study of Delinquent Gangs in Los Angeles, may shed further light in another few years.

The point has been made by Bordua that *findings* from various studies and projects tend to be limited to the geographical areas from which they emanate· It is not yet clear whether the findings of Chicago and New York pertain to Los Angeles or Seattle, to say nothing of smaller urban areas. Indeed, the *theories* which have evolved from some of the pioneer work seem also to be particularly appropriate to the area in which the work was done, and may have limited application to other areas in the nation. In view of this fact, it becomes increasingly important to bring together practitioners, researchers, and scholars in the field of delinquency in an attempt to find meaningful similarities and differences in their approaches which might lead to a better understanding of the nature of delinquency, its causes, and possible intervention strategies.

The present volume is an attempt in this direction. With the advent of the 1963 national meetings in Los Angeles of the American Sociological Association and the Society for the Study of Social Problems, the staff of the Youth Studies Center of the University of Southern California saw a rare opportunity to bring together various persons in the field of delinquency to compare findings and report on their projects and proposals. Initial conversations indicated that there was considerable interest, and the editor of this volume was asked to look into the possibility of a conference, to consider who might be available, and to determine how such a conference might be funded.

Conversations with officials of the ASA and the SSSP indicated sufficient interest to proceed with the idea. A number of people were invited to present papers at the national meetings having to do with delinquency theory, research, and action, with particular emphasis on *gang* delinquency. The Youth Studies Center received a grant from the President's Committee on Juvenile Delinquency and Youth Crime to pay for travel and other expenses for a number of the participants. This grant, #63232, was awarded to Rudy Sanfilippo and Annette Gromfin of the training staff of the Youth Studies Center.

The program for the conference consisted of four sessions. Three sessions were sponsored by the Society for the Study of Social Problems, and one by the American Sociological Association. The first session, "The Gang Member, I," was chaired by the editor. The second session, "Related Varieties of Data as Counterpoint," was chaired by LaMar T. Empey. The third session, "The Gang Member, II," was chaired by James F. Short, Jr., and the final, "Symposium on Alternative Approaches to Gang Research and Action," was again chaired by the editor. In addition to the papers presented in the second and fourth sessions, there were also discussions by Lewis Yablonsky, Daniel Wilner, LaMar Empey, and Walter Miller.

Each paper was stenotyped at the time of presentation, and typescripts were submitted to the authors for revision and editing. In several cases, most notably the papers by Koval and Polk, Tennyson, Spergel, and Rivera and Short, the authors undertook extensive revisions. Otherwise the papers are reproduced in this volume very much as they were presented at the conference. We are grateful to the authors for their fast response to requests for editing and revision.

The first goal of the entire enterprise was to bring together the various authors so that they might not only present their papers but also meet, talk, and exchange views and information both formally and informally. Our impression of this aspect of the conference was heartening, since much time was spent between sessions in discussion of matters raised in the papers. The second goal, widespread communication of theory, data, and practice, is represented by the publication of this volume. The third goal was to provide the basic content upon which curricula could be built for use in future training programs involving personnel engaged in gang intervention activity. This is, so to speak, the payoff of the grant, and work has been started by Rudy Sanfilippo and Annette Gromfin to transform materials from the papers into curriculum materials.

It is obvious that this volume could not have been brought to fruition without the aid of a great number of people. We would like to express our gratitude in particular to Virginia Burns, staff member of the President's Committee on Juvenile Delinquency and Youth Crime; to Lloyd Ohlin, Chairman of the Criminology section of the American Sociological Association; to Janice Hopper, formerly the Administrative Officer of the American Sociological Association; and to Frank Hartung, Chairman of the Committee on Crime and Delinquency of the Society for the Study of Social Problems. Without the encouragement and help provided by each of these individuals, the conference and this volume would still be only a hope. Our thanks also go, of course, to the participants and their co-authors for allowing us to use their papers in this volume and to the formal discussants who took part in the conference. We also thank colleagues on the staff of the Youth Studies Center whose enthusiasm and contribution of time and thought will, we hope, be compensated for by the knowledge that this volume will be well used in the future. Finally, we acknowledge our gratitude to Mr. Franklin A. Steinko, who arranged for the stenotyping and saw that a minimum of delay took place between the conference and the return of the papers in final form. We recommend the use of stenotyping instead of other reproduction techniques such as tape recorders for all conferences such as this. The use of stenotyping greatly reduced anticipated sources of frustration.

There is a genuine danger that the continuing specialization in the various scientific disciplines is rapidly bringing about greater gaps between specialties, between approaches, and between individual projects. Whatever our ideals of collaboration and cooperation may be, it is obvious that communication among all disciplines is a necessary first and continuing step. The value of this book will be best indicated if it becomes quickly lost in a cascade of other communicative efforts.

MALCOLM W. KLEIN

Contents

INTRODUCTION

This volume contains fifteen papers pertinent to juvenile gang delinquency and the contexts within which gang behavior must be understood. To a considerable extent each paper is self-explanatory, but if it is to achieve maximum utility, the volume as a whole also requires a context for evaluation. The question is, what sort of evaluation is called for?

The papers vary widely in subject matter, in the authors' interests and perspectives, in scope, in direct utility to theoretical and practical concerns, and in concern with verifiable statements. Each paper speaks to a different set of questions, for gang research is not yet clearly focused and gang intervention practices are not yet scientifically founded and coordinated. The base suggested here for judging these papers, both individually and as a whole, is the seemingly simple question, what do we know now that we didn't know before?

I say *seemingly* simple question because of the implied knowledge context —what indeed did we know "before" about gangs and gang behavior? A full review of the present state of knowledge about gang matters is too grandiose an enterprise for this introduction, but the brief survey which follows, although necessarily somewhat sketchy, seems to be called for. The review will then serve as the background for the assignment of the papers to their appropriate place in our present information system.

Statement of Position

First, however, let me make explicit several of my personal biases which may tend to flavor the following paragraphs. It is my conviction that the urban gang delinquent is different *in kind* from the urban non-gang delin-

1

quent. One must come to grips with the fact that only a portion of the many adolescents dwelling in an "inner-city" area who participate in antisocial behaviors become identified as gang members. There are numerous factors that bring about this selection. Some are sociological and physical—residence, school attendance, location of parks and "hang-outs," age, race, and nationality, etc. Others are psychological—dependency needs, family rejection, impulse control, and so on. And some are related to peer group factors—gang structure and cohesiveness, peer group pressures, and identification.

While many of the findings concerning the etiology of individual delinquency patterns may be *necessary* for understanding the gang member, they are not *sufficient*. If this is a fair statement, then it follows that at least two major inquiries must occupy our attention. First, what are the personological factors that direct a boy toward gang membership—needs for identification and affiliation, for example—and second, what are the group factors that affect acceptance of a member and modify his behavior? Gang members have higher police contact rates than non-members, and become involved in more serious delinquencies than non-members. What group variables can help account for this and, at a practical level, how can these variables be manipulated by enforcement and welfare agents toward the end of decreasing the delinquency involvement of group members?

There is good reason to believe that a gang's status as a *gang* and an individual member's status deriving from his *gang* membership are causally related to delinquency involvement. Gordon *et al.* (8)* have shown that gang members in Chicago differ little from non-gang boys in their evaluation and legitimation of middle class values, but that they *do rank deviant behavior values higher*. Activities which enhance *gang* status also enhance the cohesiveness of the group, and the more cohesive gang tends to be the more delinquent one. Note the emphasis here on gang as such: it is only the identification with and the status enhancement derived from the gang as a qualitatively different kind of group that concerns us for the moment.

In other words, gang research must be concerned with gang identification, status, and cohesiveness, among other variables. Gang intervention programs must be concerned with methods of *decreasing* identification, status, and cohesiveness. These are variables which can be affected directly, with some generalization of effect over many members.

Such a statement is less true of family variables or individual psychological characteristics. Neighborhood variables—economic and employment conditions, adult criminality, enforcement procedures, social and recreational facilities—can also be manipulated, but seldom by the individual worker.

---

* Numbers in parentheses refer to items in the bibliography at the end of this Introduction.

These variables call for coordinated inter-agency programs of the sort being carried out under grants from the President's Committee on Juvenile Delinquency and Youth Crime or from the Office of Economic Opportunity (the "War on Poverty"). But again, it would be helpful to look at these variables, as have Cloward and Ohlin (4), Shaw and McKay (12), and Spergel (17), in terms of their contribution to gang development and to variations in gang typologies. The existence of gangs is a function of neighborhood structure, existing gang traditions, alternative peer group opportunities, and group support factors (such as police harassment and the existence of rival gangs or even detached workers who may inadvertently perpetuate gang structure and cohesion). Gang existence is also a function of more-or-less chance factors—specific incidents, mobility patterns, school affiliations, and the like. The point being stressed here is that one medium through which these factors exert their influence on individuals is the gang itself. It is this mediating influence that has until very recently been neglected by careful empirical research.

Another "bias" of the writer is implicit in some of the foregoing, but related specifically to gang intervention procedures. It can be summed up by the question, "Do standard agent-client relationships, as taught in schools of social work or expounded in various texts, suffice for gang intervention?" I would answer this question in the negative. Casework procedures are clearly inappropriate, if only on an efficiency basis. Community organization practices are for the most part too far removed to have direct and fairly immediate effect on gang structures.

Group work practices are based primarily on attempts to employ the dynamics of group process to the advantage of the individual member. But gangs are uncohesive groups at best, with constant turnover in membership and leadership and little of the stability commensurate with good group work practice. In addition, if we are correct in stating that increasing cohesiveness leads to increasing delinquent behavior, it should be the function of the gang worker to *break up* the sources of gang cohesion, to introduce leadership *ambiguity* rather than structure, to *devaluate* group status and identification rather than to increase these for the sake of fulfilling individual needs. These suggested techniques run contrary to group work practice as ordinarily conceived.

These comments are peculiarly appropriate to the gang group because the group product of direct concern—assaults, thefts, vandalism, etc.— is undesirable, unlike most group products with which we deal. The diminution of this product should be the gang worker's first concern, the welfare of the members his second. This fact represents a challenge to the value system of many social workers and is the source of much frustration and confusion for non-enforcement agencies attempting to deal with gang problems. It is not my intention here to denigrate individual welfare goals, but rather to put them in their proper context in this particular area of practice. The fulfillment of the welfare and social needs of gang members should be seen first as means, secondarily as ends.

Another source of error in gang practice has to do with timing. Most practitioners will say in effect, "You can't move a client until he is ready to be moved." This becomes a major philosophical tenet in social intervention, and leads to slow progress while waiting for the "breakthrough" (usually conceived of in terms of client insight). But to be frank, this approach is often a rationalization employed to camouflage the fact that *we don't know how to move clients more rapidly in desired directions.* If they don't respond readily we say they are not ready. But as often as not it is we, the practitioners, who are not ready because we don't know what to do, or are threatened by too rapid improvement, or are fearful of client retrogression. It is gratifying to see just how quickly gang members *will* respond to the worker who knows where he is going and who has developed adequate resources in the community to pave the way. Needless to say, these resources must be activated. Doors do not open by themselves.

The Present State of Knowledge

These considerations, then, bring us back to our original question—how much do we know about gangs and their contexts? For purposes of organization it may be fruitful to think of delinquent behaviors and gang phenomena as part of an urban adolescent's "opportunity repertoire." That is, gang membership and attendant behavior patterns represent options to the individual boy—continuing options, regardless of whether or not he joins a gang. Given this view, the following minimal concerns confront the investigator:

1. There may exist an *internal complex of needs and motives*—a drive state, if you will—for which gang membership can provide some level of satisfaction. A number of investigators have dealt with this level of analysis. Eriksen (21) has concentrated on the natural *Sturm und Drang* of adolescence, the state of limbo between childhood and adult status that results in an often agonizing search for self-identity. Bloch (1) similarly has written of "an inversion of dependent relationships." Miller (11) and Karacke and Toby (9) have stressed values dominant in the adolescents' cultural milieu, and Spergel (17) speaks more specifically of dominant neighborhood behavior patterns. In each case, "natural" motives are involved—natural in the sense that they are normal adjuncts of emotional development or the internalization of dominant cultural norms and values as part and parcel of the socialization process.

2. These needs and motives are constantly exposed to *reinforcement*

and inhibition. In a sense, Sutherland's theory of Differential Association (7) is primarily concerned with the learning and reinforcement of the drive state exhibited in criminal or delinquent behavior. Cohen and Hodges (6) have empirically demonstrated the situation of lower class behavior patterns and life style which are self-reinforcing (and to a considerable extent self-defeating). From their account we can derive a picture of a catatonic social class—withdrawn from participation outside itself, potentially explosive at times of release, yet perfectly well aware of the "outside" world (in this case, middle class value systems). This becomes a system in which behavior patterns reinforce themselves and underlying drive states become satisfied through internal consistency.

3. There are a number of *opportunities for need satisfaction.* These have been investigated, catalogued, and discussed for decades—most recently by Clausen and Williams (3), Cloward and Ohlin (4), Cohen (5) and Spergel (16). Each of these writers views the lower class adolescent as being "in the market for a 'solution,'" to borrow Bordua's phrase (2). The most pertinent questions are why the gang solution is chosen at all, and why by some and not by others. Only the first question has been tackled theoretically with any success.

4. Each potential gang member will have *perceptions of the opportunities* in his repertoire. Miller (10) has strongly suggested that the repertoire is limited by class position, as have Cohen and Hodges (6), but he has added the view that the limitation is perceived as natural, not frustrating. In opposition, the findings of Short *et al.* (13) indicate clearly that the lower class youngster, and the gang member in particular, perceives fewer opportunities in both ends and the means to achieve those ends. To what extent the gang represents a "substitute" opportunity, and is seen as such, remains an empirical question without answer. One might even ask if a boy in some inner-city neighborhoods can realistically perceive the possibility of *not* joining the local gang.

5. One of the vexing questions implicit in the approach taken by Cloward and Ohlin has to do with the *connection between need and opportunity.* Specifically, does the delinquent *recognize* such a connection, and what does he make of it? Strodtbeck and Short (18) have made much of the "aleatory" factor, the lack of perceived connection between act and consequence. As an example, discussions of lower class Negro illegitimate births have specifically raised the question of whether a girl enters into promiscuous intercourse with the *intent* of conceiving a child because the existence of the child provides a means of acceptance back into the home. Opportunity theory is so new that this area of study has not as yet been undertaken, yet in many ways it is crucial. It relates directly to the age old problem of rationality in human behavior, the question of the adequacy of explaining behavior through the correlation of stimulus and response without recourse

to intervening perceptual variables. (See also Strodtbeck, Short, and Kolegar [19].)

6. A boy's entry into a gang can be expected to have an *effect on his perceptions, his values and expectations, his behavior.* Evaluations of such changes in attitudes are being carried out currently in the Chicago Youth Development Program. Delinquent behavior has long been assumed to increase as a function of gang membership; police response to gangs is commonly based on this very assumption. Miller (11), Short, Strodtbeck, and Cartwright (14), Short, Tennyson, and Howard (15), and Sykes and Matza (20) have all been concerned with the effect of membership in the delinquent subculture on the views and behaviors of the boys involved. In fact, if there is one area of gang research that has been most "popular" of late, it is research into the results of membership in a delinquent subculture. Still, there is much to be learned here.

7. In the same vein, it may be useful to consider *the internal reinforcers of gang behavior.* Here again, the gang "culture" is of paramount importance, as suggested by Cloward and Ohlin (4), Cohen (5), Short *et al.* (14), and the various writings on the Theory of Differential Association. It is within the gang more than anywhere else that a youngster may find forms of acceptance for delinquent behavior—rewards instead of negative sanctions. And as the gang strives for internal cohesion, the negative sanctions of the "outside world" become interpreted as threats to cohesion, thus providing secondary reinforcement for the values central to the legitimization of gang behavior.

8. Finally, as just suggested, the *community reacts* to gang behavior through its agencies and spokesmen. The McEachern and Robin articles in this volume provide examples of community response through the medium of police action. The development of detached worker programs and "area projects" provides another example of response from the community. The question is not one of documenting the existence of such responses, but rather one of the rationality and ameliorative effects of the responses. Often community reaction serves only to magnify the problem, increase its seriousness, and reinforce the presenting symptoms. Until we understand the gang member's response to the community reaction, we are in no position to plan programs for gang dissolution.

Briefly reviewing the above paradigm, we find these eight areas of concern:

1. Internal predispositions—the drive state
2. Reinforcers of the drive state
3. Opportunities for need satisfaction, including gang membership
4. Perceptions of these opportunities
5. Recognition of need-opportunity relationships

6. Effects of membership on the member
7. Reinforcers internal to the peer group
8. Reinforcers and inhibitors from outside—the response of the community

Historically, the bulk of empirical study has probably fallen in the first area, the one with greatest appeal for psychologists. Unfortunately the output here has not equaled the input of time, energy, and funds.

Recent theoretical emphases have been concentrated in the third area—opportunity systems—while the latest empirical studies, especially the work of Short and his colleagues, are concerned more with areas 4 and 7. The editor's own present work is concentrated in areas 6 and 7, emphasizing peer group variables and their relationship to member behavior.

Yet, by and large, the surface of the problem is only now being scratched. There is still much to be done. The present volume is an attempt to continue the investigative process and, as is indicated in the introductory statement preceding each paper, does speak to a number of the issues raised in the preceding pages.

Implications in This Volume

Several themes or areas of concern are common to a number of the papers. Some of these represent contributions to the field through their very explication, and others as they serve to highlight contemporary views. For instance, one recurrent theme has to do with distinguishing among various "types" of delinquents. There is no unanimity among our authors. Some have discovered or constructed useful typologies, others have failed in similar efforts, and still others—most notably Miller—maintain that concentration on the actor rather than the act is conceptually inappropriate and empirically inefficient. Calling attention to the issue—even hammering at it—is clearly a necessary prerequisite to its conceptual resolution. For the careful reader, our authors have definitely, if inadvertently, brought focus to the issue.

Also common to many of the papers is the currently prevailing notion that one of the most immediately salient variables in delinquency is cognitive patterning. Over and over, the authors investigate, speculate upon, and offer explanations for distinctive patterns of values, thought, perceptions, and aspirations of those ensnared in the delinquent subculture. Here, in the delinquent's own perspective, psychologists and sociologists alike have found common ground both for distinguishing delinquent from nondelinquent and for seeking causative explanations of deviant behavior that avoid psychological *and* sociological determinism. In many ways this "compromise" has always featured the hazy no-man's-land between the disciplines. In its formative years, social psychology was most widely defined as the study of attitudes, the individual locus of social and group forces. Only time will reveal the fruitfulness of this concentration in the cognitive area, but the very fact of such concentration bodes well for our future state of knowledge.

A third common concern is more clearly stamped with the sociologists' hallmark. It is also an area in which our authors have uniformly presented significant findings. Status and position variables—race, sex, social class— are perhaps our best current predictors of delinquency and delinquent patterns. Add family status and neighborhood setting and then analyze for *interactions* among the variables—this seems to be the common recipe, especially for the prediction of gang patterns. And for those who would concentrate on intrapsychic variables, the lesson is clear. First, control for sex, race, or minority status, and several levels of socio-economic status. These variables clearly account for more variance than any other group of factors yet isolated. Again, such a finding is hardly "news," but the relationships between these positional variables emerge far more distinctly in some of the present papers than has hitherto commonly been the case.

A fourth contribution is made by several of our authors who report data on delinquent offenses of gang members. The predominance of theft acts, the progression of delinquent offenses, and the enumeration of various offense frequencies provide highly useful guidelines for future comparative research. They also serve as antidotes to some common misconceptions of gang behavior, including that darling of the publicist, the prevalence of violence.

A similar contribution is implicit in several of the papers with respect to deprivation. We have long known that pockets of poverty, unemployment, low schooling and skill are the breeding ground of much delinquent behavior. The general assumption has been that *absolute* deprivation is the problem, but it is now becoming obvious that *relative* deprivation may be of equal importance. Thus the problem is not merely one of raising standards generally, but of decreasing the perceived gaps between levels of society. It may be the reaction to the gap rather than to one's own level which provides the motive power behind much of our urban delinquency.

Finally, for the practitioner, two major contributions can be derived from the present papers. First, there is a veritable wealth of data upon which to build action programs. Second, innovative programs *can* be introduced into delinquent-prone areas. The data presented and the programs described in this volume represent a small sample of what exists and what can be achieved. The enormity and complexity of the problem is no longer a sufficient excuse for slow or unimaginative action. What is required is attention to the available data, organization of available resources, and above all the drive and ambition to do the job.

This challenge to the change agent runs through these papers, but it does not lie alone. The theoretician is challenged also, although not in a consistent fashion. Looking only at the *data* reported in the papers, one can find evidence to refute Sykes and Matza, Cohen, Miller, Cloward and Ohlin, Yablonsky, and psychological theorists generally. Some are refuted on minor issues only. On balance, the theoretical position of Albert Cohen fares worst.

Support for perceptual approaches and for the class theorists is common to a number of the papers, but this is partially explicable in terms of the theoretical positions of the investigators themselves. Other than this, there is little to be said for the theoretical challenges contained in the volume, for by and large the papers are not designed as positive theoretical contributions (a notable exception is the paper by the Schwendingers). Rather, they tend to employ isolated theoretical propositions as taking-off points for data collection. Perhaps this fact itself is important, as it may mirror the current trend of delinquency research.

Inevitably, a collection of new papers raises numerous new questions. Each reader will tend to concentrate his attention on those questions which lie closest to his own view of delinquency and gang phenomena. However, it is the editor's advantage that he gets in the first shot, and his opportunity to shape the reader's thought is well-nigh irresistible. Accordingly, the following questions are posed for researcher and practitioner alike, but most particularly for the student newly entered into the field of gang delinquency. They are offered as questions only—as stimuli to further thought and study.

1. It is now well documented that the delinquent's view of the world about him differs in some respects from that of the non-delinquent. It is generally assumed that this view is causally related to his delinquent behavior. What are the sources and reinforcements of this difference in perception?

2. Several of the papers in this volume indicate that the delinquent's aspirations concerning his future roles and achievements are quite unrealistic—more so than those of his non-delinquent peers. Why should this be the case, and how might this relate to deviant behavior?

3. Much has been made of the preponderance of delinquency—especially gang involvement—in the lower class. Underlying this presumed fact, and many others as well, is the notion that deprivation—financial, educational, familial, psychological—somehow lies at the root of the problem. Accepting for the moment that this is a valid notion, is it the *absolute* state of deprivation which is crucial, or the *relativity* of deprivation—that is, deprivation as compared with one's peers, neighborhood, or image of "what others have"?

4. There are some specific techniques for the reduction of inter-gang fighting, including the usual bread-and-butter skills of detached workers

assigned to street gangs. But are there analogous *specific* techniques for the reduction of other categories of delinquent behavior—for theft, drug use, illegitimate sex relations, or auto theft?

5. Gangs are groups, although admittedly unusual examples thereof. As such, gangs have structures and traditions. What intervention procedures now within our repertoire can explicitly manipulate structural and tradition variables to the end of reducing gang activity?

Organization

The organization of the papers in this volume is determined primarily by the content of the questions to which they are addressed, rather than by their approaches to these questions. Part 1 includes papers describing patterns of delinquent behavior exhibited by gang members. Part 2 deals more directly with the relationships between this behavior and the values and perceptions associated with them. In Part 3 the authors are concerned with the societal or community context and response. These papers fall more directly into the area of traditional criminology, rather than social psychology, and remind us that delinquent behavior is a conceptual and definitional problem as well as a behavioral response. Finally, Part 4 includes descriptions of four attempts to deal with delinquent behavior as a social problem. These are action programs based on both implicit and explicit assumptions concerning causation, reinforcement, and the location of the most practical avenues for intervention. Part 4 provides an interesting challenge for the student—what are these assumptions, and how directly related to them are the action steps described?

This might be the appropriate spot to mention that a second volume, a companion to the present collection, is being prepared by Gilbert Geis under a training grant from the President's Committee on Juvenile Delinquency and Youth Crime. The Geis volume is a commentary on the fifteen papers presented here and an explicit attempt to draw out of them practical implications for future gang intervention programs. Included as part of that enterprise will be a comprehensive, up-to-date bibliography of gang-related literature. It is precisely this kind of integrated attack, with an interplay between theory, research, and action, that is so desperately needed at our present state of knowledge.

References

1. Bloch, Herbert A., "The Juvenile Gang: A Cultural Reflex," *The Annals of the American Academy of Political and Social Science,* CCCXLVII (May 1963), 20–29.

2. Bordua, David J., "Some Comments on Theories of Group Delinquency," *Sociological Inquiry,* XXXII: 2 (Spring 1962), 245–60.

3. Clausen, John A., and Williams, Judith R., "Sociological Correlates of Child Behavior" *62nd Yearbook of the National Society for the Study of Education,* Part I (1963), pp. 83–85.

4. Cloward, Richard A., and Ohlin, Lloyd E., *Delinquency and Opportunity.* New York: Free Press of Glencoe, Inc., 1961.

5. Cohen, Albert K., *Delinquent Boys: The Culture of the Gang.* New York: Free Press of Glencoe, Inc., 1955.

6. ———, and Hodges, Harold M., "Lower-Blue-Collar-Class Characteristics," *Social Problems,* X: 4 (Spring 1963), 303–34.

7. Cressey, Donald R., "Differential Association: An Introduction," *Social Problems,* VIII: 1 (Summer 1960), 2–5; and "The Development of a Theory: Differential Association" in Marvin E. Wolfgang, Leonard Savitz, and Norman Johnston, eds., *The Sociology of Crime and Delinquency.* New York: John Wiley & Sons, Inc., 1962.

8. Gordon, Robert A., Short, Jr., James F., Cartwright, Desmond S., and Strodtbeck, Fred L., "Values and Gang Delinquency: A Study of Street Corner Groups," *American Journal of Sociology,* LXIX: 2 (September 1963), 109–28.

9. Karacke, Larry, and Toby, Jackson, "The Uncommitted Adolescent: Candidate for Gang Socialization," *Sociological Inquiry,* XXXII: 2 (Spring 1962), 203–15.

10. Miller, Walter B., "Implications of Urban Lower-Class Culture for Social Work," *Social Service Review,* XXXIII: 3 (September 1959), 219–36.

11. ———, "Lower-Class Culture as a Generating Milieu of Gang Delinquency," *Journal of Social Issues,* XIV: 3 (Fall 1958), 5–19.

12. Shaw, Clifford R., and McKay, Henry D., *Juvenile Delinquency and Urban Areas.* Chicago: University of Chicago Press, 1942.

13. Short, Jr., James F., Rivera, Ramon, and Tennyson, Ray A., "Perceptions of Opportunities, Gang Membership, and Delinquency," paper read at annual meeting of the Pacific Sociological Association, Portland, Oregon, 1963 (mimeo).

14. ———, Strodtbeck, Fred L., and Cartwright, Desmond S., "A Strategy for Utilizing Research Dilemmas: A Case from the Study of Parenthood in a Street Corner Gang," *Sociological Inquiry,* XXXII: 2 (Spring 1962), 185–202.

15. ———, Tennyson, Ray A., and Howard, Kenneth I., "Behavior Dimensions of Gang Delinquency," *American Sociological Review,* XXVIII (June 1963), 411–28.

16. Spergel, Irving, "Male Young Adult Criminality, Deviant Values, and Differential Opportunities in Two Lower-Class Negro Neighborhoods," *Social Problems,* X: 3 (Winter 1963), 237–50.

17. ———, *Racketville, Slumtown, Haulburg.* Chicago: University of Chicago Press, 1964.

18. Strodtbeck, Fred L., and Short, Jr., James F., "Aleatory Risks vs. Short-run Hedonism in Explanation of Gang Action," *Social Problems,* XII: 2 (Fall 1964), 127–40.

19. ———, Short, Jr., James F., and Kolegar, Ellen, "The Analysis of Self-descriptions by Members of Delinquent Gangs," *Sociological Quarterly,* III (October 1962), 331–56.

20. Sykes, Gresham M., and Matza, David, "Techniques of Neutralization: A Theory of Delinquency," *American Sociological Review,* XXII: 6 (December 1957), 664–70.

21. Witmer, Helen L., and Kotinsky, Ruth, *New Perspectives for Research on Juvenile Delinquency,* U.S. Children's Bureau Publication No. 356. Washington, D.C., 1956.

Part One

PATTERNS OF GANG BEHAVIOR:
DELINQUENCY

Gang Member Delinquency in Philadelphia[1]

GERALD D. ROBIN

With all the research carried out to date on delinquent gangs, there is nevertheless a paucity of purely descriptive material on gang-related offenses. In this paper, Robin performs a valuable service by analyzing the officially recorded offenses of Negro gang members in Philadelphia. These data represent a useful baseline for comparative studies elsewhere. In addition, the author's data on individual offense patterns, progression of delinquency involvement, and time lapse between offenses have direct utility to those concerned with the development of reliable and sensitive measures of changes in offense patterns over time.

GERALD D. ROBIN, Study Director in the Social Science Department of National Analysts.

[1] A more extensive report of this study, entitled "Gang Member Delinquency: Its Extent, Sequence and Typology," appeared in the March, 1964 issue of *The Journal of Criminal Law, Criminology and Police Science*.

The Juvenile Aid Division of the Philadelphia Police Department, like several other departments in large urban areas, has a Gang Control Unit which maintains for administrative and control purposes a file of identified gangs and gang members in the city. Each member of a gang has a police delinquency record or is considered a potential source of concern to the authorities. In dealing with offenders, the Juvenile Aid Division employs two types of case dispositions: arrest and remedial. A "remedial" disposition does not result in bringing the youth to court; it is an informal adjustment of the case at the district level in which the boy is immediately released into the community by the police.

This paper reports on data for all known gang members as of January 7, 1962. On this date there were in Philadelphia twenty-seven known delinquent Negro male gangs, with a total membership of 918 persons. Obviously it was possible to include within the analysis only those youths for whom police records could be located—in this instance 711 of the 918 Negro gang members.

The ages of the gang members ranged from eleven to twenty-five years, with a mean of 17.6 years. About 53 per cent of all delinquents were adults—that is, past eighteen years of age. These figures emphasize that data were not collected on a juvenile universe, but rather on a universe of Negroes who had belonged to gangs as juveniles; this was done in order to study their law-violating behavior during that period. An additional one-fifth of the 918 Negroes were between seventeen and eighteen years old at the time of selection, so that approximately three-fourths of them had passed almost or completely through their juvenile status.

With respect to extent of delinquency, it was found that the mean number of delinquency charges against gang members was 6.2. The number of accusations ranged from one to twenty-five, with 20 per cent of the boys charged with ten or more offenses. The number of charges varied with age; the average number of delinquencies committed by twelve year olds was 3.0, compared to 6.7 for those who had completed their juvenile cycle. The average number of delinquencies for juveniles under fifteen years of age was 3.8, compared to 6.4 for those fifteen or older. The mean frequency of arrests followed a pattern similar to that of all charges: those under fifteen years of age were arrested 1.9 times, compared to 3.7 arrests for those fifteen years old or older.

It has often been suggested that the age at which a juvenile first comes into contact with a law enforcement agency has important implications for continued delinquency. To test this, a negative relationship between onset of delinquency and number of police contacts was hypothesized and received strong confirmation, as indicated in Table 1. The data in this table show a consistent decrease in the average number of delinquencies with an increased age for the onset of delinquency. While the average number of charges for all ages was 6.2, it was 9.1 for those who committed their first delinquency at six and seven years of age, compared to only 1.3 police contacts for those whose onset of delinquency was at seventeen years of age.

Table 1

AVERAGE NUMBER OF DELINQUENCIES, BY ONSET OF DELINQUENCY

	Age at Onset of Delinquency									
	6–7	8–9	10	11	12	13	14	15	16	17
No. of Delinq.	73	277	427	516	880	906	633	469	204	35
No. of Cases	8	32	46	66	120	139	113	105	57	23
$\bar{X}$	9.1	8.7	9.3	7.8	7.3	6.5	5.6	4.5	3.6	1.3

The assertion that there is a progressive involvement in delinquency in terms of severity of offense is familiar to students of crime. Unfortunately, such statements rarely specify the exact nature of this progression or the method for its determination. In an effort to measure the movement of delinquency of the gang members, each delinquent charge was ranked in terms of its seriousness: high ranks were assigned to the less serious charges, lower ranks to the more serious ones.[2] In this manner twenty-four types of delinquency charges and their corresponding ranks were established. The first delinquency of each offender was taken as the base line, and the size and direction of movement in subsequent delinquencies were measured. For example, if a gang member's first police contact was for larceny (rank six) and his second police contact was for robbery (rank three), then his first movement of delinquency was a progression of three. If this juvenile's third charge was that of assault and battery (rank seven), his second movement of delinquency was a retrogression of −4. After measuring all the movements of delinquency for an offender in this manner, the numerical values were added to yield a single value which was a general expression of whether a gang member progressed (a plus value), retrogressed (a minus value), or demonstrated no over-all movement of delinquency (a zero). The size of the value reflected the degree of progression or retrogression. This procedure was carried out for a subsample of gang members having at least two police contacts and resulted in the tabulation of 2,939 movements of delinquency.

The inadequacies in this approach at measuring movement of delinquency are recognized. With all its crudity, however, it is at least one possible way to proceed in an uncharted area. With these remarks by way of qualifica-

---

2 In general, the ranking of charges followed the order established in the *Uniform Crime Reports*. Juvenile offenses which cannot be committed by adults (e.g., truancy, malicious mischief, runaway) were considered the least serious charges and therefore given the highest ranks.

tion, attention is directed to Table 2. There we see that about 13 per cent of the gang members showed no over-all movement of delinquency, compared with 33 per cent of the offenders who retrogressed and 54 per cent who progressed in general severity of delinquent conduct. Thus, we have been able to provide some objective support for the hypothesis tested.

Table 2

DISTRIBUTION OF MOVEMENT OF DELINQUENCY

Direction of Movement	*Degree of Movement*	*Index of Movement*	*No. of Cases*	*% of Cases*
	Marked	−21 to − 15	22	4.5
Retrogression	Moderate	−14 to − 8	67	13.7
	Mild	− 7 to − 1	74	15.1
	None	0	64	13.7
	Mild	1 to 7	101	20.7
Progression	Moderate	8 to 14	96	19.6
	Marked	15 to 22	65	13.3

An important dimension of delinquency which has not received sufficient attention is its sequential characteristics—that is, the time lapse between each pair of subsequent police contacts. How much time will elapse before a juvenile again comes to police attention after committing his first offense? And having committed a second delinquency, when will a third follow, and so on? In this regard, it was hypothesized that an increase in the number of police contacts would be accompanied by a decrease in the time period between each subsequent pair of delinquencies; that is, the number of months between the second and third delinquencies would be smaller than between the first and second, and so on.

As Table 3 shows, this hypothesis was confirmed by a continuous reduction in the average number of months between consecutive delinquency accusations from the first to the tenth police contacts, after which a plateau was reached. The average time between the first and second police contacts was 14.0 months, whereas the average interval between the ninth and tenth police contacts was 3.6 months. This discovery has major implications for the prediction of delinquency: Negro gang members apprehended for illegal conduct are not only likely to engage in further delinquent behavior but, before reaching a plateau, allow less time to elapse between each successive pair of law violations. This means that the relationship between onset and extent of delinquency cannot be completely explained by the fact that the youth who begins his delinquent career early in life has more time to continue such conduct than the juvenile whose delinquency occurs later in life. Regardless of the juvenile's age at onset of delinquency, there is a noticeable tendency for subsequent delinquencies *not* to occur at regular intervals. Once delinquency begins, it is not randomly distributed in time, but instead resembles a chain reaction in which each delinquent act becomes a stimulus and signal for the commission of another delinquency within a briefer period than that immediately preceding.

Table 3

AVERAGE NUMBER OF MONTHS BETWEEN
CONSECUTIVE PAIRS OF DELINQUENCY

P.C. Interval*	No. of Months	No. of Cases	$\bar{X}$ Interval (months)
1D–2D	8819	628	14.0
2D–3D	4433	558	7.9
3D–4D	2960	486	6.1
4D–5D	2068	400	5.2
5D–6D	1498	340	4.4
6D–7D	1185	284	4.2
7D–8D	851	227	3.7
8D–9D	644	173	3.7
9D–10D	506	141	3.6
10D–11D	447	111	4.0
11D–13D	542	155	3.5
13D–16D	469	131	3.6
16D	239	65	3.7

*Police Contact Interval designation 1D–2D refers to the number of months between the first and second delinquencies, 2D–3D the number of months between the second and third, etc.

Equally if not more important than the frequency of delinquency is its typology. Studies have almost invariably contributed to destroying the popular image of juvenile crime which associates it with forcefully aggressive behavior.[3] The gang study, however, revealed that 13.4 per cent of all juvenile crimes may be described as violently person-oriented. Of the remaining typology of delinquencies, 25 per cent were property-oriented, 37 per cent general disorderly conduct, 18 per cent distinctively juvenile offenses, and 7 per cent all other offenses. Reflection on the contribution of offenses which are distinctively juvenile—that is, which cannot be committed by adults—suggests the criminal character of gang member delinquency. Moreover, with some misgivings, curfew violations were considered as delinquent charges. If curfew violations had been originally defined or redefined as non-delinquent, then the contribution of uniquely juvenile charges would be markedly reduced, since almost two-thirds (63 per cent) of the 773 juvenile charges were on this account.

[3] Joseph W. Eaton and Kenneth Polk, *Measuring Delinquency: A Study of Probation Department Referrals* (Pittsburgh: University of Pittsburgh Press, 1961), pp. 12–13.

The preceding is one possible typology of delinquent offenses. In it violently person-oriented behavior was restricted to the actual commission of such acts. However, equally significant as the prevalence of completed acts of violence is the *tendency* to resort to force and violence either in the solution of problems or as a normal pattern of response under specific conditions among certain social classes of population. Accordingly, a second typology was constructed which trichotomized delinquent behavior into: 1. Offenses Against the Person, which included homicide, forcible rape, simple and aggravated assault, robbery, threats to do bodily harm, and weapon violations; 2. Offenses Against Property, including burglary, larceny, and receiving stolen goods; and 3. General Disorderly Conduct, which included all other offenses. On the basis of this typology it was found that about 23 per cent of all delinquencies were those against the person, 21 per cent against property, and 56 per cent disorderly conduct.

Because the participation of gang members in assaultive behavior has obvious relevance, the subject was explored further. Since we were interested in the tendency to behave violently, it was appropriate to ask what proportion of the 711 gang members were *ever* charged with offenses against the person. The data reveal that 67 per cent of them had committed at least one assaultive act. This is a minimal figure since 32 per cent of the offenders who had not committed any assaultive acts were still juveniles at the date of selection of the cases. For example, 69 per cent of the sixteen year olds had been charged with at least one assault; the remaining 31 per cent still had eighteen months of juvenile status left in which they could commit delinquent acts against the person. Perhaps even more significant is the fact that 31 per cent of the gang members were charged at some time with direct, severe physical attacks upon the person—that is, with homicide, aggravated assault, or forcible rape. For those who were adults the figure was 36 per cent.

The search for stabilities in juvenile delinquency is closely related to the preceding examination of delinquent typology. Despite their similarity, however, it has been given little consideration. A study of deviant stability is typology construction applied at the individual offender level. It attempts to ascertain the tendency of an offender to commit one pattern of offense rather than another. Two problems are involved in this effort: 1. the determination of the number of offense categories, and 2. the degree of deviation from pattern, if any, that one is willing to tolerate.

To investigate stability patterns we divided all delinquent charges into offenses against the person, against property, and disorderly conduct charges. Then a pattern-of-delinquency ratio—the largest number of charges within a category divided by the total number of charges—was calculated for each offender having at least five police contacts. For example, if a juvenile had committed five offenses against the person, five against property, and ten disorderly conduct offenses, then his pattern of delinquency ratio would be 10/20 DC or .50. It was also decided that unless at least three-fourths of an offender's police contacts fell into one of the three offense categories, no pattern of delinquency would be recognized for that offender. The results of this inquiry make it clear that if stabilities in deviance exist at the adult level, as some evidence suggests,[4] they have not yet manifested themselves at the juvenile level. Even with the generous pattern ratio of only .75, just 20 per cent of the 395 offenders met this requirement. If ratios of at least .80, .90 or 1.00 are requisite for establishing a pattern of delinquency commission, then only 15 per cent, 6 per cent and 4 per cent of the offenders, respectively, could be said to have exhibited stability in their delinquency. This, of course, does not mean that the gang study delinquents are equally likely to commit acts found in all three categories; it does mean, however, that they can and do engage in all categories of delinquency relatively frequently.

As mentioned earlier, every police contact resulted in the juvenile's arrest or non-arrest (remedial) disposition. One could hypothesize that the proportion of offenders arrested for a particular offense provides a more objective and therefore superior measure of the seriousness of the act than the evaluation expressed in the *Uniform Crime Reports*. Behind such an assertion would be the conviction that the juvenile authorities, in deciding to arrest, are expressing the concern of the larger community with regard to the behavior in question. In any event, it will be informative to examine the disposition of each offender by charge, particularly with a view to determining what degree of correspondence exists between the Federal evaluation and the police decision to arrest as measures of severity of delinquency.

On a gross level, the judgment of seriousness of offenses by the FBI is supported by the external criterion of arrests: 81 per cent of those charged with Part I offenses were arrested, compared to 42 per cent of those accused of Part II offenses. Behavior which disrupts or threatens to disrupt property and economic interests or attacks the integrity of the person usually results in the arrest of the accused. This is true for both Part I and Part II offenses, as witnessed by the high arrest figures in Table 4 for those charged with assault and battery, weapon violations, threats, and sex offenses. Despite the fact that a much larger proportion of juveniles charged with Part I offenses were arrested than those charged with Part II offenses, the ranking of the seriousness of charges within Part I offenses differs slightly from that in the *Uniform Crime Reports*. On the basis of arrest of offenders, the following order is observed, from most to least serious Part I charges:

---

[4] Richard A. Peterson, David J. Pittman, and Patricia O'Neal, "Stabilities in Deviance: A Study of Assaultive and Non-Assaultive Offenders," *Journal of Criminal Law, Criminology and Police Science*, LIII (March 1962), 44–48.

homicide, robbery, rape (which includes forcible rape and assault with intent to ravish), burglary, aggravated assault, and larceny. The order established in the *Uniform Crime Reports* is: homicide, rape, robbery, aggravated assault, burglary, and larceny.

At this point it was decided to compare the disposition of the gang members with that of non-gang member delinquents, with offense held constant. Information of all police charges placed against juveniles in

Table 4

DISPOSITION OF GANG MEMBERS, BY CHARGE*

	Charge†	*No. of Offenders*	*No. Arrested*	*Per cent Arrested*
Part I	Homicide	15	15	100.0
Crimes	Robbery	205	190	92.7
	Rape	39	36	92.3
	Burglary	301	263	87.4
	Aggravated Assault	239	199	83.3
	Larceny	619	446	72.1
	Sex Offense	34	30	88.2
Part II	Weapon Violation	160	135	84.4
Crimes	Threats	39	25	64.1
	Assault and Battery	302	161	53.3
	Other offense	94	42	44.7
	Liquor Violation	116	50	43.1
	Disorderly Conduct	1,117	445	39.8
	Gambling	69	20	29.0
	Trespassing	114	29	25.4
	CLV	476	113	23.7
	Total	3,939	2,199	55.8

*Within Part I and Part II offenses, the charges appear in decreasing order of the proportion arrested for each charge.

† Curfew violations were excluded from this table because it was the policy of the Juvenile Aid Division not to arrest on this charge.

Philadelphia in 1960 was utilized as the non-affiliated delinquent comparison group.[5] The distribution of Part I and Part II charges was fairly similar in both groups: 39 per cent of the gang member charges were Part I compared with 36 per cent of the 17,571 non-gang member charges in

---

[5] This comparison is revealing, though not entirely valid, since the racial and sexual composition of the two groups differed: the gang study members consisted of all Negroes and all males, while the comparison group were 82 per cent male and 63 per cent Negro. Part of the differential disposition between the two groups, therefore, may be a result of the race and sex of the offenders rather than whether they belonged to delinquent gangs or not.

1960. However, there were some striking differences concerning the disposition of offenders. There was a conspicuous tendency to arrest a larger proportion of gang members charged with Part I offenses than of non-affiliated delinquents: 62 per cent of the 1960 comparison sample of offenders charged with Part I offenses were arrested, compared to 81 per cent of gang members. With respect to Part II charges, 28 per cent of the 1960 juvenile sample were arrested, compared to 45 per cent of the gang study delinquents. Both of these differences are statistically significant.

Upon completion of the analysis of police delinquency records, a follow-up study of those gang members who had "progressed" into adult crime was made. This study was not restricted to those with juvenile police records. It was found that 41 per cent of the 580 gang members who were adults as of October 15, 1962, had acquired criminal records, and that the gang member who did not have a police delinquency record was just as likely to "progress" into crime as the Negro who did have a police record as a juvenile.

The average number of arrests of the follow-up group was 2.5, with a range of one to fifteen. In half of the cases less than eight months had elapsed after their eighteenth birthday before they were arrested; the average age at first arrest as an adult was eighteen years and ten months, while 70 per cent of the group experienced their first adult contact with the law within one year after reaching adulthood.

Of the 595 crimes for which the follow-up Negroes were arrested, 18 per cent were aggravated crimes against the person, 22 per cent other crimes against the person, 17 per cent non-assaultive property crimes, 15 per cent liquor and intoxication violations, 19 per cent disorderly conduct and gambling, and 9 per cent other crimes. Approximately 40 per cent of all charges were for crimes against the person. Of the 151 Negroes arrested once or twice, 48 per cent had been charged with at least one crime against the person, 24 per cent with aggravated crimes against the person. Of those arrested more than twice, 86 per cent were accused of at least one crime against the person and 57 per cent with homicide, aggravated assault, or forcible rape. For all follow-up members, 36 per cent had at some time been arrested for offenses against the person and 26 per cent for aggravated offenses against the person.

Having previously discovered that there was no greater tendency for gang members with juvenile police records to acquire criminal records than for those without police records, it was decided to investigate whether, among the adult Negroes who had juvenile records, there was an inclination for the follow-up group to have been *more* delinquent than the non-follow-up. The non-follow-up group had an average of 5.9 police contacts as juveniles, while 16 per cent had ten or more charges. The follow-up group had an average of 7.4 police contacts, while 30 per cent of them had ten or more charges. These differences are significant and demonstrate a recognizable predisposition for the more delinquent delinquents to become criminals.

There is, of course, a certain inadequacy in restricting the concept of degree of delinquency ("more" or "less" delinquent) to number of police contacts. An index of degree of delinquency was needed that would also take into consideration the nature of the delinquent act itself. Accordingly, all the juvenile police contacts of the follow-up and non-follow-up groups were weighed on the basis of the differential institutional punishment provided in the Pennsylvania Penal Code. For example, the maximum penalty for larceny in Pennsylvania is five years, for aggravated assault three years, for burglary twenty years, and so on.

In a few instances it was necessary to assign arbitrary values to offenses; also, all minor charges falling into a category described as General Disorderly Conduct were given a value of one. The individual offense values were then summed for each offender to yield a total index of degree of delinquency which reflected both the number and kind of police contacts. Having carried out this procedure, it was found that the median degree of delinquency for the follow-up group was 22, compared to 17.5 for the non-follow-up group, a statistically significant difference. Thus, even when the method of determining degree of delinquency took into account more than the number of police contacts, there was a tendency for those who became criminals to have been more seriously delinquent as juveniles than those who did not become criminals.

The analysis of police delinquencies of gang members and inspection of the criminal records of those juveniles who became adult offenders have made it clear that these individuals were persistent and dangerous offenders, have shown that a large proportion of them became even more serious adult offenders, and consequently have emphasized the need for social intervention no later than at the point immediately following the juvenile's initial involvement with a law enforcement agency.

Theft Behavior
in City Gangs

WALTER B. MILLER

Miller's paper has several strengths which will inevitably have impact on the work of other gang researchers. His detailed analysis of theft behaviors reminds us that predominant juvenile offenses are not those which receive the greatest public attention. In addition to the findings presented here, Miller provides a model for analysis that lays the emphasis on the *act*, not on the individual participating in the act. This facilitates our viewing delinquent offenses as the product of an individual *as he is reacted to by others,* rather than in the cultural vacuum that often surrounds our analyses of delinquency. The author's confirmation of the importance of sex, age, race, and several levels of lower social class status, and his dramatic insistence on the "normality" of gang behavior within its own social context give his work an unusual and highly individual stamp.

WALTER B. MILLER, Harvard-MIT Joint Center for Urban Studies, Cambridge, Mass.

A bout five or six years ago, starting with Albert Cohen's provocative discussion of delinquency and culture, a new wave of sociological concern with theoretical aspects of delinquency got underway.[1] At that time there was a good deal of discussion to the effect that more data, and carefully collected data, were necessary in order to substantiate or weaken the various and often conflicting theoretical positions. Many of the papers included in this volume indicate that this discussion has been taken seriously; each represents a carefully collected body of information on delinquency in different contexts and of different types. I am particularly pleased by the fact that the present papers have attended to the important factors of age and social status—two of the major variables differentiating between kinds of delinquent behavior.

Almost any major subject in the area of crime and delinquency can be developed at great length. This is particularly so in the case of our present topic—theft behavior. Our project has been working for over a year on an analysis of theft behavior based primarily on one quite small study group of about 350 male and female gang members, and during this time we have been able to harvest only a small portion of the possible yield of our data. We have accumulated scores of charts and tables, and many pages of qualitative analyses. It is most difficult to select and condense all this information without doing great violence to the subject.

Theft behavior has emerged from our analysis as a behavioral form of striking complexity in its surface manifestations—yet one which is governed by unexpectedly regular principles. The selected conclusions reported here are based primarily on analyses of three populations of events: first, 643 behaviors in some way oriented to theft engaged in by 205 members of seven adolescent street corner groups—male and female—during a study period of approximately two years per group; second, 185 arrestable acts of theft committed by members of the same groups (here called "intensive contact" groups) during the same time period; third, 380 appearances in court on 523 charges of theft by 293 male members of fourteen corner gangs during the age period from seven to twenty-one. The accompanying tables show the size and status characteristics of the two major study groups—the seven intensive contact groups and the fourteen male gang study groups.

They also show the size of three event populations for the intensive contact groups only. Equivalent data for the fourteen male gang study group are included in forthcoming discussion, and are not contained in these tables. The tables indicate that the major units of analysis are events— theft as a form of behavior—rather than individuals. In other words, this study is essentially an analysis of theft, not of thieves.

---

[1] Albert K. Cohen, *Delinquent Boys* (New York: Free Press of Glencoe, Inc., 1955).

Table 1

EVENT POPULATIONS: SEVEN INTENSIVE CONTACT GROUPS

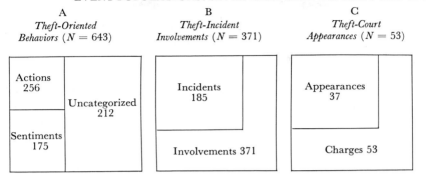

A	B	C
Theft-Oriented Behaviors ($N = 643$)	*Theft-Incident Involvements ($N = 371$)*	*Theft-Court Appearances ($N = 53$)*

Actions 256
Uncategorized 212
Sentiments 175

Incidents 185
Involvements 371

Appearances 37
Charges 53

Table 2

STUDY GROUPS

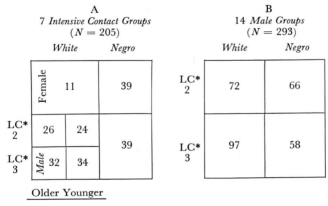

	A		B	
	7 Intensive Contact Groups ($N = 205$)		*14 Male Groups* ($N = 293$)	
	White	Negro	White	Negro
Female	11	39		
LC* 2			72	66
LC* 2 (Male)	26	24		
		39		
LC* 3 (Male)	32	34	97	58

Older Younger

*Lower class.

Each of the three populations of events—all theft-oriented behaviors, specific acts of arrestable theft, and court-recorded theft—illuminates a different facet of this complex behavioral area, and makes possible an examination of the various aspects of this phenomenon from different perspectives. But the final picture to emerge from the examination of the three event populations shows a high degree of consistency. Theft behavior by gangs in the study community emerges as a highly patterned form of behavior, regularly and consistently related to perfectly standard status characteristics (such as sex and age), engaged in by essentially normal youngsters moved by essentially reasonable motives, and comprising a distinctive syndrome of behavior which might be termed "normal lower status adolescent theft." As a form of behavior which was conventional for the studied population and which was essentially age-specific, it came into existence at predictable times, assumed characteristic forms and frequencies at predictable age periods, and diminished to negligible proportions at the close of the age period to which it was appropriate. This finding is at variance with the tendency reported by Robin[2] for a substantial group of highly criminal individuals in his Philadelphia study to continue to engage in serious crime.

Before presenting selected findings of our examination of theft, I would like to comment briefly on the role of research on theft in the study of youth crime. Theft was the dominant form of criminal behavior in Midcity gangs. During the age period from fifteen to eighteen, 37 per cent of all known illegal actions recorded for the project groups and 54 per cent of "major" offenses involved theft in one of its various forms. Acts of theft were two to three times as common as acts of assault, the next most frequent type of offense. Moreover, during the 1950s the dominance of theft among crimes was not confined to project groups, or to unofficially recorded offenses, or to the period of the Midcity study. Official court appearances by project group members during the three year study period showed the same proportion of theft to other crimes—37 per cent—as appeared in the case of "unofficial" crime. During the fourteen year age period from seven to twenty-one, court appearances for theft comprised 40 per cent of all appearances, were three times as frequent as appearances for drinking, the next most frequent type, and five and a half times as frequent as appearances for assaultive offenses, including gang fighting. The fourteen male study groups showed similar rates. Court appearances for theft during adolescence comprised about 40 per cent of all appearances, outnumbering appearances for drinking by three to four times, and for assault by four to five times.

The predominance of theft among forms of youth crime was not confined to the gangs of the Midcity study. During the decade of the 1950s theft was the dominant form of youth crime in all of Midcity, in all of Port City, in all of the state, and in all of the nation. The great bulk of crimes committed by youth were thefts, and the great bulk of thefts were committed by youths. In Port City, 65 per cent of all arrests of male juveniles in the years 1959-61 were for theft; theft arrests were eight times as frequent as arrests for vandalism, the next most frequent offense, and twelve times as frequent as arrests for assaultive offenses. In all United States cities of 2,500 or over, in the year 1961, 45 per cent of all arrests of persons under fifteen, and 39 per cent of arrests of those under eighteen, male and female, were for some form of theft. The general picture which emerges indicates that among urban United States males in the 1950s during the fourteen-to-eighteen age period, theft accounted for from 35 to 65 per

---

2 See Gerald Robin, "Gang Member Delinquency in Philadelphia," this volume.

cent of all actionable offenses, that thefts comprised about half of all officially processed youth crime, and that they outnumbered the next most frequent forms of offense by three to five times.

The fact that theft is clearly the predominant form of youth crime in the United States is not, curiously enough, reflected in the amount of attention it is accorded in contemporary writing—either popular or scholarly. "Gang violence" is frequently cited, "gang theft" seldom. The "fighting gang" or "conflict group" is a prime object of both public and professional concern; little reference is made to the "stealing gang."

What is the reason for this preoccupation with relatively uncommon forms of youth crime at the expense of its most common form? The disproportionate concern with non-theft crime derives more from characteristic emotional reactions to certain forms of crime than from documented knowledge of their actual prevalence. Four reasons for this may be cited: the high emotional shock potential of violence, the low shock potential of non-violent theft, the focus on individuals rather than on behavior, and the confusion of appropriative and aggressive aspects of crime.

The exaggerated perception of the prevalence of violent crime and the corresponding underestimation of the prevalence of appropriative crime reflect a fundamental human concern with violence and aggression as general forms of behavior. The urgency of human concern with violence strongly influences perceptions of crime prevalence. The principle governing the general perception of crime frequency might be phrased "intensity of concern converts to exaggerated perception of prevalence," or, in simpler language, the more you are concerned about it, the more common you think it is.

The reasons for this are not hard to understand. Violent or assaultive crimes pose a clear threat to the internal order of a societal unit and to the safety of its members. These are acts which, in the words of Émile Durkheim, "offend very pervasive and intense sentiments" and "shock the common conscience," and which are subject to the most severe punitive sanctions.[3] Violent crimes by youth—gang fights, gang assaults on individuals, sexual attacks—have particular power to evoke feelings of fear, threat, and danger among adults. The fact is that genuine gang fights, collective assaults on adults, and similar types of gang crime are relatively rare in any given city in any given year. For example, of more than 1,000 crimes committed by gang members of the Midcity project during the three year study period, not a single gang attack on an adult was recorded. Of fourteen threatened and partially mobilized gang fights, only one resulted in actual violence.

---

[3] Émile Durkheim, *The Division of Labor in Society, trans.* George Simpson (New York: The Macmillan Company, 1933).

This suggests the second reason for the dearth of focused concern with theft. Few events are less capable of arousing passionate responses than the constant daily flow of petty pilfering, minor shoplifting, and breaks into neighborhood stores which in fact comprise the great bulk of youth crime. The principle that perception of prevalence is influenced by emotional arousal potential applies here as well; to the extent to which nonviolent theft fails to arouse feelings of shock, indignation, and threat, to that extent is it underperceived and underreported. We have statistics which show the relative proportion of the crimes reported in the newspaper in one year and those for which legal action was taken. As one might imagine, theft crimes were badly underreported, relative to assaultive crimes.

A third reason for vagueness as to the actual prevalence of different forms of crime relates to a particular mode of viewing criminality which is prevalent among both public and professionals. One dominant approach to crime, rooted essentially in traditional religious concerns with sin and the salvation of individuals, revolves around the question, "Why do some individuals become criminals?" or, as applied to youth crime, "Why does one boy rather than another become a juvenile delinquent?" Underlying this approach is a basic conception of human nature which conceives criminality as an attribute of the individual organism; one "has" or "gets" a criminal nature or characteristic as a consequence of factors which are inherent in the organism or are implanted therein during early childhood.

If rather than asking "Why do some individuals become criminals?" one asks, "How can one account for criminal behavior?" the focus of concern shifts from individuals to behaviors, and the distinctions among widely varying forms of criminal activity become critical. Within this framework it is not necessary to decide whether particular individuals are really "true" delinquents or only "pseudo" delinquents or pre-delinquents or even non-delinquents; rather, crimes of varying types are seen as forms of behavior which can be engaged in by smaller or larger numbers of persons, with greater or lesser frequency at different ages, with differential prevalence in different sectors of the society, and so on.

A fourth reason for misperception of the actual prevalence of theft derives from a widespread failure to distinguish with sufficient clarity between "appropriative" and "aggressive" aspects of theft. The definition of theft is a most complex matter and is discussed in considerable detail in our more extensive treatment.[4] At this point I can only present our developed definition, without the extended discussion. Theft is defined as a *mode of ownership transfer which is effected without the knowledge and/or explicit consent of the assigned owner, or under circumstances involving the use or*

---

[4] Walter B. Miller, *City Gangs* (New York: John Wiley & Sons, Inc.—forthcoming).

threat of force or injury. Under this definition theft is *one mode of property transfer* which can occur under a wide variety of circumstances. Some of these circumstances involve violence, force, or the threat of force, but many do not. There is nothing in the act of theft, so defined, which involves or requires violence or aggression. And yet, within the western cultural tradition, there is a prevalent tendency to perceive "aggressive" and "appropriative" aspects of theft as organically related, and to regard an act of theft in and of itself as aggressive, malicious, and hostile. This is probably related to the particular nature of the concepts of "property" and "ownership" in western culture. It is most remarkable that in many legal codifications acts of theft are categorized as *"crimes against property,"* as if "property" were some sort of animate entity which could be hurt or offended by being appropriated.

Within this framework of perception, elements of aggression and hostility are built into the concept of theft so that it is not too surprising that theft is so often explained as a consequence of hostility. This approach is prevalent in both psychological and sociological treatments. Thrasher in his classic work on gangs classes theft as a "predatory" activity, and links his discussion of "robbing" with discussion of quite clearly hostile activities such as vandalism and malicious mischief.[5] It is important to stress that it is both possible and profitable to consider as conceptually separate the "aggressive" and "appropriative" aspects of theft. Just as there is violence without theft, and theft without violence, so there may be anger without theft and theft without anger.

The predominance of theft among youth crimes—not only in Midcity gangs but as a major characteristic of youth crime throughout the country—requires that an explanation of theft occupy a central position in any attempt to understand city gangs and their patterns of delinquency. Not only is it necessary that any theory of gang delinquency be able to accommodate theft within its general framework of explanation, but it is also necessary that theft be explained with a high degree of adequacy. Thus, for example, any theory of gang delinquency which centers on conflict or aggression must come to terms with the fact that the dominant form of crime by most gang members is not assault but theft, and that one does not account for the prevalence of theft by accounting for the existence of conflict.

If rather than asking, "What crimes are most shocking?" one asks, "What crimes are most prevalent?" and instead of asking, "Why do boys go bad?" one asks, "Why do boys commit crimes?" then the explanation of theft becomes a central task.

A sound approach to theft should involve at least two major areas of inquiry. The first should comprise a careful study in detail of the actual

---

5 Frederic M. Thrasher, *The Gang* (Chicago: University of Chicago Press, 1927).

empirical patterning of theft behavior—based on the experience of study groups with specific definable characteristics—instead of wide generalizations from the possibly idiosyncratic behavior of one professional thief or one jack-roller or one gang. It is most encouraging that more studies are now doing this, and all are examining the prevalence of specific forms of different crimes among different kinds of populations. Once we have obtained systematic information on theft behavior as *it is actually practiced* by specified populations rather than as it is imagined, we will then be in a position to address the second major question, "Why do they steal?"—in the form, "How can one account for *this particular pattern* of empirically observed theft?"

Our research is making an attempt to provide at least tentative answers to both of these extremely difficult and complex questions, and an extensive analysis of the motivation of theft has been developed. In the present paper I will only be able to report, very briefly, some of our findings in the first area—the empirical patterning of theft practiced by a designated study group.

The descriptive data of the present paper will center on three major characteristics of theft as a form of behavior practiced by city gangs—its *frequency, its patterns of participation, and its forms.* Of necessity, each of these will be discussed in highly condensed form. The *frequency* of theft will be defined as the rate of theft events per specified time period—for example, the number of theft involvements per group per contact-month, or the number of court charges per year of age. *Participation* will be defined as the proportion of a designated group or category of individuals involved in theft behavior—for example, the percentage of females known to have stolen during the study period. Under *forms* of theft, an area in which many complex distinctions are possible, only three highly simplified distinctions will be made for present purposes—theft *from* place, *from* persons, and *of* automobiles. Notice the shift in prepositions.

A major feature of the data on which our analyses are based is the availability of information of two major orders—theft behavior as recorded by field workers during the course of intensive day-to-day field contact with the study groups, and as recorded for the same and similar groups by official agencies. This makes possible some estimates as to a perennial and vexing problem of research in crime—the relation between officially recorded crime and crime as actually committed.

The fundamental body of information on which our analysis is based concerns the *frequency* of theft as a form of behavior. How often did theft occur? This question, very simple to ask, is extremely difficult to answer in any relatively uncomplicated way. Various measures of theft are possible. For example, members of one gang might engage in eight acts of theft during the course of a month—three committed by single individuals, two by pairs, two by three boys, and one by five boys. Should this be counted as eight or eighteen? We utilized both bases of counting and called the act itself an "incident" of theft, independent of the number of participants, and used the term "involvement" as a measure of incidents times participants. There are 185 incidents in Table 1B, associated with 371 involvements. That is, the average incident involved two participants.

During the contact period for the intensive contact groups—a total of 172 contact months or an average of two years per group—205 members of seven groups, five male and two female, engaged in 643 theft-oriented behaviors, were involved in 185 incidents of arrestable theft resulting in 371 individual involvements, and appeared in court thirty-seven times. (Since no female appeared in court, court data are based on male groups only.) This meant, for the full study group, that group members were involved in an average of four theft-oriented behaviors per month—male groups in about one and one-half theft incidents and about three theft involvements per month. On the level of official crimes, males were charged with theft in court on an average of once every two months during the study period.

What were the ratios of the various measures? There were three and one-half theft-oriented behaviors for every "hard" act of arrestable theft, and about ten theft involvements for every court appearance on theft charges. This is a rather surprisingly high ratio of court appearances to acts, but it still means that during the study period well over 300 incidents of theft were observed for which no official action was recorded.

How widely was theft practiced? About half of male group members were known to have stolen during the contact period, and about one-fifth of the girls. Of boys who stole at least once, two-thirds stole more than once. Eighty-five per cent of the members of the most theftive group were known to have stolen. It is noteworthy that even for the most common form of Midcity gang crime, about half of male group members were not known to have participated, nor was theft as collective as it has sometimes been pictured. Although 60 per cent of thefts involved more than one participant, 40 per cent were executed by single individuals. Groups which stole more widely, however, also stole more collectively.

What was the proportion of various forms of theft? Forms of theft may be differentiated in many ways. Our larger study, for example, developed extended analyses according to the targets of theft, the objects stolen, and the locality of commission. For present purposes we will make only three gross distinctions—theft *from* place, *from* person, and *of* automobiles. These distinctions have the advantage of being comparable to those used in national FBI arrest statistics.

A most unexpected degree of consistency in the proportion of these forms to one another emerged from the analysis, not only for the measures used for the study populations, but also for other populations. A rough ratio of two-thirds place theft, one-third auto theft, and one-tenth person theft emerged from a variety of measures. For example, on the level of observed theft—that is, the actual incidents observed by field workers during contact—theft incidents by male project group members were 64 per cent place, 22 per cent auto, and 14 per cent person. Most surprisingly, court-recorded thefts, which in Midcity are virtually coterminous with arrests, showed almost identical proportions. Court charges for the seven to twenty-one period for the fourteen male study groups showed proportions of 65 per cent place, 20 per cent auto, and 15 per cent person. By comparison, 1961 FBI arrest statistics for all cities in the United States of over 2,500 population for the fifteen-to-seventeen age period showed proportions of 75 per cent place, 23 per cent auto, and 5 per cent person. In contrast to the usual stress on the lack of correspondence between "official" delinquency statistics and actual patterns of criminal behavior, these figures would seem to indicate, at least in this one area, an unexpectedly close correspondence between statistics derived from field observation and those resulting from the screening and selecting of official agency processing. They would also suggest that in this respect, and possibly in others, findings on the patterning of theft in Midcity gangs might not be unrepresentative of patterning in many other populations.

What was the relation of each of the three characteristics of theft—frequency, participation, and form—to the status characteristics of age, sex, social status, and ethnic status?[6]

Without any doubt the single most important characteristic associated with the frequency of theft was sex. During the contact period males averaged three theft involvements per month compared to .3 per month for females. On this basis, then, male involvement in theft was ten times as frequent as female. None of the other status characteristics come close to showing differentiation of this order. Both *age* and *social* status, however, showed firm and regular relationships to theft frequency.

On the basis of contact-period theft involvement, lower class 3 groups engaged in theft three times as frequently as groups from lower class 2. During the age period from seven to twenty-one, members of lower class 3 groups appeared in court five times as often as lower class 2 groups, and six times as often during the contact-period age span. The possibility that differences of this magnitude in the court experience of two adjacent strata within the lower class would be due to differential application of justice is very remote.

Age showed a clear curvilinear relation to theft frequency. For the

---

6 Ethnic in this case refers to race, White and Negro. Social status distinctions were based on three divisions within the lower class (designated as 1, 2, and 3), using several indexes, primarily education and occupation.

fourteen male study groups, court appearances on theft charges started at the age of eight, rose steadily to a peak at sixteen, and dropped off quite rapidly by age twenty. To cite a few points on this curve: of 338 theft appearances accumulated by members of the fourteen male study groups by age twenty, 1.5 per cent occurred at age eight, 5 per cent at age twelve, 15 per cent at age fifteen, 17 per cent at sixteen, which is the peak year, 12 per cent at seventeen, and 6 per cent at nineteen. A secondary peak appearing at age twenty, largely accounted for by less than 5 per cent of the total group, could be evidence for the assumption of a different pattern of adult theft by a small subgroup.

Ethnic status taken by itself showed least relationship to theft frequency. Our data in regard to White-Negro differences are quite different from those of many other studies, which show higher rates for Negroes. Whites were somewhat more likely to become involved in theft than Negroes; on the basis both of field-recorded theft involvements and court-recorded thefts, the frequency of theft among Whites was somewhat more than one and one-half times that of Negroes. However, ethnic status showed different effects at different social status levels; among lower class 3 groups, both volume and frequency trends of White and Negro groups were very similar— both showing peak frequencies during the fourteen-to-sixteen age period. At the higher, lower class 2 level, however, Negro groups showed a peak of court appearances at age eleven-to-thirteen, while Whites did not peak until the seventeen-to-nineteen period. One important principle illustrated by these data, as well as by other data not reported here, is that characteristics such as sex and race operated differently at different status levels. At the lowest levels, the influence of social status was great enough to override other possible differentiating factors; at higher levels, differentiating factors such as ethnic differences could come into play.

Measures based on participation—that is, on the proportion of various groups which became involved in theft in various ways—proved considerably less sensitive in discriminating between various subcultural status categories than did measures based on frequency. The methodological implication of this will be commented upon later. The relationships between theft participation and status characteristics were similar to those derived from the frequency measures, but magnitudes were considerably smaller.

For each principal participation measure, the ranking of four ethnic status and social status categories was the same. Lower status Whites showed greatest participation, lower status Negroes next, higher status Whites next, and higher status Negroes least. For example, the percentage of group members appearing in court on theft charges between the ages of eight and eighteen was 55 per cent for White lower class 3, 47 per cent for Negro lower class 3, 22 per cent for White lower class 2, and 12 per cent for Negro lower class 2. Thus, 40 per cent of the Whites compared with 30 per cent of the Negroes appeared in court during this age period, and half of the lower status boys compared with a third of the higher status boys.

Taking each of three forms of theft—person theft, place theft, and auto theft—by status characteristics indicates that social status discriminated well for each type. The measure used in this case was the number of court charges of theft per individual for the age period eight to eighteen. For both place and person theft, lower class 3 groups were charged with theft approximately ten times as often as the higher status groups—a magnitude of distinction equaled only by the male-female difference in incident frequency. In the case of auto theft, however, social status differences were less pronounced, with lower class 3 boys charged with theft two are one-half times as often as higher status 1 boys. These, along with other data, would indicate that auto theft is proportionately, though not absolutely, more prevalent among higher status boys.

Form by ethnic status showed the only significant departure from the general all-theft trends. Whites were involved in both place and auto theft about twice as often as Negroes. In the case of person theft, however, Negroes were charged twice as often as whites, and, uniquely among all findings, outranked equivalent status Whites at both status levels. Even with this reversal, however, lower status Whites showed six times the person theft frequency of higher status Negroes.

Form of theft was also related regularly to age. Each of the three forms was more prevalent during particular periods of adolescence. This measure was also based on court charges during the eight to eighteen age period. Place theft reached its peak earliest, rising smoothly to age thirteen to fourteen, then diminishing smoothly. Person theft showed a peak at fifteen. Negro groups, however, showed a secondary peak at twenty which was absent for the Whites. Auto theft also showed a smooth curve for both ethnic groups, peaking at age fifteen to seventeen.

It would thus appear that some combination of age, sex, and ethnic and social status data could quite accurately predict theft frequency, form, and participation.

Before concluding, I would like to cite briefly a methodological point of some importance to the study of criminal behavior. Our study utilized, among others, two commonly employed measures of behavioral prevalence—"frequency" and "participation." The "frequency" measure asked the question, "How many times during a specified time period did a behavioral event occur?" The "participation" measure resembled the questionnaire item type of question used frequently by investigators such as James Short: "Have you ever engaged in, or do you now engage in, behavior *x*?" Our concurrent use of both these kinds of measures permitted comparison of the two. At least two conclusions emerged. First, these two measures were often related to quite different things. Second, and more important, the "participation" measure, "Have you ever," or "Do you," proved most insensitive in making some of the most vital discriminations of the study; it tended to wash out or minimize differences between categories which emerged with great clarity on the basis of the frequency measure. One example will illustrate this. For one of our lower status female groups, the proportion who ever engaged in theft during the study period was 55 per cent; for a higher status male group the proportion was 49 per cent. However, the *frequency* of theft acts for the females was .4 thefts per month and for the male group 2.4 per month—*six* times that of the female group. These figures might support a finding that theft *participation* at lower status levels could be more responsive to social status, and theft *frequency* more responsive to sexual status. The point is that if participation alone had been used as a measure of theft prevalence, results would not only have been incomplete, but would actually have supported a *reverse* finding regarding the relative influence of sex and social status.

These data on the form, frequency, and participation patterns of theft behavior, along with much other data not here presented, show that theft, as a culturally patterned form of behavior in this study group, had specifiable and distinct characteristics: it was mostly place theft; both form and frequency were regularly related to age, with peak frequencies occurring during the fourteen to seventeen age period; it had a strong utilitarian component; it was far more frequent than any other form of crime, but even so was not universally engaged in; it was predominantly a male activity; its frequency bore little relation to being White or Negro; its patterning was so decisively related to social status that status differences as small as those between lower class 2 and 3 had marked influence on its frequency.

It is, therefore, these characteristics of Midcity gang theft which both weaken the possible validity of certain kinds of explanations—for example, the idea that theft is largely a response to resentment of racial discrimination—and give positive clues to more adequate explanations. For example, in Midcity there was something about being male, being in middle adolescence and of lower social status which was conducive to more frequent stealing, and something about being female, of higher status, and a non-adolescent which was conducive to less frequent stealing. It is along these lines that we are developing our conclusions on the motivation of theft behavior.

Deviant Patterns and Opportunities of Pre-Adolescent Negro Boys in Three Chicago Neighborhoods

IRVING SPERGEL

This report dovetails with the previous paper by Miller, for it too emphasizes substrata within the lower class as related to deviance. However, Spergel's viewpoint derives from the "opportunity structure" theory of Cloward and Ohlin, and consequently lays more stress on relative states of deprivation as related to the neighborhood setting. A major modification of the Cloward-Ohlin approach is provided by the demonstration of an interaction effect between socio-economic status and age in their relationship to delinquency. Practitioners should pay special attention to the final pages of this paper which relate the data directly to possible emphases in action programs.

IRVING SPERGEL, School of Social Service Administration, University of Chicago.

T his exploratory ex post facto research was conducted within a framework of anomie and opportunity theories as formulated by Merton[1] and Cloward and Ohlin.[2] It was also conducted specifically to test the relevance of two apparently contradictory notions about the development of delinquent subcultures.

Cohen and Short[3] have formulated the concept of "parent male" delinquent subculture which is described as "non-utilitarian, malicious, negativistic, versatile, and charatcerized by short run hedonism and group autonomy." They have suggested that the "common core" subculture generates other types of subculture: "conflict oriented," "drug addict," and "semi-professional theft." The Cohen-Short formulation is not a clear one and is difficult to operationalize, particularly since the age of the young people subscribing to the "parent male" subculture is not specified. It is not clear whether the "parent male" subculture precedes or in some other way conditions the development of specialized delinquent subcultures.

Cloward and Ohlin[4] reject the "parent male" subculture idea and assume that "the social milieu affects the nature of the deviant response whatever the motivation and social position (i.e., age, sex, socio-economic level) of the participants in the delinquent subculture." They believe that "the local cultural and social structure impinges upon and modifies deviant responses from the very onset."

It is very difficult to test these opposing points of view; first, because the concept of subculture may not mean precisely the same thing to the two sets of authors; second, because the methodological problems of determining to what extent or degree an individual or group subscribes to certain values, norms, beliefs, and actions are extremely complex; third, because the conceptual and methodological problems of relating certain key variables such as perception of opportunities to actual opportunities available for achieving middle class or success status have not been sufficiently addressed.

This research, conducted as a student project in the School of Social Service Administration,[5] University of Chicago, relied primarily on measure-

---

1 Robert K. Merton, *Social Theory and Social Structure* (rev. ed.) (New York: Free Press of Glencoe, Inc., 1957), pp. 131–94.

2 Richard A. Cloward and Lloyd E. Ohlin, *Delinquency and Opportunity* (New York: Free Press of Glencoe, Inc., 1960); see also Irving Spergel, *Racketville, Slumtown, and Haulberg: An Exploratory Study of Delinquent Subcultures* (Chicago: University of Chicago Press, 1964).

3 Albert K. Cohen and James F. Short, Jr., "Research in Delinquent Subcultures," *Journal of Social Issues,* XIV: 3 (1958), 24ff.

4 Cloward and Ohlin, *op. cit.,* pp. 159–60.

5 Miss Diane Porter assisted during the summer of 1963 in further analysis of the interview data. The following students participated in the collection and partial analysis of data: Joan Ackerman, Paul E. Blackstone, Angela Blumberg, Rosalie Blumberg, Barbara Bunsis, James Christianson, Paul D. Cohn, Jordon Devlin, Louise Doss, Geraldine K. Gordon, Alvin E. Green, Richard W. Hoekstra, Walker W. Hudson, Ruth Klau, Gary Nolder, Frances E. Popek, Beatrice R. Scheid, Henry R. Scheunemann, John R. Schuerman, Karen Shulman, Walter Scott, Jr., David N. Seiberling, Dominie Shortino, Kenneth N. Viggers, and Susan Workoff.

ments of individual behavior as an index of the existence of delinquent subculture. The research attempted to assess patterns of deviant behavior, mainly of Negro boys, eight to twelve years old, but also of older youths and young adults in three Chicago neighborhoods. In addition, the researchers were interested in differences in aspiration and expectation levels, and in perception of certain types of opportunity available to conformist and deviant children eight to twelve years old. Only partial findings will be reported here.

Method

Three neighborhoods were selected, each almost exclusively Negro in population but differing in relative socio-economic status as measured by per capita family income, occupation, and education of adults. The West Woodlawn neighborhood was classified roughly as upper lower class, the East Woodlawn neighborhood as middle lower class, and the North Lawndale neighborhood as lower lower class.[6]

In regard to significant social and ethnic transitional characteristics of the neighborhoods it was noted that West Woodlawn, the upper lower class neighborhood, was the oldest and most stable of the three Negro areas. It had been settled solidly by a middle class Negro population for more than three decades. Some of the old time residents remained, but in the past decade a large influx of lower class persons has taken place. The median age of the population was highest in West Woodlawn (ULC) and lowest in North Lawndale (LLC). Also, family size was smallest in West Woodlawn (ULC) and largest in North Lawndale (LLC).

East Woodlawn (MLC) and North Lawndale (LLC), formerly all white, lower middle class areas, had been settled recently by Negroes. A change in ethnic composition of these two neighborhoods from all white to almost all Negro had occurred in the past decade. Mobility rates were higher and home ownership rates were lower in East Woodlawn (MLC) and North Lawndale (LLC) than in West Woodlawn (ULC). East Woodlawn (MLC), in the south of Chicago, was considered a more desirable place to live than North Lawndale (LLC) and was, to some extent, a stopping place for upwardly mobile Negroes moving out of the slums. Finally, in terms of relative strength and number of organized community groups, West Woodlawn (ULC) would probably rank highest and North Lawndale (LLC) lowest.

---

[6] The Negro lower class groups appeared to fall into three fairly distinct categories rather than the two categories of upper lower (working) and lower lower class commonly utilized. See for example, August B. Hollingshead and Frederich C. Redlich, *Social Class and Mental Illness: A Community Study* (New York: John Wiley & Sons, Inc., 1958).

A previous study,[7] using 1960 arrest and institutional data, found that young adults in the two Woodlawn neighborhoods (middle lower and upper lower class) were engaged in more sophisticated or acquisitive but less violent criminal behavior—such as burglary, larceny, and fraud—as compared with young adults in the North Lawndale neighborhood (lower lower class) who were engaged in more violent crimes such as rape, assault, and robbery, but less theft or acquisitive behavior. The same patterns held for older teenagers in each of the neighborhoods. These findings were, in general, successfully replicated as part of the present study, using 1962 and 1963 arrest data.[8] Differences were statistically significant ($p<.05$) (see Tables 1, 2, and 3).

Table 1
DISTRIBUTION OF TYPE OF OFFENSE:
TEENAGE AND YOUNG ADULT*

Neighborhood and Age of Offender	Type of Crime		
	Assaultive†	Theft‡	Total
East Woodlawn (MLC)			
16–19 years	109 (55.1%)	89 (44.9%)	198 (100%)
20–29 years	315 (67.6%)	151 (32.4%)	466 (100%)
North Lawndale (LLC)			
16–19 years	52 (69.3%)	23 (30.7%)	75 (100%)
20–29 years	108 (78.8%)	29 (21.2%)	137 (100%)

*Chicago Police Department Statistics, May 1962 through March 1963.
†Includes arrests for murder, non-negligent manslaughter, forcible rape, robbery, aggravated assault, other assaults, weapons—carrying, possessing.
‡Includes arrests for breaking or entering, larceny, theft (except auto theft), auto theft, forgery, counterfeiting, embezzlement, fraud, stolen property—buying, receiving, or possessing.

Table 2
DISTRIBUTION OF TYPE OF OFFENSE:
TEENAGE (16–19 YEARS)*

Neighborhood	Assaultive†	Theft‡
East Woodlawn (MLC)	109 (55.1%)	89 (44.9%)
North Lawndale (LLC)	52 (69.3%)	23 (30.7%)

* Chicago Police Department Statistics, May 1962 through March 1963.
† Includes arrests for murder, non-negligent manslaughter, forcible rape, robbery, aggravated assault, other assault, weapon—carrying, possession.
‡ Includes arrests for breaking or entering, larceny, theft (except auto theft), auto theft, forgery, counterfeiting, embezzlement, fraud, stolen property—buying, receiving, or possessing.
$X^2 = 4.02$; $p < .05$

[7] Irving Spergel, "Male Young Adult Criminality, Deviant Values and Differential Opportunities in Two Lower Class Negro Neighborhoods," *Social Problems*, X: 3 (Winter 1963), 237–50.
[8] The Chicago Police Department supplied relevant statistics.

Table 3
DISTRIBUTION OF TYPE OF OFFENSE:
YOUNG ADULT (20–29 YEARS)*

Neighborhood	Assaultive*	Theft‡
East Woodlawn (MLC)	315 (67.6%)	151 (32.4%)
North Lawndale (LLC)	108 (78.8%)	29 (21.2%)

* See note *, Table 2.
† See note †, Table 2.
‡ See note ‡, Table 2.
$X^2 = 5.86$; $p < .02$

In the present study, a youth serving agency was selected from each neighborhood[9] and the populations of boys eight to twelve years old regularly attending the agency's programs in January 1963 were interviewed. These boys were regarded as representative of neighborhood boys, particularly of boys living in the immediate vicinities of the agencies.

An interview schedule of seventy-two items was the primary source of data. It contained mainly fixed alternative questions, along with some probe and projective items. A total of 131 interviews was collected and analyzed. Of these, forty-eight were from North Lawndale (LLC), fifty-four from East Woodlawn (MLC), and twenty-nine from West Woodlawn (ULC). Nineteen-sixty census tract and 1962 and partial 1963 police arrest data were also gathered and analyzed.

For purposes of the study *deviancy* was defined as behavior which did not conform to legal or social standards. Such behavior included various forms of theft, riding in stolen cars, attacking an adult, gang fighting, extortion, truancy, vandalism, running away from home, and "acting up" behavior in the classroom serious enough to warrant being sent to the principal's office. Those children interviewed who had commited one or more deviant acts in the previous twelve month period were classified as deviant; those not committing such acts were classified as conformist. Furthermore, the category of deviant children was subdivided into three subcategories: the school deviants, who had committed antisocial acts in school only; the neighborhood deviants, who had committed antisocial acts in the neighborhood but not in school; and the extreme deviants who had committed antisocial acts both in and out of school. Comparisons were made between conformists and various types and combinations of deviants, and mainly between East Woodlawn (MLC) and North Lawndale (LLC) children. Comparisons

---

[9] The Woodlawn Chicago Boys Club, Parkway Community House, and BBR-Chicago Youth Centers were fully cooperative in permitting interviews of children in their programs.

between West Woodlawn (ULC) and neighborhood children were not generally made because of small sample size.

Findings

Of 131 boys interviewed, eighty-three or 63.4 per cent were classified as deviant and forty-eight or 36.6 per cent as conformist. In each of the neighborhood agencies more of the boys were classified as deviant than conforming. The agency in the lower lower class neighborhood had the highest proportion of deviant boys. Although it also had the highest proportion of eleven and twelve year old boys, the difference in age distributions of boys among the agencies were not statistically significant; when age was held constant the distribution of responses did not change.

BEHAVIOR PATTERNS

The evidence based on interview responses and police arrest statistics indicated that patterns of conflict (including acts of assault and extortion) and of theft behavior (including larcenies and auto theft) were similar for eight to twelve year old deviants in the lower lower class and the middle lower class neighborhoods (see Table 4). Police data for the calendar year 1962 indicated that 68.5 per cent of the arrests of eight to twelve year old Negro males in East Woodlawn and 74.4 per cent of the arrests in North Lawndale had been for various acts of theft.

Table 4
DISTRIBUTION OF TYPE OF OFFENSE OF CHILDREN 8–12 YEARS*

Neighborhood	Assaultive		Theft	
	Police Arrest*†	Interview Data§	Police Arrest*‡	Interview Data‖
East Woodlawn (MLC)	34 (31.5%)	10 (71.4%)	74 (68.5%)	4 (28.6%)
North Lawndale (LLC)	22 (25.6%)	100 (75.8%)	64 (74.4%)	32 (24.2%)

* Chicago Police Arrest Statistics, January through December 1962; Interview Data.
† See note †, Table 1.
‡ See note ‡, Table 1.
§ Includes each instance of a gang fight, assault on an adult, and extortion reported by children ($n = 54$ in East Woodlawn; $n = 48$ in North Lawndale).
‖ Includes each instance of theft, burglary, and riding in a stolen car reported by children.

The interview responses based essentially on the same categories of delinquent acts were similar for the two neighborhoods. However, there were two important differences. In both areas interview responses revealed greater evidence of violent behavior than did police arrest statistics. In the LLC neighborhood 75.8 per cent of deviant acts were of a violent nature; in the MLC neighborhood 71.4 per cent of the deviant acts were of a violent nature. In other words, the police arrest data indicated a dominant orientation toward theft while the interview responses indicated a dominant orientation toward violence in the two areas. However, it should be noted that the police data represented arrests for entire neighborhoods; the interview data represented self reports of deviant acts by youngsters attending selected agencies in the three neighborhoods. It is possible that youngsters this age tend to overreport participation in acts of violence. Nevertheless, the presumed discrepancies in patterns of deviant behavior as indicated by police arrest and interview data deserve more investigation and analysis.

In any case, for each set of statistics employed, patterns of deviant behavior appeared to be similar for children eight to twelve years of age in East Woodlawn and North Lawndale—i.e., in both lower lower and middle lower class neighborhoods.

Of further interest is the fact that police arrest data (see Table 5) indicated no significant difference in patterns of behavior in each of the two neighborhoods under the age of fifteen years. However, at age fifteen, and particularly at age sixteen significant differences clearly arose. Male teenagers at sixteen through nineteen years of age in the LLC neighborhood were arrested for relatively more acts of violence than were teenagers in the MLC neighborhood. On the other hand, male teenagers sixteen through nineteen years old in the MLC neighborhood were arrested for relatively

Table 5

DISTRIBUTION OF TYPE OF OFFENSE OF CHILDREN
UNDER 15 YEARS, 15 YEARS, 16 YEARS*

Neighborhood and Age	Type of Offense		
	Assaultive†	*Theft‡*	*Total*
East Woodlawn (MLC)			
Under 15	51 (27.0%)	138 (73.0%)	189 (100%)
15	24 (42.9%)	32 (57.1%)	56 (100%)
16	27 (44.3%)	34 (55.7%)	61 (100%)
North Lawndale (LLC)			
Under 15	22 (34.9%)	41 (65.1%)	63 (100%)
15	19 (65.5%)	10 (34.5%)	29 (100%)
16	22 (81.4%)	5 (18.6%)	27 (100%)

* Chicago Police Department Statistics, May 1962 through March 1963.
† See note †, Table 1.
‡ See note ‡, Table 1.

Table 6

DISTRIBUTION OF TYPE OF OFFENSE OF CHILDREN UNDER 15 YEARS*

Neighborhood	Type of Offense	
	Assaultive†	*Theft‡*
East Woodlawn (MLC)	51 (27.0%)	138 (73.0%)
North Lawndale (LLC)	22 (34.9%)	41 (65.1%)

* See note *, Table 2.
† See note †, Table 2.
‡ See note ‡, Table 2.
$X^2 = .69$; $p < .50$ (not significant)

Table 7

DISTRIBUTION OF TYPE OF OFFENSE OF CHILDREN 15 YEARS OF AGE*

Neighborhood	Type of Offense	
	Assaultive†	*Theft‡*
East Woodlawn (MLC)	24 (42.9%)	32 (57.1%)
North Lawndale (LLC)	19 (65.5%)	10 (35.5%)

* See note *, Table 2.
† See note †, Table 2.
‡ See note ‡, Table 2.
$X^2 = 3.07$; $p < .10$

Table 8

DISTRIBUTION OF TYPE OF OFFENSE OF CHILDREN 16 YEARS OF AGE*

Neighborhood	Type of Offense	
	Assaultive†	*Theft‡*
East Woodlawn (MLC)	27 (44.3%)	34 (55.7%)
North Lawndale (LLC)	22 (81.5%)	5 (19.5%)

* See note *, Table 2.
† See note †, Table 2.
‡ See note ‡, Table 2.
$X^2 = 9.05$; $p < .01$

more acts of theft than were teenagers in the LLC neighborhood (see Table 1).

Thus the police arrest data strongly suggested differential patterns of delinquent behavior for teenagers sixteen years of age and over in the two neighborhoods. Differences persisted at least through young adulthood.

However, patterns of delinquent behavior of males under fifteen years old, and particularly between the ages of eight and twelve years, inclusive, showed relatively little difference.

It is possible on the basis of these findings to speculate that the deviant behavior patterns of male children particularly twelve years of age and under in low income areas tend to be relatively independent of patterns developed by older teenagers and young adults. These findings would tend to support Cohen and Short's idea of a common core subculture as a generating condition for various specialized delinquent subcultures. Alternatively, the type of deviant behavior of children under a certain age may be much less a response to a delinquent subculture and more directly a response to pressures mainly emanating from home and school. The idea of delinquent subculture may not be relevant for the eight to twelve year old child since the peer culture does not exert its dominating influence until an older age. On the other hand, the Cloward-Ohlin hypothesis which suggests that the social milieu affects the nature of the deviant response regardless of age appears not to be supported for pre-adolescents. It should also be noted that neither theory correlates types of delinquent subculture or patterns of deviant behavior with different levels of lower class population.

Aspirations—Expectations

The present research also attempted to differentiate conformist and deviant children using concepts and propositions derived from anomie and opportunity theories. The exploratory research endeavored to test the anomie hypothesis that deviants internalize success goals but do not have the means to achieve these goals. Thus the anomie condition presumably provides certain pressures conducive to delinquent activity. It was expected that deviants would have high aspiration levels in terms of academic and occupational achievement. Furthermore, it was anticipated that they would have relatively low expectation levels for actual achievement. Expectation levels were assumed to be dependent, at least in part, upon the means or opportunities perceived by the deviants as available to them.

Findings on aspiration and expectation levels were similar in each of the neighborhoods. In response to the question, "How high would you *most like* to go in school—graduate high school, college, or some other type of school," 77.0 per cent of the conformist group and 68.7 per cent of the deviant group aspired to graduate from college. However, in response to the question, "Do you *think you will* graduate high school, college, or some other type of school," 68.8 per cent of the conformists as opposed to 50.6 ı er cent of the deviants responded yes to college graduation. Only 4.2 per cent of the conformists and 15.7 per cent of the deviants aspired for but did not expect to achieve college graduation (see Table 9).

Table 9

ASPIRATIONS AND EXPECTATIONS: GRADUATION FROM COLLEGE

Type of Youngster	Aspires for College Graduation and Expects to Achieve It	Aspires for College Graduation but Does Not Expect to Achieve It	Other Combinations*
Conformist (n = 48)	31 (64.6%)	2 (4.2%)	15 (31.3%)
Deviant (n = 83)	43 (51.8%)	13 (15.7%)	27 (32.5%)

* Includes mainly aspiration for less than college graduation and expectation for achieving it. It should be noted that two of the conformists had expectations but not aspirations for college graduation.

$X^2 = 4.15$; df $= 2$; p < 20

The difference was not statistically significant. However, while comparison of the responses of the extreme deviants (those who had committed antisocial acts in and out of school) with those of the conformists revealed a similar pattern of educational aspiration—Seventy-two per cent (18 out of 25 boys) aspired for college graduation—expectations of the extreme deviants for graduation from college were very low. Only 36 per cent (9 out 25 boys) expected to graduate from college. The difference between the response of conformists and extreme deviants on expectations was statistically significant ($X^2 = 5.94$; p$<$.02).

Noteworthy were the high aspiration levels for educational achievement by children, whether conformist or deviant, from each of the low income neighborhoods and the relatively lower expectation levels of deviant youngsters for achieving such aspirations. Actually, only 3 or 4 per cent of the adult population in these neighborhoods graduated from college. The median school years per adult twenty-five years old and over in the various neighborhoods ranged from 8.6 to 10.4 years.

Feelings of frustration on the part of the deviants, probably resulting from the disparity between high aspirations and considerably lowered expectations for college graduation, may have been further intensified by their greater perception of the prevalence of college oriented role models in the neighborhood. Deviants perceived significantly more often than did conformists the presence of college oriented teenagers in their neighborhoods. Seventy-one and one tenth per cent of all the deviants but only 58.3 per cent of the conformists knew adolescents who were planning to go to college ($X^2 = 4.20$; p$<$.05). It is possible to speculate that deviants were at least as aware, if not more aware, of the importance of a college education than were conformists, but they were clearly less confident about their ability or the availability of actual or perceived opportunities to achieve a college education.

The researchers were interested, in addition, in the source or sources of possible pressure on the child for internalization of success goals which emanated from the home environment. Did the child, for example, perceive parents or parent substitutes as desiring them to graduate from college? The data revealed that the majority of children, conformist or deviant, regarded this to be the case. Patterns of response were almost identical for conformist and deviant children. Seventy-five per cent of the conformists and 73.5 per cent of the deviants viewed their mothers or mother substitutes as wanting them to complete a college education. Apparently not as many fathers or father substitutes were perceived as desiring this for them. Sixty-four and six tenths per cent of the conformists and 62.7 per cent of the deviants responded that their fathers (or father substitutes) wanted them to obtain college degrees.

Data on occupational as well as educational aspirations and expectations were also obtained. When the question, "What job would you *like* or *wish most* to have when you are grown up (adult)?" was asked, 60.4 per cent of the conformist group responded with a preference for professional, technical, managerial, or proprietor occupations; 54.2 per cent of the deviants responded with a preference for these types of job. However, when the question, "What job do you think you *will have* when you are grown up (adult)?" was asked, 52.1 per cent of the conformist group but only 39.8 per cent of the deviant group believed it was possible to attain such aspirations. As compared with only 4.2 per cent of the conformists, 19.3 per cent of the deviants aspired for but did not expect to achieve middle class occupational status. The difference was statistically significant (see Table 10).

Table 10

ASPIRATIONS AND EXPECTATIONS: ACHIEVEMENT OF MIDDLE CLASS OCCUPATIONAL STATUS (PROFESSIONAL, TECHNICIAN, MANAGER, PROPRIETOR)

Type of Youngster	*Aspires for Middle Class Occupation and Expects to Achieve It*	*Aspires for Middle Class Occupation but Does Not Expect to Achieve It*	*Other Combinations**
Conformist (n = 48)	25 (52.1%)	2 (4.2%)	21 (43.8%)
Deviant (n = 83)	31 (37.3%)	16 (19.3%)	36 (43.4%)

* Includes mainly aspiration for lower class occupation and expectation of achieving it. It should be noted that two of the deviants had expectations but not aspirations for middle class occupations.

$X^2 = 6.94$; df = 2; $p < .05$

Of interest was the fact that twenty-five children or 19.8 per cent of all children aspired to be doctors. Also noteworthy was the fact that only 2.6 per cent to 7.0 per cent of the adults in these neighborhoods held professional, technical, managerial, or proprietor positions of any kind.

The data on aspirations and expectations showed unusually high aspiration levels for all groups of youngsters relative to the actual status of adults currently present in the neighborhood. Expectations for achieving success status were generally greater for conformist than for deviant youngsters. Deviant youngsters appeared to be less optimistic in regard to educational and occupational goal achievement by middle class standards. The findings on aspirations and expectations thus suggested support for the anomie propositions.

Opportunities

FAMILY SYSTEM

Explicit in the anomie hypothesis is the sociological notion that the (acute) disparity between goals and means creates a condition of normlessness conducive to deviant behavior. However, also implicit is the psychological notion that a severe disparity between aspirations and expectations produces a condition of frustration which may be conducive to a deviant adaptation. In this connection a limited effort was made to determine whether a facilitative home environment was or was not present for the various types of interview subject. It was assumed that the sheer presence in the home of a set of natural parents tended to establish grossly for children a positive or enabling environment for the achievement of a variety of basic psychological satisfactions and social goals, including directly or indirectly the attainment of success goals as defined by the larger society. In both psychological and sociological senses, the family could be regarded as an opportunity system.

The findings indicated that deviant children came more often—although not significantly more often—than did conformist children from "broken" families (see Table 11). It was possible to speculate that deviants lacked the opportunity of an "intact" family system through which to obtain the training and guidance in role expectation and role performance necessary for or at least associated with success-goal achievement. Furthermore, it is worth reporting that more deviant children in the relatively more socioeconomically secure neighborhood, West Woodlawn, came from "broken" families than in the most deprived neighborhood, North Lawndale. It could be hypothesized not only that deviant children came more often from

Table 11

FAMILY STRUCTURE

Neighborhood and Type of Child	"Intact" Family*	"Broken" Family*	Total
West Woodlawn (ULC)			
Conformist	8 (72.7%)	3 (27.3%)	11 (100%)
Deviant	7 (38.9%)	11 (61.1%)	18 (100%)
East Woodlawn (MLC)			
Conformist	16 (72.7%)	6 (27.3%)	22 (100%)
Deviant	20 (62.5%)	12 (37.5%)	32 (100%)
North Lawndale (LLC)			
Conformist	9 (60.0%)	6 (40.0%)	15 (100%)
Deviant	17 (51.5%)	16 (48.5%)	33 (100%)
Total			
Conformist†	33 (68.8%)	15 (31.2%)	48 (100%)
Deviant†	44 (53.0%)	39 (47.0%)	83 (100%)

* "Intact" family: natural mother and father living together with child(ren) in the home; "broken" family: at least one of natural parents not present in the home.

† $X^2 = 2.49$; $p < .20$

"broken" families but that they tended to come most often from "broken" families in the Upper Lower Class neighborhood and least often from "broken" families in the Lower Lower Class neighborhood. On the other hand, it was possible to speculate that conformist children from "broken" families were more likely to be found in the Lower Lower Class area. Larger samples are needed to test this hypothesis more adequately.

SCHOOL SYSTEM

Similar to an "intact" family, a "good" school system could be considered as providing opportunities facilitative of achievement of success goals in American society. One measure of the adequacy of the school system is the helpfulness of the teacher in contributing to the learning of the child. In the present research the child was asked to indicate whether his teacher was very helpful, somewhat helpful, a little helpful, or not at all helpful in his learning of his school work. The findings revealed that deviants, generally, regarded teachers as less helpful than did conformists. However, the difference was not quite statistically significant. At the same time a comparison of conformist and extremely deviant children did reveal a statistically significant difference in the expected direction. Thirty-nine of forty-eight or 60.4 per cent of the conformist children but only six out of twenty-five or 24 per cent of the extremely deviant children viewed their teachers as very helpful ($X^2 = 7.34$; $p < .01$). Thus, it could be hypothesized that deviant children, in effect, perceived the school, represented by the teacher, as a frustrating and limited opportunity system.

HOUSING CONDITIONS

"Good" housing conditions represent an opportunity providing the security, comfort, and convenience necessary to or at least associated with success-goal achievement in various aspects of the human daily life struggle. For the child, constriction of space or noisy and inadequate accommodations for study and play constitute not only a source of personal frustration but a handicap—for example, to the fulfillment of the role of successful student in school.

The research anticipated that deviant children would be exposed to more limited opportunities, including worse housing conditions (particularly crowding), than would be conformist children, even in slum areas. The findings did not support this expectation. Indeed, slightly more conformist than deviant children had to share a room with two or more other persons. Deviant children were clearly not at a disadvantage relative to conformist children in regard to housing opportunity. On the other hand, deviant children *perceived* crowded home conditions significantly more often than did conformist children. Thirty per cent of all the deviants but only 4.4 per cent of the conformists saw their homes as crowded ($X^2 = 4.65$; $p < .05$).

While it is true that a minority of both groups of children viewed their housing as crowded, at the same time it also is obvious that the presence or absence of opportunities—for example, housing opportunity—per se may not be a sufficient explanation of pressure leading to or even associated with deviance. What is likely in the responses of children about the adequacy of their housing is that the deviants were using a different standard of adequacy than were the conformists. In other words, it is the condition or opportunity relevant to some standard or norm of that which is "good" which qualifies the condition and permits judgment of it as useful for the attainment of a goal. Thus it is not only possible that aspirations are high and opportunities limited for deviants, but also that opportunities are perceived as limited when in fact they are relatively adequate for the attainment of success goals. The conditions under which institutional means or opportunities are perceived as available or unavailable for achieving goals have been insufficiently addressed in anomie and opportunity theories. It would seem that propositions dealing with the significant factors contributing to judgment of the adequacy or availability of opportunity must be integrated into a theory which purports to explain deviance.

Neighborhood Orientation and Illegitimate Opportunities

With the limitation on actual or perceived family, school, and housing opportunities available to deviants, it was expected that they would seek alternative opportunities by which to attain success status more often than would conformists, and that they would be oriented to neighborhood persons, especially delinquents and criminals who might be considered a source of alternate opportunities, more often than would conformists. The data suggested that indeed this was the case. Deviants said they knew more adults who could teach them criminal roles.[10] The difference between the conformists and extreme deviants was statistically significant ($X^2 = 6.16$; $p < .02$). Deviants, especially extreme deviants, had more acquaintance with teenagers oriented toward strong-arm activity and shoplifting. They more often knew teenagers who were in trouble with the police and who were gang leaders. None of these differences, however, was statistically significant at the .05 level. Nevertheless, it was plausible to expect that the transition to the roles of adolescent delinquent and adult criminal would be more readily managed by those youngsters with greater familiarity with performances of such roles than by youngsters who did not have such contacts.[11]

In general, deviants were more oriented to neighborhood adolescents, delinquent and non-delinquent, than were conformists. Deviants, more often than conformists, wanted to hold jobs, both conventional and illegitimate, which neighborhood adolescents held ($X^2 = 6.51$; $p < .02$). It was possible to speculate that while conformists were more oriented to or had greater access to opportunities at home and in school, deviants were more oriented to or had greater access to neighborhood adult and peer relationship opportunities.

Summary and Action Implications

1. The findings failed to support the Cloward-Ohlin notion that the social milieu affects the nature of the deviant response regardless of age. 2. The existence of differential deviant behavior patterns among children twelve years of age and under, and possibly up to fifteen years of age, in different types of lower class neighborhoods was not found. However, differential

---

[10] The interview question was, "Do you know any adult in the neighborhood who could teach you to be a strong-arm man?" Yes____ No____. "A shoplifter?" Yes____ No____. "A racketeer? (specify)" Yes____ No____.

[11] Edwin A. Sutherland, *Principles of Criminology* (rev. 4th ed.) (Philadelphia: J. B. Lippincott Co., 1947), pp. 6–8.

older teenage delinquent and young adult crime patterns continued to be found in the various neighborhoods. 3. Support for the Cohen-Short notion of common core delinquent subculture seemed more likely but still was not clearly obtained.

Aspiration levels of conformist and deviant children for success goals were high in lower class neighborhoods. A major source of pressure to achieve high educational aspirations probably emanated from parents. Expectation levels for achievement of success goals were lower for deviant than for conformist children. The disparity between high aspirations and substantially lowered expectations might constitute a pressure for deviance among children in lower class neighborhoods.

Deviants appeared to have less access to conventional opportunities than conformists. The condition of "broken" families is possibly more often associated with the deviant than the conforming child, particularly in the higher socio-economic or upper lower class neighborhood than in the lower lower class neighborhood. The school situation as represented by the teacher seemed to provide the deviant with a less useful learning situation than was perceived by the conformist. However, question was raised whether in fact there was more limited opportunity available to the deviant child. Despite the deviant's perception of more limited opportunities, deviants in fact may not have been more disadvantaged than conformists—at least in regard to available housing space. Finally, it was apparent that more deviants were oriented to neighborhood persons, particularly criminal adults and older delinquent youths, than were conformists.

Speculations about action implications for practitioners seeking to treat or control the problem of delinquency include the following:

1. Since differential patterns of deviant or delinquent behavior may exist on an age graded and neighborhood basis, programs to modify delinquent behaviors should vary. Programs appropriate for one age group or type of lower class neighborhood may not be appropriate for another. Also, attention to family conditions may be more important in the case of deviants from a less deprived neighborhood than from a highly deprived neighborhood. Furthermore, efforts should be made to modify the orientations and relationships of deviants to adolescent and adult deviants in the area.

2. The high level of aspirations of children suggests the importance of two kinds of program, particularly in the lower lower class neighborhood:

    a. A massive community development program to provide means or opportunities whereby children may ultimately attain desired success goals.

    b. A concerted effort by parents and key community socializing agents—e.g., teachers—both to reduce interpersonal and cultural pressures on children for attainment of success goals in middle class terms and to remove or alleviate psychological and perceptual conditions interfering with the utilization of existing opportunities.

Finally, one cannot overstress the need for a great deal more systematic research in the area of delinquency utilizing class, neighborhood, age, opportunity, and perception variables and, particularly, the importance of the development of action programs on the basis of available knowledge and theory about *differential* delinquent patterns of young people.

Part Two

RELATED PATTERNS
OF PERCEPTION AND BEHAVIOR

Family Structure
and Delinquent Behavior

RAY A. TENNYSON

In this paper, Tennyson uses Chicago data to test fundamental propositions developed in Boston by Walter Miller. The question of the relationship between female dominance in the lower class family and the delinquent behaviors of lower class gang members has intrigued researchers for some years. Tennyson's analysis suggests that the relationship is far weaker than has been maintained, but further analyses with more refined delinquency data seem to be in order.

RAY A. TENNYSON, Washington State University.

This paper[1] attempts to demonstrate: 1. relationships between family structure, group membership, and reported behavior, and 2. relationships between selected social psychological factors and behavior patterns. The position taken is that family structure has not been explored adequately in terms of its varieties, nor have the assumed consequent behavior patterns been adequately related to these structural forms.

The literature demonstrates that the normative system of family structure in America is one in which the presence of a husband-father male is quite normal, desirable, and necessary.[2] The tendency is to label other types of family structures as deviant and consequently productive of deviant behavior patterns.

If most family structures were in fact without males or contained males who were not functioning within the structure, what would the expectations for delinquency be? "Higher delinquency," say those of us fathers who try to salvage our concept of self. There is ample evidence, however, that the male-based family is far from universal. Murdock's materials indicate that about 21 per cent of all cultures have matrifocal, or what we will later call female-based, household systems.[3] The 1960 census reports that in the United States 22.7 per cent of *all* families with children eighteen years of age or under have a female as head of household.[4] It may be suggested that the one to four ratio of female to male head-of-household families is surely too large not to be regarded as an institutionalized form. The female-based household is in fact an established family system in the United States; further, it is in a form that has established processes for maintaining and perpetuating itself as a family system in at least some strata or segments of our society. Descriptions given by Frazier of the Negro family argue for the existence among Negroes in the United States of a female-based family system.[5] Anthropological works of a recent vintage point to patterns of female dominated households among the Caribbean countries.[6] One can cite the Mescalero Apache reservation and, most recently, Walter Miller's state-

---

1 This research was completed under sponsorship of NIMH grant number M–3301 conducted at the Youth Studies Program, University of Chicago, under the directorship of Dr. James F. Short, Jr., to whose assistance much is owed.

2 For selected references to "Family-Delinquency" literature, see especially Chapter 10, "The Home and Family," in E. H. Sutherland, *Principles of Criminology* (Philadelphia: J. B. Lippincott Co. 1947); and Section VI, "The Family Setting," in Marvin E. Wolfgang, ed., *The Sociology of Crime and Delinquency* (New York: John Wiley & Sons, Inc., 1962).

3 G. Murdock, "World Ethnographic Sample," *American Anthropologist*, LIX (August 1957), 675–86.

4 *Statistical Abstract of the United States*, 1961, p. 39.

5 E. Franklin Frazier, *The Negro Family in the United States* (New York: Dryden Press, 1951).

6 Peter Kunstadter, "A Survey of the Consanguine or Matrilocal Family," *American Anthropologist*, LXV: 2 (February 1963), 56–66.

ments about the prevalence and functions of female-based households in large urban American communities.[7]

Regarding family structures, Miller notes that the female-based household occurs in 20 to 30 per cent of the households in urban slum areas. His view is that customary patterned ways of acting or behaving have built a system among the lower classes in which there is little expectation that the male parent will remain in the family setting due to the economic inadequacy of the male. This absence of the male from the family setting creates pressures upon the female to provide ways for the boys in the family to achieve masculine status. How is this achieved? Miller says:

> Although mothers attempted to the best of their ability to acquaint their sons with an image of estimable manhood, their capacity to present a consistent model of customary male behavior or to teach specific masculine skills and behaviors was necessarily limited. Thus, while on one level mothers deplored the tendency of their pubescent sons to spend an increasing amount of time out on the corner with "them bums," on another level they recognized that the gang was able to provide for their sons superior training in the difficult task of becoming a "real man."[8]

Up to the age of eleven or twelve, the major portion of the boy's life is within an orbit of female nurturance with the presence of the male being at best sporadic. In this grouping of adolescent males, the boy Miller describes learns about the masculine qualities of toughness, fighting prowess, and hardness. "Most boys from female-based households at a fairly early age adopt as their primary reference group and learning milieu a set of peers raised under similar circumstances."[9]

It appears that Miller's position is something like this: the female-based household places pressures on male adolescents to "achieve masculinity." In achieving masculinity, a boy associates with other boys in the context referred to as the gang, through which aggressive male acts reflecting high masculine assertiveness take place. It is expected, then, that in these groups delinquency should primarily involve behavior reflecting aggression or masculine assertiveness.

If Miller is correct then we would predict the following differences: 1. a class difference in the number of adult males present in the family setting—

---

[7] Walter Miller, "Implications of Urban Lower Class Culture for Social Work," *Social Service Review,* XXXIII (September 1959), 219–36; Walter Miller, "Male Sexual and Mating Behavior," in *City Gangs: An Experiment in Changing Gang Behavior* (New York: John Wiley & Songs, Inc., forthcoming).

[8] Miller, "Male Sexual and Mating Behavior, *op. cit.,* p. 19.

[9] Miller, "Implications of Urban Lower Class Culture . . . ," *ou. cit.,* p. 10.

specifically, there will be fewer males present in urban slum families; 2. class differences in the dominance of the female in the family setting, especially in the lower class household; 3. a direct relation between adult male absence and gang membership or, stated differently, a positive relation between female dominated households and gang membership of male adolescents.

Questions in addition to those precipitated by the above comments on family structure are: What is to be expected if the male is present but not psychologically the head of household, and, what about the psychological dimension of parental attachment? Shouldn't the association of a child and his mother or father be considered an intervening quality between family structure and participation in groups and/or subsequent delinquent behavior?

This paper will present data on the type of family structure, the presence of male or female dominant patterns within the family structure, and a measure of attachment to male or female parent and/or guardian, from data collected on 538 members of sixteen delinquent gangs assigned to detached workers by the Program for Detached Workers of the YMCA of Metropolitan Chicago.[10] The gangs studied ranged in size from sixteen to sixty-eight members, on the basis of workers' judgments concerning who should and who should not be considered members. Gangs were selected by the YMCA on the basis of troublesome character to the community, and by a University of Chicago research program in fulfillment of research design requirements related to studying gangs representative of "delinquent sub-cultures." An interview schedule was administered to a "catch-as-catch-can" sample of members of these gangs, with considerable aid by their detached workers. Interviewing was "catch-as-catch-can" because it was impossible to interview some gang members who were in jail or unavailable for other reasons. Behavioral data comparing boys who were and were not interviewed suggest that no significant biases were introduced by the selection process. Interview questions were asked of Negro and white gang boys, as well as of a selection of boys described as non-gang boys from lower class origins who lived in the same communities as the gang boys studied. Lower class non-gang boys were located by detached workers, other agency social workers, or gang boys in these areas who acted as witnesses to the fact that boys chosen as non-gang boys did not belong to gangs. Members of middle class Negro and white YMCA groups also were interviewed for comparative purposes. For what are considered obvious reasons, no approximation to random process was made in collecting any portion of the sample in this study.

Interviewers were research assistants with the Youth Studies Program

---

[10] James F. Short, Jr., Ray A. Tennyson, and Kenneth I. Howard, "Behavior Dimensions of Gang Delinquency," *American Sociological Review*, XXVIII (June 1963), 411–28.

and others at the University of Chicago. All were trained by the YSP. Questions asked which have to do with family structure are: a. "Who have you lived with during most of your life?" Responses were categorized as 1. mostly with both parents; 2. with father; 3. with mother; 4. with married couple; 5. with female to whom related; 6. with male to whom related; 7. with married couple to whom not related; 8. with male to whom not related; 9. with female to whom not related. b. "Which of the following statements comes closest to describing your own family while you were growing up?" 1. "It was a family in which the man was definitely the head of the house, and he ruled the house with an iron hand." We will call this a male dominated household. 2. "It was a family in which the man was definitely the head of the house but in which the woman made some important decisions too." 3. "It was a family in which both the man and the woman were the head of the house, and they made decisions together." We call this a sharing family. 4. "It was a family in which the woman was the head of the house, and she made the important decisions." This will be called a female dominated family.

Parental attachment was questioned in the following manner: "How would you describe the amount of attachment between you and your father (stepfather, male guardian)? Would you say you are 1. very close to him; 2. there is a good deal of attachment; 3. only a moderate amount of attachment; 4. very little attachment; or 5. there is no attachment at all?" The same question was repeated with reference to mother (stepmother, female guardian). Numerous other family questions were asked and are to be considered in subsequent reports.

Two relevant questions about police contacts and arrests were worded as follows: "About how many times have policemen warned you about something you have done without doing anything about it?" and "How many times have you been brought to the police station for something you have done and then released without going to court?"[11]

The logical temporal sequence assigned to variables in this analysis are deduced from the literature as proceding from the end product, behavior, back to the primary precipitator, family structure. We view race and class as antecedent to family structure and suggest that any analysis of the variables on which we have data must proceed from race→class→family structure (physical)→family structure (psychological—here defined by the dominance question)→attachment to parents→gang-non-gang→police warnings. The position of variables in this temporal sequence is not to be regarded as invariant, but, hopefully, reflects a position which is compatible with that suggested by the literature. The complete analysis of this

---

11 Future analysis will contain detached worker reports of behavior as found in the Short, Tennyson, Howard paper and official police records of the respondents (see footnote 10, above).

ordering requires elaboration beyond the scope of this paper. However, summary data will be reported and cross tabulations of these variables will be made against police warnings (as a behavioral end product) as a basis for assessment of conditional statements found in the literature. Ten tables form the basis for analysis of the relationships between variables.

Table 1 describes masculine-feminine dominance. It shows that the joint husband-wife sharing relationships predominate among all groups. In only the Negro lower class and white gang boy groups does the figure fall below 50 per cent. Within race, noticeably more sharing families occur among middle class groups, but white lower class non-gang boys report a higher percentage of "sharing" parents than do Negro middle class boys. The most striking variation in male dominant families occurs for white gang boys, among whom 18 per cent so reported. Such reports are exceptionally rare among other white groups and comparatively so among all Negro groups. Female dominant households—although our measure differs from that of the census—approach the U.S. Census figures previously cited (22.7 per cent) for lower class groups of both races, with Negro gang boys reporting the highest incidence of any group (26.3 per cent). Variations in all patterns by race, holding constant social class, generally are small.

Table 1

PERCENTAGE RESPONSES TO THE QUESTION ABOUT FAMILY DOMINANCE PATTERN BY RACE, CLASS, AND GANG STATUS

	Negro Gang	*Negro Lower Class*	*Negro Middle Class*	*Total*	*White Gang*	*White Lower Class*	*White Middle Class*	*Total*
	205	*89*	*26*	*320*	*89*	*75*	*53*	*217*
Male dominant	5.4	6.7	7.7	5.9	18.0	1.3	1.9	8.3
Male dominant but female makes some decisions	18.0	24.7	23.1	20.3	16.9	16.0	22.6	17.9
Husband-wife sharing	50.2	47.2	57.7	50.0	44.9	61.3	73.6	57.3
Female dominant	26.3	21.3	11.5	23.8	19.1	21.3	1.9	15.6
Unknown	——	——	——	——	1.1	——	——	0.5

Female dominance in gang families manifests itself in reports from detached workers such as: "The Mrs. is the dominant figure in the house. She's the tough one. . . ." Such dominance becomes especially apparent when boys get into difficulty with the law, for then the mother's importance directs detached workers to her. There are many accounts from workers such as: "I informed Joe's mother that he was in jail. She said she would go right down and see what the trouble was and see if she could get him out."

Table 2 provides distributions of responses to the question, "Whom did you live with while growing up?" This family structure evidence favors the presence of both parents more or less continuously (rows 1 and 2 in the table) for all groups, with gradations in frequency running from a high of 98 per cent among white middle class boys to a low of 55 per cent for Negro lower class boys. The Negro-white difference, cutting across class, shows that 25 per cent more white boys had both parents present. Other relatives apparently provided residences for more Negro gang and Negro lower class boys. Negro middle class boys accounted for over half of the "father only" instances. Among Negroes percentages for boys living with mothers alone are somewhat higher than the U.S. Census figure of 22.7 per cent for families with children having female heads of household. For our population, female presence appears to be both psychological—that is, "she does wear the pants"—as well as physical in a family structural sense. A mother rears 26 per cent of Negro gang boys, 29 per cent of Negro lower class boys, and 15 per cent of Negro middle class boys. The figures for white gang and white lower class are 12 and 15 per cent, respectively. Table 2 also demonstrates that when the nuclear family is disrupted, child rearing functions are relegated to females. Fathers alone combined with fathers and stepmothers in the family account for less than 3 per cent of Negro family structures and only 1.8 per cent of white groups.

Table 2

PERCENTAGE RESPONSES TO THE QUESTION: "WHOM DID YOU LIVE WITH WHEN GROWING UP?" BY RACE, CLASS, AND GANG STATUS

	Negro Gang	Negro Lower Class	Negro Middle Class	Total	White Gang	White Lower Class	White Middle Class	Total
	205	89	26	320	89	75	53	217
Both parents continuously	44.4	40.4	61.5	44.7	58.4	61.3	92.5	67.4
Mostly both parents	11.7	14.6	11.5	12.5	21.3	17.3	5.7	16.1
Father	3.4	——	3.8	2.5	3.4	1.3	——	1.8
Mother	26.3	29.2	15.4	26.3	12.4	14.7	——	10.1
Stepparents	0.5	2.2	——	0.9	1.1	1.3	1.9	1.4
Foster parents	0.5	——	——	0.3	——	——	——	——
Other relative	12.2	13.5	7.7	12.2	3.4	4.0	——	2.8
Unknown	1.0	——	——	0.6	——	——	——	——

The first two tables, then, suggest that boys' perceptions of their family settings agree with Miller's contention that there are class differences in the proportion of male-present families and female dominant families. With respect to family structure, however, racial differences are as great as are differences between classes. These tables also demonstrate that there is no clearly defined relationship between adult male absence from the family and/or female dominance and gang membership, as Miller hypothesizes. The data suggest relatively similar patterns of family structure and dominance for gang and non-gang lower class boys within race, but with Negro boys more frequently reporting mothers and other relatives as family heads. The male dominant family pattern is more often reported by white gang boys, which again is contrary to Miller's prediction.

Tables 3 and 4 reflect the measure of attachment a boy has to his mother and/or father. Clearly, boys universally *like* their mothers, with Negro gang boys being especially high in this respect, as compared with their white counterparts. Detached-worker accounts of "doing" and "buying things for Mom" by gang boys tended to focus around "special" days, the

Table 3
PERCENTAGE RESPONSES TO THE QUESTION: " HOW WOULD YOU DESCRIBE THE AMOUNT OF ATTACHMENT BETWEEN YOU AND YOUR FATHER (MALE GUARDIAN) ? " BY RACE, CLASS, AND GANG STATUS

	Negro Gang	Negro Lower Class	Negro Middle Class	Total	White Gang	White Lower Class	White Middle Class	Total
	205	89	26	320	89	75	53	217
High	58.0	60.7	57.7	58.8	51.7	62.7	86.8	63.8
Medium	13.7	14.6	23.1	14.7	23.6	18.7	13.2	19.3
Low	13.2	7.9	19.2	12.2	19.1	8.0	——	10.6
Unknown	15.1	16.9	——	14.4	5.6	10.7	——	6.0

Table 4
PERCENTAGE RESPONSES TO THE QUESTION: "HOW WOULD YOU DESCRIBE THE AMOUNT OF ATTACHMENT BETWEEN YOU AND YOUR MOTHER (FEMALE GUARDIAN) ?" BY RACE, CLASS, AND GANG STATUS

	Negro Gang	Negro Lower Class	Negro Middle Class	Total	White Gang	White Lower Class	White Middle Class	Total
	205	89	26	320	89	75	53	217
High	95.1	92.1	92.3	94.4	83.1	88.0	88.7	85.8
Medium	2.4	6.7	——	3.4	11.2	8.0	9.4	9.6
Low	1.0	1.1	7.7	1.6	4.5	4.0	1.9	3.7
Unknown	1.0	——	——	0.6	1.1	——	——	0.5

time of Christmas being most "special." Christmastime gestures were many. One gang boy obtained a job delivering furniture, and then, while on a delivery run, "dropped off" for "Mom" an overstuffed chair, reporting to the store owner later that the chair had fallen off the truck somewhere. The "heisting" of Christmas trees for "Mom" was frequently reported, also.

Paternal attachment is noticeably less than maternal attachment for all except middle class white boys, whose fathers are occupationally the most "successful."[12] The finding is consistent with data reported by Gold for Flint, Michigan, and may reflect, in addition, the relative discontent of Negro middle class boys whose fathers have achieved success relative to other Negroes, but who nevertheless continue to occupy relatively low status positions.[13] These families probably are the most mobility conscious of all who were studied. White boys follow a reverse pattern to that of the Negro boys. White gang boys have the least attachment to fathers, one of every two acknowledging other than high attachment to his father.

Self reports of police warnings and arrests are utilized in this paper as a rough index of police contact necessary for official definition of delinquency. The literature suggests that behavior of the type which produces police attention and/or arrest is more likely to occur among gang boys from female-based households. Therefore, we expect: 1. that female dominant households will produce more delinquent type behaviors within gangs than outside of them; and 2. that high male parental attachment should act as a constraint upon official contact with police.

Table 5

PERCENTAGE RESPONSES TO THE QUESTION: "HOW MANY TIMES HAVE POLICEMEN WARNED YOU ABOUT SOMETHING YOU HAVE DONE WITHOUT DOING ANYTHING ABOUT IT?" BY RACE, CLASS, AND GANG STATUS

	Negro Gang	Negro Lower Class	Negro Middle Class	Total	White Gang	White Lower Class	White Middle Class	Total
	205	89	26	320	89	75	53	217
Never	21.5	37.1	34.6	26.9	5.6	25.3	54.7	24.3
Once or twice	25.4	36.0	42.3	29.7	12.4	28.0	32.1	22.5
Three or four times	18.5	13.5	7.7	16.3	10.1	14.7	5.7	10.6
More than four times	34.6	13.5	15.4	27.2	71.9	32.0	7.5	42.2
No response	——	——	——	——	——	——	——	——

---

[12] See Ramon Rivera and James F. Short, Jr., "Occupational Goals: A Comparative Analysis," this volume.
[13] See Martin Gold, *Status Forces in Delinquent Boys* (Ann Arbor: Institute for Social Research, 1963).

Table 6

PERCENTAGE RESPONSES TO THE QUESTION: "HOW MANY TIMES HAVE YOU BEEN BROUGHT TO THE POLICE STATION FOR SOMETHING YOU HAVE DONE AND THEN RELEASED WITHOUT GOING TO COURT?" BY RACE, CLASS, AND GANG STATUS

	Negro Gang	*Negro Lower Class*	*Negro Middle Class*	*Total*	*White Gang*	*White Lower Class*	*White Middle Class*	*Total*
	205	*89*	*26*	*320*	*89*	*75*	*53*	*217*
Never	26.3	59.6	73.1	39.4	33.7	57.3	92.5	56.0
Once	32.2	31.5	19.2	30.9	19.1	24.0	7.5	17.9
Twice	15.6	5.6	7.7	12.2	9.0	8.0	——	6.4
Three times or more	25.9	3.4	——	17.5	38.2	10.7	——	19.3

Table 7

PERCENTAGE COMPARISONS* OF POLICE WARNINGS AND ARREST, WITH RELEASE, BY RACE AND GANG STATUS

Negro Gang Warnings	*Arrest*				*White Gang Warnings*	*Arrest*			
	Never	*Few*	*Many*	*N*		*Never*	*Few*	*Many*	*N*
Never	29.6	46.3	24.1	54	Never	13.3	33.3	53.3	30
Few	19.7	44.9	35.4	127	Few	2.9	25.7	71.4	35
Many	12.5	33.3	54.2	24	Many	——	——	95.8	24
				205					89
	Negro Lower Class					*White Lower Class*			
	Never	*Few*	*Many*	*N*		*Never*	*Few*	*Many*	*N*
Never	45.3	47.2	7.5	53	Never	34.9	44.2	20.9	43
Few	25.7	51.4	22.9	35	Few	16.0	40.0	44.0	25
Many	——	(100.0)	——	1	Many	——	(42.9)	(57.1)	7
				89					75

*Parentheses indicate that base for percentage is very small.

Tables 5, 6, and 7 contain data supporting what has been frequently demonstrated in the literature—i.e., that class differentials are an indicator of variation in police contact and arrest. These data also indicate that gang boys are more likely to engage in police attention-getting behavior than non-gang boys or middle class boys, exclusive of race. When arrests and warnings are cross tabulated, white gang respondents report considerably more arrests without having received warning than do Negro gang boys (Table 7). This condition also holds for non-gang lower class white boys.

When police warnings are cross tabulated with categories of adults lived with while growing up (Table 8), one again finds slim evidence for the Miller view. This table indicates that a few more white gang boys than

Table 8

PERCENTAGE COMPARISON* OF "WHOM LIVED WITH WHILE GROWING UP?" AND POLICE WARNINGS BY RACE AND GANG STATUS

Family	*Negro Gang*				*White Gang*			
Situations	*Never*	*Few*	*Many*	*Total*	*Never*	*Few*	*Many*	*Total*
Both parents	19.8	41.5	38.8	116	4.3	20.3	75.4	69
Father	(42.9)	(28.6)	(28.6)	7	(33.3)	(33.3)	(33.3)	3
Mother	20.4	50.0	29.6	54	(9.1)	(18.2)	(72.7)	11
Stepparents	——	——	——	1	——	——	——	1
Other relative	24.0	52.0	24.0	25	——	(33.3)	(66.7)	3
Total	44	90	71	203	5	20	64	87

Negro Lower Class					*White Lower Class*			
	Never	*Few*	*Many*	*Total*	*Never*	*Few*	*Many*	*Total*
Both parents	36.7	51.0	12.2	49	29.3	41.4	29.3	58
Father	——	——	——	0	——	——	(100.0)	1
Mother	34.6	42.3	23.1	26	(18.2)	(54.4)	(27.3)	11
Stepparents	——	(100.0)	——	2	——	(50.0)	(50.0)	2
Other relative	(50.0)	(50.0)	——	12	——	(33.3)	(66.7)	3
				89				75

* Parentheses indicate that base for percentage is very small.

Table 9

PERCENTAGE COMPARISON* OF FAMILY SITUATION AND POLICE WARNINGS BY RACE AND GANG STATUS

	Negro Gang (205)					*White Gang (89)*				
	Police Warned?					*Police Warned?*				
Family		*Few*	*Many*	*Un-*			*Few*	*Many*	*Un-*	
Situation	*Never*	*(1–4)*	*(>4)*	*known*		*Never*	*(1–4)*	*(>4)*	*known*	
					Total					*Total*
Male dominant	18.2	27.3	54.5	——	11	——	25.0	75.0	——	16
Male dominant and share	13.5	45.9	39.5	——	37	13.3	20.0	66.7	——	15
Husband-wife share	22.3	45.6	32.0	——	103	7.5	25.0	67.5	——	40
Female dominant	25.9	42.6	31.5	——	54	——	17.6	82.4	5.9	17

Negro Lower Class (89)	Never	Few (1—4)	Many (>4)	Un-known	Total	White Lower Class (75) Never	Few (1—4)	Many (>4)	Un-known	Total
Male dominant	(66.7)	(33.3)	——	——	6	(100)	——	——	——	1
Male dominant and share	31.8	45.5	22.7	——	22	15.4	46.2	38.5	——	13
Husband-wife share	38.1	52.4	9.5	——	42	30.4	39.1	30.4	——	46
Female Dominant	31.6	52.6	15.8	——	19	13.3	53.3	33.3	——	15

* Parentheses indicate that base for percentage is very small.

non-gang boys living with mothers only report more police warnings. These slight differences between gang and non-gang data lead us to conclude that white family structures have more of a differential impact on behavior (as reflected in reported police warnings) than do Negro family structures. The hypotheses likewise fail to receive support in Table 9, comparing police warning rates by family dominance patterns. Among the white gang boys, both male dominant and female dominant families are reported to have more police contact than either husband-wife sharing or male dominant and sharing families.

Low paternal attachment is positively related to white gang boys' reports of frequent police contact (Table 10), but almost two-thirds of these boys

Table 10

PERCENTAGE COMPARISON* OF ATTACHMENT TO FATHER AND POLICE WARNINGS BY RACE AND GANG STATUS

Negro Gang Attachment	Police Warnings Never	Few	Many	Total	White Gang Attachment	Police Warnings Never	Few	Many	Total
High	24.4	42.0	33.6	119	High	10.9	26.1	63.0	46
Medium	28.6	35.7	35.7	28	Medium	——	20.0	80.0	20
Low	22.2	59.3	18.5	27	Low	——	25.0	75.0	16
Unknown	3.2	45.2	51.6	31	Unknown	——	——	(100.0)	7
				205					89
	Negro Lower Class					White Lower Class			
Attachment	Never	Few	Many	Total	Attachment	Never	Few	Many	Total
High	35.2	55.6	9.3	54	High	27.7	40.4	31.9	47
Medium	38.5	38.5	23.1	13	Medium	21.4	42.9	35.7	14
Low	(42.9)	(42.9)	(14.3)	7	Low	(16.7)	(66.7)	(16.7)	6
Unknown	40.0	40.0	20.0	15	Unknown	(25.0)	(37.5)	(37.5)	8
				89					75

* Parentheses indicate that base for percentage is very small.

who stated they were highly attached to their fathers also acknowledged many police warnings.

Future analysis will utilize the variables in this paper which will be cross tabulated with reported behavior items specifically chosen to evaluate the importance of "masculine" aggressive behavior. Official police records will also be used, much as police warnings have been in this paper. Age and sibling position are also to be included in further analyses.

In summary, data presented in this paper suggest that those relative differences which were found were most influenced by whatever factors contribute to our category of race. Miller's tendency to treat behavior problems as lower class phenomena per se obviously needs extension—as he undoubtedly would agree—to include variations attributable to ethnicity.

Occupational Goals:
A Comparative Analysis

RAMON J. RIVERA
JAMES F. SHORT, JR.

The following work contains much significant material. It confirms earlier findings by Short and his colleagues in Chicago that the gang member truly represents the lowest rung on the adolescent social ladder. The focal point this time is occupational goals and expectations, and it is interesting to note that these are related to the very same variables as were delinquency patterns in the preceding papers. Again, the practitioner is referred in particular to the final section in which the authors attempt to draw from their data some suggestions for dealing with the actual and perceptual occupational discrepancies with which gang boys must deal.

RAMON J. RIVERA, Washington State University, and JAMES F. SHORT, JR., Sociological Research Laboratory, Washington State University.

This paper will report upon the status of origin and the occupational goals of Negro and white adolescents. Our data lend themselves to the analysis of three related questions.

Initially we shall examine the SES background of groups of Negro and white youngsters contacted in the course of a large scale study of juvenile delinquency in Chicago. Many of the adolescents interviewed belonged to delinquent gangs; the others were members of non-delinquent peer groups within the same areas in which these gangs were found. These samples will first be compared to each other in terms of social origin. Then the Chicago samples will be re-examined against a much broader background provided by information from a national probability sample of some 800 youngsters—both Negro and white.[1]

Our initial task, then, is to offer a brief profile of the status of origin of groups of delinquent and non-delinquent urban adolescents.[2]

Our second focus concerns the problem of occupational goals—the employment expectations of the Chicago delinquents, their neighborhood controls, and also those young men in the national sample.[3]

Finally, variation in occupational goal levels will be related to certain aspects of local structures of opportunity.

Table 1 indicates the size and mean age of each category of respondent. Lower class boys interviewed in Chicago by the staff of the Youth Studies Program[4] are designated as either NG (Negro gang), WG (white gang),

[1] The Chicago samples were surveyed by the Youth Studies Program of the University of Chicago (now located at Washington State University). The National Institute of Mental Health financed the collection of this portion of data (M–3301). The national data were made available by the National Opinion Research Center. The Carnegie Corporation provided funds for the larger study of which the adolescent and young adult sample is a part.

[2] There is an extensive literature on the relationship between socio-economic status and delinquent behavior: cf. for example, Cletus Dirksen, *Economic Factors in Delinquency* (Milwaukee: Bruce Publishing Co., 1948); Ernest W. Burgess, "The Economic Factor in Juvenile Delinquency," *Journal of Criminal Law and Criminology*, XLIII (May–June 1952), 29–40; Albert Cohen, *Delinquent Boys: The Culture of the Gang* (New York: Free Press of Glencoe, Inc., 1955); Richard A. Cloward and Lloyd E. Ohlin, *Delinquency and Opportunity: A Theory of Delinquent Gangs* (New York: Free Press of Glencoe, Inc., 1959); Albert J. Reiss, Jr., and Albert L. Rhodes, "The Distribution of Delinquency in the Social Class Structure," *American Sociological Review*, XXVI (October 1961), 720–32.

[3] Basic references concerning this problem include A. B. Hollingshead, *Elmtown's Youth* (New York: John Wiley & Sons, Inc., 1949), especially Chapter 2, pp. 267–88; H. H. Hyman "The Value Systems of Different Classes: A Social Psychological Contribution to the Analysis of Stratification," in Reinhard Bendix and Seymour M. Lipset, eds., *Class, Status and Power* (New York: Free Press of Glencoe, Inc., 1953), pp. 426–42; G. Knupfer, "Portrait of the Underdog," Bendix and Lipset, *op. cit.*, pp. 255–63; R. K. Merton, *Social Theory and Social Structure* (rev. ed.) (New York: Free Press of Glencoe, Inc., 1957), pp. 131–94.

[4] The Youth Studies Program was the research arm of the Detached Worker Program of the YMCA of Metropolitan Chicago. As street workers were assigned to additional gangs in this action program, research activities were also expanded. The

NLC (Negro lower class control), and WLC (white lower class control).
The mean age of these samples ranges, roughly, from sixteen to seventeen
years. Two additional groups provided by the National Opinion Research
Center include all Negro and white respondents, both male and female,
from a 1962 national probability sample of all persons aged seventeen to
twenty-four in the continental United States.[5] There is an age difference

Table 1

SAMPLE GROUPS: THEIR SIZE, MEAN AGE, AND SOURCES
OF THE DATA

Sample	Size	Age	Source	
NG	205	17.1	YSP	(Chicago)
WG	89	17.3	YSP	(Chicago)
NLC	89	16.3	YSP	(Chicago)
WLC	75	16.7	YSP	(Chicago)
Negro	111	20.3	NORC	(National)
White	692	20.2	NORC	(National)

between the Chicago and national samples—a mean difference of about
three to four years. As we proceed it will become obvious that *other* differences exist as well. We will not argue for strict comparisons at every point,
but we will compare the sets of data wherever it seems appropriate to do so.

Our measure of social status in this report—both status of origin and
expected status—is a quantitative index of social position developed by
Duncan.[6] The unit scored is an occupation; the score assigned to any

interviewing phase of the Youth Studies Program was thus a rather long-term operation, beginning in the summer of 1960 and lasting well into 1961. For an overview
of all data gathering activities of the Youth Studies Program and a summary of
early findings, cf. James F. Short, Jr., "Street Corner Groups and Patterns of Delinquency: A Progress Report," *American Catholic Sociological Review,* XXIV (Spring
1963), 13–32.

[5] The actual case base of the National Opinion Research Center sample is 698.
Certain categories of adolescents were systematically undersampled, however, and a
weighting procedure brought the case base to 813. In this weighted sample there are
111 Negroes and 692 whites available for analysis (see Table 1). In the early tables
of this analysis, data derived from females as well as males are employed as we
attempt to fix SES norms for each race. This was done in an attempt to compensate
for the general underrepresentation of males in the national sample, probably due
to the effect of military service. It should be noted that there is no difference in the
SES position of the males and females sampled by NORC. If only males were to
appear in the final columns of Table 3, for example, neither figure would vary by
more than two tenths of a decile and all comparisons would attain exactly the same
levels of statistical significance.

[6] Duncan's scale is presented in Albert J. Reiss, Jr., *Occupations and Social Status*
(New York: Free Press of Glencoe, Inc., 1962), pp. 263–75.

occupation is a function of both the education attained and the income received by all males so employed in the civilian labor force in 1950. Duncan has provided the decile rank of 425 occupations, indicating the particular tenth of the labor force into which the position falls. A selected list of these is presented in Table 2. While only mean decile ranks will appear in the tables to follow, more exact gradations can be inferred from the final column of the table, which presents the original index scores on which the decile ranking is based.

Turning to Table 3 and to the initial topic of substantive interest, let us first examine the social position of the families of the Chicago adolescents.

Table 2
SELECTED OCCUPATIONS BY DECILE RANK AND SOCIO-ECONOMIC INDEX

Occupation	*Decile*	*Socio-Economic Index*
Lawyer	10	93
Manager—banking and finance	10	85
Electrical engineer	10	84
Accountant	10	78
Social worker	9	64
Real estate agent	9	62
Athlete	9	52
Sales clerk	8	47
Electrician	8	44
Policeman	8	40
TV repairman	7	36
Plumber	7	34
Piano tuner	7	33
Bus driver	6	24
Welder	6	25
Shipping clerk	6	22
Auto mechanic	5	19
Bartender	5	19
Operative (manufacturing)	4	17
Waiter	4	16
Cook	4	15
Laborer (metal industry)	3	14
Farm owner or tenant	3	14
Elevator operator	2	10
Taxi driver	2	10
Janitor	2	9
Construction laborer	2	7
Porter	1	4

Section A of the table is staggered to facilitate comparison of the recorded

Table 3

OCCUPATION OF MAIN EARNERS

A. MEAN DECILE RANKS

NG	*WG*	*NLC*	*WLC*	*Negro*	*White*
3.6		4.2		3.9	
(196)		(82)		(99)	
	5.0		5.1		5.9
	(88)		(75)		(664)

		N = 441			N = 763
		NA 17			NA 40
	Total N (Chicago)	458		Total N (national)	803

B. INTERGROUP COMPARISONS: LEVEL OF SIGNIFICANCE
OF OBSERVED DIFFERENCES

Sample	*NG*	*WG*	*NLC*	*WLC*	*Negro*	*White*
NG		.05	.05	.05	NS	.05
WG			.05	NS	.05	.05
NLC				.05	NS	.05
WLC						.05
Negro						.05
White						—

mean scores. Looking initially at the Negro samples we can observe a significant difference in the status of origin of gang and non-gang Negro boys. The pattern is *not* repeated among white adolescents, where the difference is negligible. A more systematic relationship can be seen in the superior position that all white groups hold over their Negro peers. Further comparisons are available from the NORC material.

In the national survey all respondents were requested to identify their father's occupation or, if he were deceased, his final occupation before his death. In Chicago, because we correctly anticipated a high rate of family disorganization, respondents without working fathers were permitted to identify as their breadwinner the adult who had most recently supported them, even if they were not directly related.[7] For both sets of adolescents, therefore—Chicago and national—interviewing procedures were adapted

---

[7] Note that this procedure allows us to assign an SES score to those breadwinners currently receiving public welfare: the decile rank of the breadwinner's *most recent* type of employment. In areas where the public assistance rate is as high as 165.5 per thousand, it became necessary to devise *some* procedure, however abitrary, to locate these families on the SES decile scale. Duncan discusses comparable problems in Reiss, *op. cit.* pp. 146–51.

to the populations under study. As a result we cannot report complete overlap of procedure, but the SES scores obtained are at least roughly comparable. Returning to Table 3 we note that the relatively deprived position of Negroes is even more pronounced in the national comparison. Inspecting the full range of scores for the Negro groups we note an unexpected pattern. In terms of status of origin, neither our gang nor our lower class samples can be differentiated from the larger Negro young adult population; yet, as already noted, the groups from Chicago *can* be differentiated from one another. Thus, for Negro adolescents above and beyond their original status disadvantage (compared to whites), there is a *second* sorting out process *within their urban communities* which operates to assign only the most deprived youngsters to delinquent careers. In terms of status of origin these delinquents are no different from Negroes generally, but they *are* different from those boys in their local communities who are *not* in gangs. Among whites the picture is reversed. *Both* Chicago samples fall *below* the national white status norm; yet compared to each other they are *equivalent* in status of origin. For white adolescents, then, the SES sorting process related to delinquency would seem to occur only *once,* and then it is within a more inclusive status universe. These data suggest that if social status is to be employed as an explanatory variable in theories of delinquent behavior, then *race* must be controlled as a conditional variable whatever the social level—community or nation—at which explanations are sought.

The balance of this paper explores certain dimensions of the occupational expectations of lower status adolescents. For these purposes we abstract from Table 3 only one central finding: making all possible between-group comparisons, it is obvious that *all categories of Negroes rank below all categories of whites in terms of social status.*

Let us now address the question of occupational expectations, or goals. Here we borrow definitions from Empey;[8] we shall examine these goals in both an *absolute* and *relative* sense. *Absolute* goals refer simply to the occupational level an adolescent defines as attainable; *relative* goals specify the *amount of mobility beyond status of origin* which our respondents expect to achieve. For the Chicago samples both measures have been derived from answers to the question: "...thinking realistically, what sort of work do you actually think you'll be doing ten years from now?" The answers received are presented in the first four columns of Table 4. Three major patterns emerge from these data.

First, all groups expect to attain positions well above their present status. Second, within both the gang and non-gang categories racial differences

---

8 LaMar T. Empey, "Social Class and Occupational Aspiration: A Comparison of Absolute and Relative Measurement," *American Sociological Review* XXI (December 1956), 703–9.

are now either less pronounced or actually reversed. Note in particular that non-gang Negroes expect to occupy higher occupational levels than non-gang whites.

Finally, with race controlled, the expectations of gang boys are lower than those of non-gang boys, considering their status of origin. There is a difference of six-tenths of a decile between the initial status of gang and non-gang Negro boys; yet the observed difference in their occupational expectations is more than three times this figure. The fact of gang membership appears to be associated with a relative reduction of occupational goal levels.

Table 4

OCCUPATIONAL EXPECTATIONS

A. MEAN DECILE RANK

NG	WG	NLC	WLC	Negro	White
5.3		7.2		7.2	7.9
(204)		(39)		(29)	(224)
	5.9		6.8		
	(87)		(75)		

N = 455		N = 253	
		NA (female)	447
NA (expectations)	3	NA (indefinite)	71
Total N (Chicago)	458	NA (expectations)	32
		Total N (national)	803

B. INTERGROUP COMPARISONS: LEVEL OF SIGNIFICANCE
OF OBSERVED DIFFERENCES

Sample	NG	WG	NLC	WLC	Negro
NG		.05	.05	.05	—
WG			.05	.05	—
NLC				NS	—
WLC					—
White					→ NS

Among these findings there is no obvious reason to select any one as intrinsically more meaningful than any other. The most *surprising* finding, however, concerns the extremely high goal levels of the Negro adolescents. Given the inexperience of our respondents as objects of survey research, and acknowledging the possibility that some of them might have willfully distorted their responses, it was inevitable that the general problem of reliability should force itself upon our attention. Could similar results be obtained from other, perhaps more representative, groups of youngsters?

The NORC material answers this question, although it approaches the problem somewhat differently. All respondents in the national survey were dichotomized into two groups—those with quite concrete notions concerning their anticipated occupational fields and those whose plans were at least somewhat indefinite. The question, "What do you think you'll probably end up doing?" was asked of only the "definites"—those young people already committed to a particular line of work.

The answers given by all Negro and white males to this item are presented in the fifth and sixth columns of Table 4. Please note that the question was *not* asked of all respondents and that *no* females appear in this tabulation. These figures *cannot* be compared to those available for the Chicago samples, but they can quite appropriately be compared to each other. The statistical comparison is available in section B of the table, and we note that the Chicago findings are confirmed. *The goals of these young men, Negro and white, are not significantly different.*

Since we already know that the racial groups differ quite sharply in status of origin, we can perhaps correctly anticipate their performance in terms of *relative expectations*—the distance *beyond their status of origin* that the youngsters expect to move. The appropriate subtractions were performed on all individuals for whom both measures were available; the resulting mean decile ranks—measures analagous to the notion of social or occupational distance—appear in Table 5. Again, let us maintain a clear distinction between our sources of data: the four Chicago samples can be compared *only* to each other; and NORC's whites and Negroes can also be compared *only* to each other.

Table 5

DISPARITY SCORES: OCCUPATIONAL EXPECTATIONS—
MAIN EARNERS' OCCUPATION
A. OBSERVED DISPARITY IN DECILES

NG	WG	NLC	WLC		*Negro*	*White*
1.7		3.1				
(195)		(82)			3.2	1.8
					(27)	(215)
	0.8		1.7			
	(86)		(75)			

	N = 438				N = 242	
					NA (female)	447
NA (expectations)	3				NA (indefinite)	71
					NA (expectations)	32
NA (father's					NA (father's	
occupation)	17				occupation)	11
Total N (Chicago)	458				Total N (national)	803

B. INTERGROUP COMPARISONS: LEVEL OF SIGNIFICANCE
OF OBSERVED DIFFERENCES

Sample	NG	WG	NLC	WLC	Negro
NG		.05	.05	NS	—
WG			.05	NS	—
NLC				.05	—
WLC					—
White	──────────────────────────────────────→				.05

Both sets of comparisons, however, yield the same over-all pattern: within all comparable categories Negroes anticipate a substantially greater amount of upward mobility than whites. For the Chicago samples, the difference is most pronounced among non-delinquent boys, suggesting from yet another perspective that, within these racial groupings, gang membership is incompatible with extreme mobility expectations. As before, the NORC data serve to resolve any problem that may be raised concerning the reliability of the over-all racial trend.

Our findings may now be reconsidered in terms of the problem of status deprivation, or position discontent, as it may be related to juvenile delinquency. According to Albert Cohen[9] and the more recent work of Cloward and Ohlin,[10] one important element in the genesis of lower class delinquency lies in the frustration of the early motivations of deprived youngsters to achieve conventional success. Cohen attaches special importance to the reaction of such adolescents to situations where middle class values and behaviors are paramount. Cloward and Ohlin broaden this perspective to include settings related to illegitimate channels of opportunity. In both formulations subcultural delinquency is conceived to an important degree as *a reaction to actual or anticipated conventional failure.*

From our own data it is clear that high mobility expectations are widespread among adolescents. Although there are variations related to social origins, race, and gang membership, at this early age no group can be characterized as giving serious thought to the possibility of actual failure.

Albert Cohen clearly specifies how delinquent behavior might ultimately effect these attitudes. He would argue, we think, for a widespread *denial* of the value of such behavior among delinquents. Even granting that our gang members appear to be less committed to the norm of mobility than others, our data do not reflect a "reaction formation" against the middle class concern with occupational mobility. To the contrary, we find general acceptance among all lower class adolescents of the supposedly middle class dictum that substantial social mobility be achieved. To the extent that the works of Cohen and Cloward and Ohlin (and the relevant work of Walter

---

9 Cohen, *op. cit.*
10 Cloward and Ohlin, *op. cit.*

Miller[11]) offer competing formulations in this area, the Chicago findings are most congruent with Cloward and Ohlin. Yet the "fit" is far from perfect, for nowhere in their work have we been led to anticipate the *extreme emphasis placed upon social mobility by all Negro adolescents.*

A "rational" model of factors influencing differential goal levels would stress differential structures of opportunity. To Cloward and Ohlin the existence of such opportunities implies "access to appropriate environments for the acquisition of the values and skills"[12] associated with adult roles. We have attempted to specify several dimensions of such opportunities and, after defining these, we will note their effectiveness in inducing significant variation in legitimate occupational goal levels.

Lipset and Bendix have argued that "all factors which intensify the involvement of a child with his parents or other adults...increase the likelihood that he will be upwardly mobile."[13] At first glance this statement rings true. Yet any person familiar with the urban slums in which the Chicago groups were found would certainly demand qualifications. For these youngsters it seems more sensible to expect a state of *alienation* between upwardly mobile adolescents and a major segment of their adult environments. The mobile adolescent in these communities is more likely to be highly *selective* in his contacts with older persons; he may be forced to become a "free agent" ready to abandon virtually all close ties at the local level, perhaps including those to his own family.

With these qualifications in mind, let us briefly hypothesize a profile of the mobile lower class adolescent, employing five variables derived from the recent literature, especially from the work of Cloward and Ohlin. This profile will then be tested against data provided by the Youth Studies samples from Chicago.

FATHER FIGURES

Initially, let us consider the family. The general conclusion of previous research in this area suggests that the presence of a strong father figure within the home is fatal to high mobility goals.[14] The father—the person who is probably the most *salient* occupational role model in the environment of the child—inspires extreme mobility goals only when he does not dominate family interaction. Given the unique character of the Chicago

---

11 Walter B. Miller, "Lower Class Culture as a Generating Milieu of Gang Delinquency," *Journal of Social Issues,* XIV (April 1959), 5–19.

12 Cloward and Ohlin, *op. cit.,* p. 148.

13 Seymour M. Lipset and Reinhard Bendix, *Social Mobility in Industrial Society* (Berkeley and Los Angeles: University of California Press, 1960), pp. 239–40.

14 Cf., for example, W. Lloyd Warner and James C. Abegglin, *Big Business Leaders in America* (New York: Harper & Row, Publishers, Inc., 1955); Fred L. Strodtbeck, "Family Interaction, Values and Achievement," in McClelland, *et al., Talent and Society* (Princeton, N.J.: D. Van Nostrand Co., Inc., 1958), Chap. 4, pp. 135–94.

samples, we are in a position to explore the effect of extreme cases of inhibited male authority—that is, the effect of the complete *absence* of a man in the home.

From the questionnaire material we have identified all boys living in households which contained any male at least fifteen years older than the child. These adult males we term "father figures," although there is at times no relationship by blood between these persons and the boys we interviewed. They are simply persons who are in a position to function as a father in providing an initial definition of an occupational role. In considering the influence that such individuals might have upon mobility expectations, it was hypothesized that *youngsters exposed to the influence of adult males in their homes would tend to entertain lower occupational goal levels.* It was thus anticipated that the absence of a father figure would encourage expectations of upward mobility. Attention is directed to the first column of Table 6, which indicates, for each Chicago sample, the percentage of youngsters living in homes containing a male who qualifies as a "father figure" by this definition.[15]

Table 6

PER CENT OF EACH CHICAGO SAMPLE GIVING A POSITIVE
RESPONSE TO OPPORTUNITY STRUCTURE VARIABLES

Sample	Father Figure Present (1)	Know High Status Adults (2)	Local Role Model (3)	Legitimate Opportunities Open (4)	Illegitimate Opportunities Open (5)
NG	51.2	26.2	47.3	25.9	70.2
	(203)	(172)	(201)	(205)	(205)
WG	66.7	32.2	44.1	31.5	41.6
	(87)	(59)	(86)	(89)	(89)
NLC	64.0	50.0	31.4	43.8	55.1
	(89)	(82)	(86)	(89)	(89)
WLC	74.6	53.0	52.0	68.9	28.4
	(75)	(66)	(75)	(74)	(74)
N	454	379*	448	457	457
NA	4		10	1	1

Total N = 458

* Asked only of groups participating in community studies.

---

15 The percentage distribution of boys living with their natural fathers is also of interest and runs as follows: NG = 44 per cent; WG = 64 per cent; NLC = 42 per cent; WLC = 71 per cent. By subtracting these figures from the per cent with "father figures" we can generate a gross index of each sample's *rate of recovery* from broken homes. The NLC sample is outstanding in this respect. Comparison with Table 6 indicates that 22 per cent of these youngsters were living in homes containing adult males who were *not* their natural fathers. An extensive analysis of the families of all respondents has been undertaken by Ray A. Tennyson of Washington State University.

HIGH STATUS ADULTS

Soon after our interviewing program was begun it was decided to undertake community studies of the areas in which our groups resided, using for respondents adults who were nominated by the boys themselves. Accordingly, most of the Chicago youngsters were asked to identify the *four* adults with whom they had "the most contact." Each boy's immediate family was excluded from nomination though they might be nominated by another boy, and the names of persons—such as school teachers—who did not live in the same neighborhoods as the boys were accepted. We aimed specifically at those adults outside the boy's family whom he knew well enough to identify. The occupation of each nominee was determined and coded according to the Duncan index.

The decision to prepare these inventories of adults was somewhat delayed in terms of the adolescent interviewing program, yet some 379 respondents, or 83 per cent of the lower class adolescents interviewed, contributed the names, addresses, and occupations of those older persons with whom they had especially high contact. Our coverage is virtually complete except for a number of Negro and white gang boys who were among those first contacted by our interviewers. The second column of Table 6—"Know High Status Adults"—indicates the per cent of each adjusted sample nominating three or four adults who could be ranked above the mean national socio-economic (or occupational prestige) level as determined by the Duncan index. We hypothesized that *individuals maximizing contact with high status older persons would have higher goals than their peers.*

LOCAL ROLE MODELS

Most central to the Cloward-Ohlin thesis is the proposition that locally available role incumbents serve as models for the anticipated behavior of youngsters in their communities. To tap this particular dimension of adult-adolescent integration it should be useful to consider the number of boys who have taken for their occupational goal a job which is actually held by some local adult whom the boy knows. Accordingly, after each boy had identified the job he expected to hold in ten years, he was asked if he could think of anyone in his community who actually worked at such a position. The third column of Table 6 characterizes each Chicago sample according to the per cent of adolescents aiming for an occupation which is known to be held by at least one local adult familiar to the boy. The column is labeled "Local Role Model."

For lower class boys the selection of a local role model may well reflect a more pervasive commitment to their home communities. Accordingly, we hypothesized that *lower class boys integrated into their communities in this fashion will typically be oriented to lower occupational goals.*

Up to this point we have discussed differential contact with adults, and have proposed indices to measure it. We have assumed that such indices may provide useful measures of differential exposure to legitimate structures of opportunity. We turn now to local opportunities *in general*—as the boys perceive them—and to their relation to personal occupational goal levels.

LEGITIMATE AND ILLEGITIMATE OPPORTUNITIES

Cloward and Ohlin dichotomize "opportunity structures" into legitimate and illegitimate realms. Our interview schedule contained a series of true-false items devised to test perceived access to these alternate avenues of achievement. Generally speaking, each major structure of opportunity, both *legitimate* and *illegitimate,* was approached with the question: is this route to success viewed as *presently accessible to neighborhood adolescents?* A summary scoring procedure was devised which enabled us to differentiate our samples into groups defining opportunities as either *open* or *closed*.[16] For present purposes legitimate and illegitimate opportunity structure items were scored separately, yielding *two* scores for each boy—one score for each avenue of achievement. The fourth and fifth columns of Table 6 indicate the per cent of each sample offering *open* definitions for legitimate and illegitimate opportunity structures, respectively.

The impact of such definitions on occupational goals is difficult to assess theoretically. To assume any significant impact at all, one must accept the proposition that perceived restrictions on group or general opportunity seriously effect *private* judgments of one's fate as an individual. The assumption seems safe enough at face value and we shall tentatively accept it. We would hypothesize that *high occupational goals are positively related*

---

[16] In scoring the true-false items the following procedure was employed: answers suggesting that opportunities were open were assigned 1 point; all other responses were scored 0 points. Ten items were combined in this fashion to yield a legitimate oppotunities open score with a possible range of 0 to 10. An illegitimate opportunities open score was developed in exactly the same manner. Seven items were employed which generated a range of scores from 0 to 7. The responses of special samples of middle class Negro and white adolescents were originally pooled with those of the gang and non-gang boys. After examining the scores for all boys interviewed (N = 537), cutting points were selected to yield groups of roughly equal size. This was done separately for each measure. Examples of the items employed to define perceptions of legitimate opportunities (where the false entry indicates perceptions of opportunities as *open* and assigned 1 point) are:

    a. College is too expensive for most of the guys in the area. (False)

    b. It's hard for a young guy in our area to get a good paying honest job. (False)

Examples of the items used to specify illegitimate opportunities (where true implies *open*) are:

    a. There are connections in this area for a guy who wants to make good money illegally. (True)

    b. Young guys can learn a lot about crime from older people in the area. (True) *to definitions of legitimate opportunities as open and illegitimate opportunities as closed.*

Let us summarize our hypotheses:

1. We anticipate that adolescents from households which do not contain an adult male will be oriented to relatively higher goal levels.

2. Adolescents who maximize contact with high status adults are expected to have higher occupational goals.

3. Lower class boys who have not selected local role models will have higher goals.

4. Finally, relatively high occupational goals will be positively related to definitions of legitimate opportunities as open and illegitimate opportunities as closed.

Father figures—The data indicate that adult household males are more often present in white than in Negro households. Negro gang boys illustrate an extreme case of family disorganization—a bare majority reporting father figures, in contrast to a minimum of 64 per cent among the other groups. Although even among the non-gang boys fathers or father substitutes are more frequently found among whites, the very generosity of our definition of "father figure" serves to focus special attention on the Negro gangs.

High status adults—Contact with high status adults is most characteristic of non-gang boys. While gang membership is most effective in reducing the probability of such contact, there is also a slight but consistent racial differential, with white boys reporting more such contact than Negroes.

Local role models—The extent to which boys expect to achieve an occupation which is held by a local adult does not vary systematically by either race or gang membership. Between one-third and one-half of each sample had accepted such a model. Considering the SES characteristics of main earners and other adults for these samples, however, we see no reason to abandon the assumption that such a choice is likely to reflect the distribution of role models that is actually available on the local scene.

Legitimate and illegitimate opportunities—Perceptions of the relative closure of opportunities show strong and consistent differences. Perception of *legitimate opportunities* is powerfully influenced by *gang status,* while perception of *illegitimate* avenues of achievement is powerfully influenced by *race*. The net effect of these patterns is such that among Negro gang boys illegitimate avenues of achievement are more than twice as salient as legitimate means, while lower class white boys, at the other extreme, find conventional rather than illegal paths to success more available by roughly the same ratio.

The unequivocal patterns generated by most of our opportunity structure variables suggest that they will prove to be effective predictors of differential goal levels *within* communities—or *within* samples. We note, however, that these opportunity structure variables shed no light on the major problem presented by our earlier findings. That is, they do not explain the extremely high goal levels of deprived Negroes. We must therefore abandon the question at this point, leaving it to future research.

Our final task is to observe the effect of our opportunity structure variables *within* samples, the degree to which such community level variables—with known distributions *across* samples—operate to account for *within*-sample differences in level of occupational goals. Relevant data appear in Table 7.

Our first three opportunity structure variables—concerning father figures, high status adult contacts, and local role models—can be placed under the general heading of *social relationships.* These three variables are taken as direct measures of exposure to legitimate channels of opportunity at the community level. Our final two variables are measures of the *perceptions* adolescents report concerning local opportunities—legitimate and illegitimate.

In three out of four instances hypothesis number one is confirmed— *boys without fathers or father substitutes are more frequently oriented toward higher levels of occupational success.* Yet the fact that Negro gang

Table 7

DECILE RANK OF OCCUPATIONAL GOALS BY OPPORTUNITY STRUCTURE VARIABLES: CHICAGO SAMPLES

Sample	Father Figure Present (1)		Know High Status Adults (2)		Local Role Model (3)		Legitimate Opportunities Open (4)		Illegitimate Opportunities Open (5)	
	Yes	No	Yes	No	Yes	No	Yes	No	Yes	No
NG	5.6		5.9		4.9		5.1		5.2	
		5.0		4.9		5.7		5.4		5.6
L.S.	.05		.05		.05		N.S.		N.S.	
WG	5.6		5.4		5.3		6.1		5.7	
		6.5		5.4		6.3		5.8		6.0
L.S.	.05		N.S.		.05		N.S.		N.S.	
NLC	6.7		7.5		6.7		7.4		7.3	
		8.1		6.6		7.4		7.1		7.1
L.S.	.05		N.S.		N.S.		N.S.		N.S.	
WLC	6.7		7.5		6.1		6.9		7.0	
		7.3		6.1		7.6		6.5		6.8
L.S.	N.S.		.05		.05		N.S.		N.S.	
N	454		379*		448		455		455	
NA	4				10		3		3	

Total N = 458

* Asked only of groups participating in community studies.

boys demonstrate both the highest incidence of such family disorganization and constitute a clear (and statistically significant) reversal of the trend for all other groups suggests that the rationale supporting our hypothesis may be re-examined with profit.

Our second hypothesis is also confirmed in three of four comparisons. Two of the observed differences are statistically significant and, with the exception of white gang boys, we may conclude *that adolescents who maximize contact with high status adults have higher occupational goals than their peers.*

Hypothesis 4 is confirmed by these data as well. *Goals are especially high for those lower class adolescents whose contacts and orientations are directed to persons and occupations beyond those represented within the local community.*

The observed effects of boys' perceptions of available opportunities are in the hypothesized direction in five out of eight instances. Given the dramatic percentage distributions of these variables across samples, however, one is struck by the fact that there were three reversals to the anticipated pattern and in no instance was the hypothesized difference sufficiently strong to achieve statistical significance. On one hand, we may point to a slight tendency for lower class adolescents to modify personal goals in terms of generally restrictive conditions on group mobility; yet the trend is slight enough to warrant some consideration of the possibility that lower class boys are also victims of a countervailing tendency to see themselves as personally somewhat immune to restrictions on their peers.

We are thus forced to reconsider two of our four original hypotheses. We shall introduce no new variables as we do this; our re-evaluation is therefore highly tentative, and offered in the hope of highlighting problems which demand more systematic research attention.

A review of all variables under consideration indicates that family organization, as such, is only tenuously related to the type of community-level influences which we have taken as our central concern. It may be useful, therefore, to reconsider the role that the family might play at this more inclusive level.

One such family role may be that of integrating family members into the local community. The image we offer here is that of a family, itself integrated into its local social context, acting to direct the attention and commitments of its children toward the immediate milieu. To perform this function most effectively the family inself should be stable. Here we do not use stability in its conventional sense. We mean instead that the family, to best perform as an integrating agent, should reflect that level of stability or type of organization which is prevalent and taken as normal at the community level. We assume that strategic aspects of community life are at least partially a function of that type of family organization locally prevalent, and it is hypothesized that for lower class adolescents extensive integration acts to minimize expectations of upward mobility.

Returning to Table 7 and to the three samples which behaved as hypothesized (WG, NLC, WLC), we would reinterpret our findings to this extent: families which most nearly approximate the locally prevailing type of household organization are best equipped to integrate their children into this larger social setting. When the integration that occurs is integration into a lower class milieu, it tends to be associated with a lowering of mobility expectations.

These speculations are, of course, little more than a preface for an examination of our one seemingly deviant group—the Negro gang sample. The literature on the Negro family consistently emphasizes its traditional matriarchal structure. Kvaraceus and Miller have described this particular type of social origin—the female-based household—as a family unit in which "a male acting in the father role is either absent from the home; only sporadically present; or, when present, only minimally or inconsistently involved in the support and raising of children."[17] For Negro gang boys, then, we might well ask "what constitutes a *typical* or normal family?" Half of these boys have "father figures," half do not, and we are led to believe that the proportion able to claim an adult household male *is likely to fluctuate widely over time.*

The hypothesis which is suggested is that the matriarchal family unit is "normal" for a Negro gang boy and, perhaps, the most stable form of household organization available in his environment. *As such, we expect that it should operate most effectively to integrate the adolescent into this environment and, therefore, to depress his occupational goals.*

Paradoxically, then, it is the Negro gang boy from a family which reflects the modal American type who expresses substantial mobility expectations. For other deprived but mobile youngsters the opposite condition obtains— their homes are likely to be "broken" by conventional standards. If one accepts the element of relativity which we have made the cornerstone of our interpretation (that the state of organization of household units must be examined in terms of community rather than national norms), it is obvious that *both groups of boys are products of ineffective families.* And these families are ineffective in a very special sense—they cannot maximize for themselves and for their sons "typical" social relations at the community level. Furthermore, because family and community do not mesh, they cannot effectively control adolescent allegiances. In situations such as these, adolescents may successfully *evade* acts of commitment to the local milieu

---

[17] William C. Kvaraceus and Walter B. Miller, *Delinquent Behavior: Culture and the Individual* (Washington, D.C.: National Education Association, 1951), p. 95.

and entertain options concerning certain types of behavior. They can at least dream of being upwardly mobile.[18]

Concerning perceptions of opportunities, let us briefly recapitulate our findings. It was noted that the availability of alternate avenues of achievement was defined quite differently among our samples. The distribution of legitimate means, as reported by the boys, was most effected by gang membership; the perception of illegal opportunities was most responsive to race. Both relationships were dramatic and implied that strong within-sample differences would also be responsive to such perceptions. Yet the observed within-sample effects were weak. We have underlined the fact that our measures were designed to reflect *definitions of common fate*—i.e., judgments that opportunities (of either type) were or were not available for *neighborhood youngsters as a group.* It appears that such judgments concerning general restrictions on group mobility *are only tenuously related to personal occupational expectations, at least within the lower class.*

Quite suggestive in this respect are the recent findings of Gordon and Short, employing data from the Youth Studies Program (yielded, in fact, by many of the same boys who were interviewed for this analysis). They noted that lower class boys tended to devaluate their peers:

---

[18] Our interpretation assumes that many important differences in community level interaction are associated with the SES differences already noted between gang and non-gang Negro adolescents. It is necessary, in fact, to maintain this assumption (which is partially supported by our data) while simultaneously acknowledging the fact that the two samples were drawn from the *same* communities. Our conception of the Negro neighborhoods in which these boys were found thus emphasizes their internal heterogeneity, and would stress such factors as overcrowding and artificial restraints on physical mobility in accounting for their more diverse SES "mix." These speculations are supported by data from the most comprehensive study of Chicago Negroes available—Otis and Beverly Duncan's *The Negro Population of Chicago* (Chicago: The University of Chicago Press, 1957). The Duncans employ the index of dissimilarity to specify differences in the areal distributions of occupational groups. Taking an extreme example, we note that the delta yielded in comparing professionals and laborers (both white and non-white) was 54. This indicates that 54 per cent of Chicago's professional workers would have to change their residence to make their spatial distribution identical to that of laborers. Considering only non-whites, the delta yielded was 33. If proportionately *fewer* non-white professionals would be displaced in such a movement, it is correct to infer that proportionately *more* of them are presently sharing their living space with laborers. The professional-laborer comparison is suggestive of a general trend that applies to other occupations as well. When all possible occupational comparisons are made, the mean index value for both races is 32.1; for non-whites it is 18.4. (The deltas for both races appear in Table 3 of the Duncan's "Residential Distribution and Occupational Stratification," *American Journal of Sociology,* LX (March 1955), 498. The figures for non-whites only appear in the larger work, *op. cit.,* Table 69, p. 295.) We recognize that there is a countervailing tendency which operates to draw substantial numbers of high status Negroes to the perphery of the "Black Belt"; this point is impressively documented by the Duncans. Our own research, however, underlines the significance of socio-economic heterogeneity *within* smaller areal units of Chicago's Negro ghetto.

...the lower the social level, the less "good" one described his peers as being....
[Also], it was noted that lower class and gang boys feel themselves to be "better"
than their peers, while middle class boys feel their peers are equal to or "better"
than themselves. This suggests an invidious comparison in which lower strata
boys see themselves as being not of the same sort as their peers and perhaps as
having, on the average, less of an inclination to cause trouble.[19]

Seeing oneself as having "less of an inclination to cause trouble" may be
still another aspect of viewing oneself as a knowing but uninvolved and
unaffected witness of those more general "troubles" that do occur. Yet to
be specified are those particular areas in which such disassociation from
peers is likely to be translated into actual behavior. Our own data suggest
that for lower class adolescents, occupational goals, at least, are apt to bear
little relation to one's image of what is likely to occur to others within the
local community.

More generally, what our opportunity structure variables have taught us
is that social relationships with adults make a *difference* in occupational
goal levels while perceptions of the mobility chances of neighborhood
peers do not. However strong their present commitment to the adolescent
culture, there is a strong implication that youngsters are highly responsive
to the influence of adults as they orient themselves to future occupational
roles.

Implications for Action

To the extent that the maintenance of high goal levels implies a readi-
ness among delinquents and other lower class boys to grow toward a better
life, action implications are clear. What is necessary is a sustained effort
to introduce a *measure of variety* into the *occupational horizons* of these
youngsters. For if mobility goals are to be heightened, then these adolescents
must be taught that better worlds exist and that these worlds are populated
with flesh-and-blood people with whom they may interact. Persons such
as detached workers and school teachers fit the bill quite nicely. The
problem lies in the task of getting close enough to the boys to be taken
seriously and in encouraging a sense of emulation and a willingness to seek
a more pervasive and final separation from the neighborhood milieu.

Gang boys have the additional handicap of their identification (by others
as well as themselves) and involvement with gang activities. Other data
from this same survey tell us that gang boys are less successful in school than
are their non-gang counterparts. Police data indicate much greater involve-

---

19 Robert A. Gordon and James F. Short, Jr., "Social Level, Social Disability and
Gang Interaction," unpublished manuscript (1963) Youth Studies Program (mimeographed).

ment in delinquency among gang than non-gang boys. The employment experience of these gang boys is extremely unstable.

In each of these areas of adjustment the gang is an important influence. The gang represents, in effect, a further tie to the neighborhood milieu which depresses occupational goals and, for a variety of reasons, increases involvement in delinquency. Observational data from the Youth Studies Program suggest that the gang actively tends to discourage serious discussion of goals in a number of areas—e.g., family planning and responsibility, employment, and school.[20] Students of the gang, at least since Thrasher,[21] have pointed to the fact that "long-term involvement in the 'free undisciplined' street life with money at hand from petty theft and with the days devoted to play was not exactly ideal preparation for the humdrum life of the job."[22] In addition, experience of the YMCA detached worker program in Chicago suggests that for some boys the hold of the gang is so strong that they will refuse or quit jobs which interfere with gang life, and that for others, long hours on the corner with its customary pursuits of wine, women, and "rep" are involved in tardiness and absenteeism which contribute to job failure.

The problem goes deeper than this, of course. For lower class boys, Negroes particularly and gang members particularly, available jobs are rarely above unskilled or semi-skilled levels, and job ceilings are painfully low. Opportunities for education and training, even if the boys remain in school, are inferior to those which are readily available to middle and upper class youngsters. While we do not have comparable observational data for non-gang boys, it seems likely that gang boys are more apt to have illegitimate role models and opportunities for at least minor positions in organized criminal pursuits. Even the latter are likely to pay more than the menial legitimate jobs which are available. The matter is complicated further by predatory credit practices which encourage boys who have dropped out of school and secured any type of job to incur indebtedness beyond their ability to manage. The quality of on-the-job experience for school dropouts is likely to be less conducive to adequate vocational preparation because of

---

[20] A dramatic example of gang disparagement of individually held conventional views of family planning and responsibility is reported in James F. Short, Jr., Fred L. Strodtbeck, and Desmond S. Cartwright, "A Strategy for Utilizing Research Dilemmas: A Case from the Study of Parenthood in a Street Corner Gang," *Sociological Inquiry*, XXXII (Spring 1962), 185–202. Similarly, detached workers and research observers have reported instances of devastating "razzing" by other gang members of individual members who wish to talk seriously of vocational plans and school.

[21] Frederic M. Thrasher, *The Gang* (Chicago: University of Chicago Press, 1927).

[22] David J. Bordua, "Delinquent Subcultures: Sociological Interpretations of Gang Delinquency," *Annals of the American Academy of Political and Social Science,* CCCXXXVIII (November 1961), p. 134.

the unstable nature of many such jobs (many are seasonal or in the "casual labor" category) and by reason of other hazards.[23]

Some of these problems go to basic characteristics of the society and require action at that level. Some can be addressed by programs working with gang boys, individually and collectively. The process of weaning boys away from the gang requires more than provision of a job. Boys can be helped to better vocational preparation, to more rational financial management, and to better skills in the interpersonal relations which may often disrupt job performance. Even more basic, in terms of the larger picture, gang boys can be given greater incentive for staying and performing well in school.[24] Boys can be given status as adults for "putting it down" (stopping fighting and other delinquency), and for helping other boys do the same.[25] In the long run, such programs seem likely to be more important to the adjustment of gang youngsters than are efforts which are concerned directly and immediately with delinquency prevention.

---

[23] Witness, for example, one of our Negro gang respondents who secured a job as a dishwasher, only to find that his two fellow employees were homosexuals who propositioned him almost immediately. He quit the job after talking the situation over with his detached worker, on the grounds that he felt quitting was better than giving in to his homosexual antagonists or "beating the shit out of them" and getting himself in trouble with the police.

[24] The Chicago YMCA program provides tutors from area colleges and gives trophies and other awards for school attendance, scholarship, and participation in extracurricular activities in much the same manner as it does for program-sponsored athletic activities.

[25] Again, the Chicago YMCA program provides an apposite example. Under terms of a grant from the Ford Foundation, gang leaders are paid small salaries to aid the program in its delinquency prevention activities. For a report of this and other aspects of the YMCA program, see Charles N. Cooper, "The Chicago YMCA Detached Workers: Current Status of an Action Program," in this book.

Delinquent Stereotypes of Probable Victims

HERMAN SCHWENDINGER

JULIA SCHWENDINGER

The Schwendingers' paper has several strengths not to be found elsewhere in this volume. First, it is theoretically oriented throughout. While some of the other papers use theoretical propositions extant in the field as foci for data collection, none attempts so directly as this work to build and amplify a particular conceptual viewpoint. Second, the Schwendingers have adopted experimental techniques to the testing of hypotheses—in this case dealing with rationalizations of deviant responses. This combination of experimental and field approaches to theory construction is, sad to say, unusual in the area of delinquency. The result of the combination in this instance is a definite step forward in our understanding of the delinquent's perceptual processes and sources of value reinforcement.

HERMAN and JULIA SCHWENDINGER, School of Criminology, University of California, Berkeley, California.

What values are held by delinquents? Are they similar or different from those of other youth? Is there a unique delinquent view of life? To date, these questions have been answered in divergent ways. Albert Cohen has suggested that delinquent values are the inverse of those held by middle class persons.[1] Solomon Kobrin speaks of two antithetical value systems in high delinquency areas; one held by delinquents, the other reflected in the activity of conforming youth.[2] Walter Miller presents a description of lower class youth concerned about being in trouble with the police and maintaining a tough, masculine image of themselves.[3] In Walter Miller's view, these values are continuous with traditional lower class culture. In contrast, Sykes and Matza stress the continuity between delinquent values and an ethos of prior leisure or upper class relationships.[4]

Most of these beliefs about the nature of delinquent values and views of life are predicated on the researcher's personal impressions, on a review of the literature, or on observations made by social workers. Thus, theoretical accounts of delinquent perspectives are generally marked by analysis of data from secondary sources, the presence of highly impressionistic categories, and the absence of controlled measurement. This state of affairs is primarily dictated by enormous difficulties in obtaining responses from delinquents under controlled experimental conditions.

In a previous paper we presented a study of experimentally controlled delinquent and non-delinquent verbal responses to the same set of conditions; namely, instructions to imagine themselves in a debate about victimizing a person.[5] The participants were instructed first to argue about, and then to decide to victimize particular kinds of people. The analysis focused on statements that might be made if an act of victimization were to be discussed and questioned among small groups of closely associated adolescents.

Thirty-nine role plays were conducted among fifty-four delinquent and non-delinquent youths.[6] Each role play enactment contained no less than three subjects. Almost all the fifty-four adolescents acted in three role plays each and performed a total of 162 roles. The delinquents were non-institutionalized youth and among them were boys who were currently

---

1 Albert K. Cohen, *Delinquent Boys* (New York: Free Press of Glencoe, Inc., 1955).

2 Solomon Kobrin, "The Conflict of Values in Delinquency Areas," *American Sociological Review*, XVI (October 1951), 653–61.

3 Walter B. Miller, "Lower Class Culture as a Generating Milieu of Gang Delinquency," *Journal of Social Issues*, XVI (1958), 5–19.

4 David Matza and Gresham M. Sykes, "Juvenile Delinquency and Subterranean Values," *American Sociological Review*, XXVI: 5 (October 1961), 712–19.

5 Herman and Julia Schwendinger, "Delinquent Stereotypes of Probable Victims, Part I," read at Pacific Sociological Association Conference, Sacramento, April 1962.

6 The delinquents were selected from lowest strata youth in a community. For definition of the term "lowest strata," see Herman Schwendinger, *The Instrumental Theory of Delinquency,* unpublished doctoral dissertation, University of California at Los Angeles, 1963.

active but non-apprehended thieves, drug users, and participants in acts of violence—to mention only a few of the types of illegalities involved.

Although the deviant status of these groups was known as a result of extensive participant observation of delinquent cliques, crowds, and clubs from different communities over several years, a questionnaire was administered which was composed of items developed by Nye and Short.[7] These items provided the degree to which the respondent admitted engaging in different types of thieving and fighting, up to the time the questionnaire was administered. The analysis of responses, as summarized in Table 1, indicates the increasing involvement in fighting and thievery as one moves from Group A to Group E.

Table 1

AVERAGE OF GROUP MEMBERS RESPONSES TO FIGHTING
AND THIEVING QUESTIONS

Group	Fighting Alone	Rank	Fighting Gang	Rank	Theft $2.00	Rank	Theft $2.00 to 5.00	Rank	Theft Over $50	Rank	Sum of Ranks
A	2.1	1	1.1	1	2.1	1	1.5	1	1.0	1	5
B	2.4	2	1.4	2	2.3	2	1.9	2	1.2	2	10
C	3.3	4	1.9	3	2.5	3	2.1	3	1.5	3	16
D	3.0	3	2.0	4	3.1	4	3.0	4	1.7	4	19
E	3.8	5	4.2	5	3.3	5	3.1	5	2.8	5	25

Rank Correlation: .97 (Kendall coefficient of concordance)

At the beginning of each role play some of the male subjects were instructed to argue for and against proposals to commit specified deviant acts. Those who were assigned roles against the deviant act will be referred to in this paper as *Objectors*. The role players justifying the act will be called *Proponents*. The participants were given the following instructions:

> I want you to act out this story; some teenagers are arguing over whether they should beat up an Outsider who insulted their club. An Outsider is someone outside their circle of friends. Those who are in favor of beating him up argue with the others about it. The others are finally *convinced* that the Outsider should be beaten up by the *entire* group.

The same general format was followed in additional enactments involving victimization of a Rich Teenager and a Businessman, with the following modifications in instructions:

---

[7] F. Ivan Nye and James F. Short, Jr., "Scaling Delinquent Behavior," *American Sociological Review*, **XXII** (June 1957), 326–31.

Some teenagers are arguing over whether to take advantage of a teenager in order to get money to go to Disneyland, or Pacific Ocean Park, or get club jackets. Those who are in favor...

Some teenagers are arguing over whether to rob a local businessman's store. Those who are in favor...

The role play dialogues were taped and transcribed and the dialogues of each group were analyzed.

In the earlier paper, referred to above, we presented findings which were felt to be contradictory to Sykes and Matza's interpretation of the function of delinquent rationalizations. It was pointed out that if these authors were correct, we would find some moral ambivalence, or a sensitivity to a "societal generalized other."[8] It was reasoned that if this sensitivity among delinquents exists, at least the delinquent Objectors would seize upon moral issues in challenging the legitimacy of the delinquent act. They would take the standpoint of the conventional moral perspective and utter such statements as "its not fair," "put yourself in the other guy's shoes," "he worked for his money and has a right to keep it," or "where would we all be if everyone stole from each other?" These utterances mirror the moral implications of the act which Sykes and Matza believe are situationally neutralized by delinquent rationalizations.

However, the *delinquent* Objectors were almost entirely concerned with tactical rather than moral issues. They countered the Proponent's arguments with such tactical problems as possible defeat at the hands of the Outsider's friends, apprehension by the police, or stakes too small for the risk involved in robbing the businessman. In contrast, it was in the dialogues of the *non*-delinquent Objectors that concern for moral issues was revealed.

Since the non-delinquent dialogues manifested the dynamics that Sykes and Matza believed would take place among delinquents, it was concluded from these findings that these authors, like our non-delinquent actors, might have unwittingly placed themselves in the roles of the delinquents. They may have fashioned their theoretical dynamics of delinquent behavior out of the moral concerns aroused while imagining themselves in these roles.

In the prior paper we also attempted to show that the moral utterances of delinquent and non-delinquent role players could only be explained by assuming the existence of two different working ethics, and two different modes by which moral utterances were structured. A mode of moral utterances consists of basic assumptions about the nature of human relationships which are deeply rooted in our culture and which usually unwittingly influence the form in which good reasons for conduct are shaped. For

---

[8] Gresham M. Sykes and David Matza, "Techniques of Neutralization: A Theory of Delinquency," *American Sociological Review*, **XXII** (December 1957), 664–70.

example, in earlier religious rhetorics deviant persons were often defined as instruments of the devil or persons fallen from the grace of God.

Today, most conforming persons construct their good reasons for moral activity out of what might be called a "rhetoric of egoism." A model of this rhetoric has been described more fully elsewhere.[9] There are other rhetorics organized around kinship, religious, political, or humanistic principles. However, the rhetoric of egoism is the most commonly shared mode of discourse, even though tacit shifts are often made between it and other modes. We will also refer to the rhetoric of egoism as the "conventional mode of moral discourse."

The underlying assumptions contained in the conventional moral rhetoric are that all men possess inherently egoistic interests; human relationships consist of atomistic individuals who are competitively arraigned against each other; and each man confronts the other as an equal and engages in myriad interactions in which goods and services are exchanged. The general form of these exchanges is an acquisitive, laissez-faire society. In this framework, the moral weight of any man's decision is seen to rest on free choice; therefore, he is responsible for his own actions. In this rhetoric, the weight of moral decision is placed on responsibility to fulfill obligations inherent in the definition of the rules governing conduct. Moral conduct is lawfully regulated conduct, and society would disintegrate without moral contracts. There are other principles which underlie this rhetoric, but these are sufficient to understand the relationship between the rhetoric of egoism and the mode by which the rationalizations of our non-delinquents were constructed.

The rhetoric of egoism can be used to justify legal activity. This is primarily achieved by placing emphasis on the legitimacy of the conventional *rules* of the game. In objecting to the illegal means *and* ends—for no means is completely divorced from ends—the users of this rhetoric invoke the legitimacy of "playing fair," of "going by the rules," "keeping up one's obligations," or "acting right because if we acted wrong then where would we be?"

Another way in which this rhetoric structures the utterances of those who support conventionally governed activity is by maintaining the moral worthiness of possible victims. (The "self" cannot easily justify abrogation of typical rules, especially when "others" have maintained their obligations.)

Finally, this rhetoric can be used to justify conventionally governed activity by reweighing the comparative value of the ends that may serve to legitimate an illegal means. One can then claim that the ends are not worth the price that may have to be paid for the use of an illegal means. In order to do this in the company of like-minded peers, one has to question the value

---

[9] Herman Schwendinger, *op. cit.* See Chapter 3, Section V, "Models of Rhetoric and Linguistic Structures of Moral Conversations," pp. 164–93.

of the ends served by the means. In the role plays, for example, the values of club honor and money must be brought into question.

The user of this rhetoric can also justify a questionable, deviant act in terms of this mode. This is done by construing a deviant act as an act of moral sanction, or as an act not governed by those rules stipulating "typical" responses, or as an act which is justified in terms of the value of the ends involved.

One can see examples of this use of the rhetoric in Cressey's study of men who have committed the act of embezzlement for the *first* time.[10] The paradigm which is used by some of them to structure the relation between themselves and their victims is that of two persons competing for a value. In their justifications, the victim is defined as a deviant in order to maintain a typically moral self-definition. In this sense, the criminal defines his criminal act as an act of a morally indignant man.

In the course of the role plays, the non-delinquent Proponents fashioned the image of the Businessman to be that of a "monopolistic miser" or a "dishonest merchant" who cheats his customers and therefore *deserves* to be victimized. The illegal act was defined as an act of moral indignation. In response to this, the non-delinquent Objectors countered with positive images of the victim; images of worthy, compassionate, and moral human beings.

Through a content analysis of the dialogues we found that it was the *non*-delinquent Objectors who structured their discourse in terms of the rhetoric of egoism. They were more likely to invoke the conventional rules governing conduct, to question the value of the ends to be served by the deviant act, to refer to the image of the victim in positive terms. On the other hand, the delinquent Objectors were more likely to raise the tactical issues, to *affirm* and not question the value of club honor or money even while objecting to the act, and to ascribe negative attributes to the victim.

In the main, the delinquents *were indifferent to* the concerns that seemed to have shaped the non-delinquent dialogues. We tried to show with these findings that a different kind of moral rhetoric structured the delinquent dialogues. We termed this the *instrumental rhetoric*.

In another mode of discourse, the humanistic rhetoric, persons are defined in terms of an ever widening potentiality. In the conventional, egoistic rhetoric, individuals are ideally seen in a contractually governed exchange relation bounded and judged in terms of their obligations. In the instrumental rhetoric, the images of human beings are stripped of all humanistic or conventional sentiment and their definitions are carved solely out of their utility for the private ends of those powerful enough to command their use. In its most systematic form, the instrumental rhetoric depicts a world of Givers and Takers, and the Takers are accorded superior status. The

---

10 Donald R. Cressey, *Other People's Money* (New York: Free Press of Glencoe. Inc., 1953).

habituated delinquent fashions his interpretation of the moral character of his act out of the assumption that successful persons achieve their positions in life primarily through the manipulation of less powerful human beings. This view of life emerges when habituated delinquents conceptually abstract the internecine character of their interpersonal milieu and generalize it to all social relationships. Older career delinquents often share this view of life.

Of course, not every delinquent subscribes to a systematic and general instrumental view, but such variation is unimportant on the level of analysis dealt with here. Even though there may be many delinquents who do not stereotype a large range of persons, it is suggested that these youth are publicly constrained to frame their reasons for acting in terms of an instrumental ideology. Otherwise these reasons would be evaluated either as false or incomprehensible by delinquent audiences. Further, even though they may not privately subscribe to their public utterances, it is suggested that they *act* on the basis of their public rather than their private vocabularies of motive.

We analyzed the statements of those who were given the role of Objectors to show that they were constrained to express those rationalizations which were believable from the standpoint of the working ethic of these groups. In this sense, for example, even though both delinquent and non-delinquent Objectors might have challenged the legitimacy of the act by referring to the victim as a person who did not deserve to be victimized—that is, by maintaining a positive image of the victim—the delinquents were more likely to say "I *know* he is a *punk*, but we shouldn't swing him because we'll get caught." There seemed to be a tacit agreement among the delinquents from the very beginning of the plays that the victim was a worthless human being.

This paper presents additional data that reinforce the assumption that delinquents tacitly hold a common attitude toward the victim. These data are based upon the use of semantic differentials to measure the existence of stereotypic definitions of victims.[11]

The theoretical reasoning that gave rise to the construction of the differ-

---

11 A stereotypic relation, as defined here, is a special case of an institutionalized role-axis. In this case, the definition of the other is fashioned so as to legitimate specific manipulations, often but not always illegal. Two major types of definitions exist. The first is fashioned out of the attributions of inferior virtues; the second is constructed solely along the dimension of the relative power that distinguishes the victimizer from the victim. This latter type is functionally more rational to the institutional structures that develop among older delinquents. We use the term "role-axis" as it is conceived by Ralph H. Turner, "Role-Taking: Process Versus Conformity" in *Human Relations and Social Processes: An Interactionist Approach,* ed. Arnold M. Rose (Boston: Houghton Mifflin Company, 1962), pp. 20–40. For application of this concept to criminal-victim role-axis, see W. Phillips, "Criminal Self-Conceptions and the Respectable Others," an unpublished manuscript. For the investigation of stereotypic conceptions of outgroup members under conditions of adolescent intergroup rivalry, see Muzafer Sherif and Carolyn W. Sherif, *Groups in Harmony and Tension* (New York: Harper & Row, Publishers, 1953).

entials is that delinquents tend to develop stereotypic definitions of social types early in their careers. However, *along with their deviant motives,* these definitions do *not* emerge *prior* to experiencing deviant behavior. Instead, they develop out of this experience.

As they engage in initial forms of deviant activity, youngsters legitimate their behavior by developing consensually validated images of victims. At this stage, some youth focus on the moral issues involved and fashion the images of the victim out of the conventional moral rhetoric. After this stage, however, the stereotypic images become standardized in the form of metaphors which catalogue persons by typical kinds of victim terms; words like Punk, Chump, Box, Pigeon, and Fag emerge and represent the standardization of the typical moral relations with the victim as perceived from the standpoint of the victimizer's ideology. These terms do not emerge in isolation from others, but rather through social processes in which peers are persuaded by prestigeful members to engage in deviant activity.

As such, these terms are created in the first place because they function as linguistic coordinates for collective activity. It is suggested that for most youth these terms function as symbolic coordinates for the individual, as part of his personal belief system, after the terms have been standardized in collective usage.

Most delinquents stereotype persons in the context of delimited situations. Certain honorific codes specify the conditions under which persons are legitimate objects of victimization. However, particularly under those conditions wherein illegal marketplace activities exist,[12] the career delinquent tends to define everyone as a probable victim; society itself is seen as one vast assemblage of instrumentally defined persons. The instrumental rhetoric obtains its most systematic form under these marketplace conditions, and even in-group members are stereotyped in the proverbs and maxims that abound among these youth. Examples of pithy commentaries on the nature of reality are:

> It's fuck your buddy week, fifty-two weeks of the year.
> Do unto others as they would do unto you. . .only do it first.
> If I don't cop (steal) it. . .somebody else will.
> You know man, everybody's got their little game.

To obtain evidence of the existence of stereotyping processes among the delinquents, three semantic differentials were presented to the subjects prior to any hint as to the nature of the role plays. These differentials contained

---

12 Julia and Herman Schwendinger, "The Illegal Marketplace Among Adolescents," read at Pacific Sociological Association Conference, Portland, Oregon, May 1963.

possible meanings of the types of persons who served as the victims. We shall refer to these differentials as the Outsider, Rich Teenager, and Businessman differentials.

The subjects were asked to define an "average" Outsider, Rich Teenager, or Businessman on the differential. Thus, the first differentials defined these persons as general types. A differential was then presented to them after the decision to victimize was reached and the subjects were asked to respond to it from the viewpoint of the actor whose role they played. These differentials corresponded to the specific plays; the Outsider differential was given to the role players after the enactment about the Outsider, the Rich Teenager differential after the enactment about the Rich Teenager, and so on. Finally, after the actors had filled out the differential the second time, they were asked to respond to a third differential of the same type. At this third time, they responded to the differential from their own personal perspective—that is, as they "really" saw the social type. Usually, the subjects would complain that they did this the first time. However, we insisted that they do it again.

In brief, the subjects filled out three differentials. Each social type was defined as an "average" type prior to the instruction for the first play; that is, players were not to think of a particular individual. Then after each play, a differential based on the victim represented in the play was defined from the standpoint of the actor. When this was done, we asked the subjects to define the type of victim from their personal point of view.

The differentials were constructed in the following way: we obtained adjectives from a selected group of delinquent "jive studs" who described the following types in the delinquent lexicon—the Punk, the Chump, and a powerless Dealer. Once this was done, we attached an antonym secured from our informants to each adjectival term. These polar adjectival dimensions were used as the semantic dimensions of the differentials. The dimensions which the informants used to describe the Punk were used for the Outsider differential, the terms based on the word Chump were used for the Rich Teenager differential, and those related to the Dealer were used for the Businessman differential. The words Punk, Chump, and Dealer did not appear at all on the differentials. Rather, the semantic dimensions which could be used to define these terms appeared under the words: Outsider, Rich Teenager, and Businessman.

For example, the Outsider could be defined as a "worthless," "untrustworthy," "cowardly" person who "should be taken advantage of" and who "deserves no sympathy." These were the most negative meanings possible in defining this type. On the other hand, the Outsider could be defined in opposite terms: as a "valuable," "trustworthy," "courageous" person who "should not be taken advantage of" and who "deserves sympathy."

By standardizing the response scores that most closely approximated the negative meanings at zero, we obtained a differential profile score that represented the same meanings that had been used to define a Punk, or Chump, or Dealer. All other profile scores were also standardized so that they would range between the most negative and positive meanings; any actual score represented a quantitative distance from the standard stereotypic score—i.e., zero.

The first hypothesis tested with the use of this instrument was that before the role play instructions were first given to the actors, delinquent groups would tend to stereotype the Outsider, Rich Teenager, and Businessman (when defined as general social types) more negatively than would the non-delinquents. This hypothesis is confirmed in Table 2.

Table 2

GROUP MEANS OF STANDARD STEREOTYPE
FIRST DIFFERENTIAL SCORES

Differential	Group A	Rank	Group B	Rank	Group C	Rank	Group D	Rank	Group E	Rank
Outsider	8.95	1	8.51	2	7.96	3	6.93	4	6.35	5
Rich teen	6.15	2	7.14	1	5.78	3	3.19	5	3.70	4
Businessman	5.52	1	5.05	2	4.81	3	3.35	4	3.30	5
Sum of ranks		4		5		9		13		14

Rank correlation: .91 (Kendall coefficient of concordance).

The range of scores possible for any differential is dependent upon the number of semantic dimensions it contains. The Outsider differential contained five dimensions and the range of scores could vary from zero to 13.42. The Rich Teenager differential contained four dimensions and the range was from zero to 12.0. The Businessman differential contained three dimensions and the range was from zero to 5.19.[13]

The mid-points of the differentials (6.7, 6.0, and 5.1) represent the undecided boundary which separates the positive from the negative profiles. It can be seen that the delinquent responses, although more negative than the non-delinquent ones, are either clustered around the "undecided" mid-point and therefore represent problematic concepts to the delinquents, or they are on the negative side of the mid-point.

We have indicated that the role plays performed by the delinquents began with a tacit assumption regarding the stereotypic nature of the victim. In light of this, whether or not the social types were problematic—that is, as

---

13 The dimensions of the Rich Teenager differential were: Hep(wise)-Gullible, Can be Used-Can't be Used, Flunkey-Independent, Sympathetic-Unsympathetic. The dimensions of the Businessman were: Unselfish-Out for Himself, Dishonest-Honest, Sympathetic-Unsympathetic.

they appeared prior to the plays where they were defined in terms of "undecided" responses—we would expect the delinquents to sharply define the types negatively as actors when the role plays were terminated.

We also have indicated in our analysis that the non-delinquents, confronted by the problem of legitimating their deviant decision, constructed images that legitimated such a decision out of the rhetoric of egoism.

It is assumed that the symbolic content that has been long standardized in the development of many delinquents is now created by the non-delinquents in their role plays. It was expressed, argued about, and standardized in their dialogues. For a short moment they were like new delinquents who developed categories of the victim in some ideal isolation from older deviant youth.

In line with these interpretations, the second hypothesis is that all groups, delinquent and non-delinquent, will define the victim more stereotypically at the end of the role play, when they respond to the second differential as actors. Table 3 indicates that all groups do shift negatively without exception.[14]

Table 3

DIFFERENCE BETWEEN GROUP MEANS OF SEMANTIC DIFFERENTIALS ADMINISTERED BEFORE (FIRST DIFFERENTIAL) AND AT THE END (FROM THE VIEWPOINT OF THE ACTOR) OF THE ROLE PLAY

Group	Differential	First	Second (Actor)	Difference
A	Outsider	8.948	4.609	−4.339
	Rich teen	6.151	4.588	−1.563
	Businessman	5.519	3.503	−2.016
B	Outsider	8.510	5.340	−3.170
	Rich teen	7.130	4.780	−2.350
	Businessman	5.050	2.510	−2.499
C	Outsider	7.955	4.895	−3.060
	Rich teen	5.782	4.193	−1.589
	Businessman	4.808	4.531	−0.277
D	Outsider	6.930	0.110	−6.820
	Rich teen	3.192	0.560	−2.632
	Businessman	3.345	3.170	−0.175
E	Outsider	6.350	4.930	−1.420
	Rich teen	3.700	2.190	−1.510
	Businessman	3.300	2.848	−0.452

Summary: All groups shifted negatively toward greater stereotypy.

[14] The lower magnitude of the negative shifts among delinquents is an artifact. Since the delinquent differentials were less positive to begin with, the degree to which the shifts were possible is smaller than the non-delinquent shifts.

The third hypothesis, which involves the selective reinforcement effects of the role play experiences and the theory underlying it, cannot be discussed within the limits of this paper.

Certain theoretical observations and conclusions can be drawn from this study.

The psychoanalytic tradition has long pointed to the discrepancy between the justifications that persons express for their action and the "real" underlying motives. However, while the psychoanalysts utilize the frustrated motive as the independent variable for deviant behavior, Sykes and Matza point instead to the rationalization. On one level, both these authors and the psychoanalysts fragment the motive and the rationale as a "mechanism" or "technique" which expiates individual guilt, or, in Sykes and Matza's terms, "neutralizes the moral implications of the act." But on another level, while utilizing similar components in their scheme, one theoretical approach uses the rationale as the causal locus, while the other uses the frustrated motive.[15]

In order to ascribe a causal role to the rationalization, Sykes and Matza indicate that other symbolic relationships—such as values, moral imperatives, or attitudes of delinquents—are similar to those of "dominant society." In their words:

> It is by learning these techniques [of neutralization] that the juvenile becomes delinquent *rather* than by learning moral imperatives, values or attitudes standing in direct contradiction to those of the dominant society.[16]

We have tried to show that if dominant society is mirrored in the moral standpoint of our non-delinquents, then differences in values, moral impera-

---

[15] The major theories of delinquency today contain references to the *necessary* function of repression or "neutralization" of guilt in the development of delinquent careers. However, we feel that such processes, while important in some cases, are still not necessary for understanding factors effecting other delinquent career-lines. Some youth are ideologically marginal and subscribe to both conventional and instrumental perspectives simultaneously. Their guilt is never fully "neutralized" throughout their entire career. Because important interests are at stake, they act in consort with delinquent others irrespective of the guilt they feel. Other youth (very early in their play group experiences) come into contact with stereotypic definitions that have been highly stabilized in the community for many years. They quickly learn these definitions from older youth. In fact, delinquent relationships around them may be so stabilized and pervasive, that the age-graded transition in perspectives occurs with very little concern as to contradictory moralities. Finally, there exist youth who have never subscribed to a conventional moral perspective to begin with. Instead, they have learned to define conventional moral relations in stereotypic terms (and all "respectable" persons as hypocrites) from earliest family experience. These youth do not repress guilt that is allegedly aroused by the thoughts of their immoral conduct. They have never felt guilty in the first place.

[16] Sykes and Matza, *op. cit.*, p. 666; our emphasis.

tives, definitions of persons, and mode by which rationalizations are structured exist between our non-delinquent and delinquent subjects. This has been shown in the analysis of the collective rhetorics of these youths.

A relationship between the institutional arrangements within which delinquent biographies are enacted and the institutions of society at large can be shown once one has stipulated the institutional sources of humanistic, religious, egoistic, and instrumental rhetorics. To do this, one must analyze the very different kinds of moral relationships that exist within our society. These moral relationships do not have their locus within small groups of frustrated individuals or imitative patterns of past leisure class relationships. They emerge in concrete religious, economic, political, and other institutions, and they cut across class lines.

In light of Davis and Moore's suggestion that social class relations of any society be analyzed in terms of dominant institutional frameworks,[17] one might say that the structuring of social class relations primarily around values of competition and invidious ownership of commodities, combined with the use of these values as guides to the estimation of human worth, represents the pervasive influence of economic institutions on the formation of status groups in our society. Among Elmtown adults, for example, Hollingshead has pointed out that occupational achievement, stocks, bonds, property, and money are the prevailing criteria by which honor is estimated.[18]

Youth, however, are not directly involved in economic institutions. The institutional effects of the market which they experience are mediated through the occupational ideologies subscribed to by their parents, or by mass communications media. They perceive and interpret life from the standpoint of their own childish consciousness, and instead of conventional property, it is styles of dress, transistor radios, customized cars, and owning relationships with the opposite sex that are among the many commodities serving as guides to human worth.

From seven to fourteen years of age, status groups begin to emerge among youth who give preeminent subscription to values of this sort. By junior high, the system composed of these status arrangements begins to differentiate into various strata. It becomes most differentiated within communities with families of heterogeneous social class composition. In these communities, two major adolescent strata, and often an intermediary one, emerge.

The proportional sizes of these strata vary considerably from community to community. In some communities this system is populated by almost three

17 Kingsley Davis and Wilbert E. Moore, "Some Principles of Stratification," *American Sociological Review*, X (April 1945), 242–49.

18 August B. Hollingshead, *Elmtown's Youth* (New York: John Wiley & Sons, Inc., Science Editions, 1961), pp. 449–50.

quarters of the youth inhabiting the area; in other communities only one third may be so involved. While there is an overlap between this system of strata and those youths outside of it, the majority of conforming youth are not within the system.

Besides the overlapping between those inside the system and those outside of it, there are youth who take on different strata roles at different times and shift between the strata. In order to analytically grasp the constancies of this highly fluctuating and ephemeral system, one has to perceive it independently of these fluctuations—as a set of institutional arrangements independent of the fluctuations of the individuals who move about within it and separate from the private attitudes of those who assume its roles.

For example, Short, Strodtbeck, and Cartwright[19] have pointed to the discrepancy that exists in regard to public and private attitudes expressed by delinquent boys. They found that the attitudes expressed in private to adult interviewers (regarding marriage and relations with girls) were much different from the attitudes expressed in public among peers. The privately expressed views were highly conventional, while the publicly expressed attitudes supported deviant sexual relationships. It was the *public rhetoric* that closely approximated the kinds of attitudes facilitating their delinquent activity.

We had become aware of this profound schism between public and private attitudes of delinquents early in our investigation of delinquent behavior. It not only exists in regard to their attitudes toward sexual relationships, but is also characteristic of their attitudes toward a large number of persons and relationships. The schism arises, in part, out of the conflict between their public views and more conventional perspectives. Since their relationships are never wholly independent of conventional ones, we can expect to find that, among some youth, extreme shifts between conventional and deviant modes of discourse are, under certain conditions, characteristic not only of their public but also of their private rhetorics.

It is believed that one cannot begin to understand the complexities involved until delinquent behavior is lifted out of reductionist frameworks and first understood as institutionalized forms of behavior. In doing this, the personalistic categories that involve only the relationships between the individual and his motives, rationales, and acts should be replaced with such sociological categories as ideology, vocabularies of motive, and institutional arrangements.

In the context of prevailing modes by which deviant behavior is interpreted, delinquent biographies are made comprehensible primarily by

---

19 James F. Short, Jr., Fred L. Strodtbeck, Desmond S. Cartwright, "A Strategy for Utilizing Research Dilemmas: A Case Study from the Study of Parenthood in a Street Corner Gang," *Sociological Inquiry,* XXXII: 2 (Spring 1962), 189.

constructing theoretical models of atomistic, troubled youth and setting these models into motion with categories of frustrated motives or learned mechanisms, by which guilt is expiated. However, once the broader institutional class patterns are made clear, it can be seen that deviant motives and rationales for action only emerge when youth have already experienced deviant relationships and have conceptually grasped them through acts of conversation among peers.

Stake Animals, Loud-Talking, and Leadership in Do-Nothing and Do-Something Situations

HANS W. MATTICK
NATHAN S. CAPLAN

More than any other work in the book, this report gives
one some of the "feeling" of gang work and the excitement
of field research with gangs. The "Stake Animal" is a
recognizable type of individual—once he is pointed out—
and the strategy for using him flows directly from the
recognition of his place in the group. The analysis points
out once more the practical advantages to gang intervention programs of understanding basic elements of the group
and interpersonal structures which direct a considerable
portion of gang behavior and gang response to adult
workers.

Hans W. Mattick and Nathan S. Caplan, Chicago Youth
Development Project, Institute for Social Research, University of
Michigan and Chicago Boys Clubs.

Introduction

The source data for the three behavioral conceptualizations to be discussed were derived from the street club work program of the Chicago Youth Development Project. The CYDP is an action-research project designed to prevent and control juvenile delinquency in two inner-city areas of Chicago. It is a joint project of The Chicago Boys Clubs and the Institute for Social Research of the University of Michigan and is financed by a Ford Foundation grant for a period of six years, commencing in 1961.

Although there has been a good deal of joint planning, cross-fertilization, and feedback between the action and research components of the project, there is a definite division of labor between them. The major responsibility for developing and conducting the action phase of the project belongs to the Chicago Boys Clubs, and more particularly to the CYDP staffs of the two Chicago Boys Clubs units located in the experimental areas where the action program is being implemented. The major responsibility for devising the research designs and making the investigations to evaluate and study the effectiveness of the action program lies with the Institute for Social Research, and more particularly with its Chicago research staff. It is one of our purposes here to illustrate, by ways of these three conceptualizations, how a research team, whose primary responsibility is evaluative research, may yet make contributions to the goals of an action program so as to provide important insights of consequence to the attainment of those goals.

Stake Animals

From a social-psychological point of view, there is a certain amount of conceit in sending a street club worker out into the community to establish relationships with youth groups and confidently expecting that he will exert influence over them in a unilateral fashion. This is especially the case when the worker is a relatively young man with a relatively middle class set of values and the youth group is a delinquent gang reflecting not only a lower class set of values but a definite orientation toward the antisocial and criminal opportunities afforded by a deprived community. Such a set of relationships, in such a context, is fraught with all kinds of ambiguous possibilities. The most obvious possibility is the one that has probably never happened—at least it is outside our realm of experience—and that is that the street club worker goes over to the other side, so to speak, and joins the gang. The possibility of corrupting the worker is not, however, limited to the constant testing of his motives toward venality; in fact, the possibilities are multifarious and sometimes insidious. Among the more seductive modes of corrupting the street club worker are those that fix upon his impulses toward generosity, humanitarianism, and sentimentality, as well as those that play upon his desire to elicit conventional responses from his gang-member clients. After two years of observing the interaction between our seven street club workers and the members of thirty-five different youth groups, it seemed to us that the problem of corruption through sentimentality was of sufficient frequency and magnitude to call for a serious review of our street club work methods.

It was repeatedly observed in the field, and reflected in the daily activity reports of the workers, that in working with a youth group of perhaps eight to fifteen members, too many of our workers had become too deeply involved and overcommitted with a particular kind of a boy who seldom evidenced any positive behavioral changes despite the excessive efforts devoted toward helping him. Such an application of the worker's time and talent tended to reduce what should have been group work methods to a species of private case work with one boy, while the behavior and needs of the remaining group members, who were present, went relatively unobserved and unaddressed.

A special investigation of several such boys who seemed to have such an overweening fascination for the worker revealed that they tended to share some common characteristics. They were the ones who were really problem-laden. The social pattern from which they emerged and the personality type that they tended to exhibit were strikingly similar in most cases. Their parental families were broken or highly disorganized, or both. Drunken fathers and mothers with quick tempers and violent methods of discipline, crowded home situations, grinding poverty, dependence on relief, and rejection of the boy round out the picture. The boy himself is either a school drop out or a frequent truant who is even more frequently expelled. He has a history of delinquency, drinks to excess when he gets the chance, and has no real inclination to work. On top of it all, more frequently than not, he freely retails all his problems to anyone who will listen, especially the street club worker.

We have labeled such boys "Stake Animals." The term comes from big game hunting and refers to an injured or helpless animal that is staked out to lure an unsuspecting quarry. As ordinarily conceived, and to stay within the bounds of the metaphor, in street club work the worker is usually considered the hunter and the delinquent gang, or at least its delinquent tendencies, are his legitimate quarry. In the case of the stake animals, however, the hunter becomes the prey. The stake animal's many delinquent and dependent characteristics divert the worker's attention from his legitimate quarry, the group, and entrap most of his time, energy, and resources. What is so seductive about the stake animal to the street club worker is that he seems to be almost rotten-ripe with the musk of potential reform. At least, that seems to be the way the street club worker perceives the stake animal for a considerable period of time before disillusion or demoralization sets in.

The role of the stake animal *vis-à-vis* the street club worker and the rest of the group is also an interesting one. At first it seemed to us that there was a conspiracy on the part of the group to push the stake animal off on the worker in order to keep him happy and occupied. While this may have been true in some cases, the situation was really more complex. What seemed to occur was a three-way "deception" based on an inadequate appreciation of the degree to which a street club worker could be helpful to a stake animal type of boy. Sometimes the gang members would actively solicit the worker's attention and focus it on the one whom they knew, better than anyone else, needed the most help. Sometimes the gang members seemed to do the same thing out of cynical motives, in order to exploit the worker. At all times it seemed to us, at least in our preliminary analysis, that the street club worker was self-deceived by seriously entertaining the notion that he was going to have any positive and lasting effect on a stake animal.

Regardless of the motives of the parties involved, however, the objective situation and the constructive possibilities of the relation between the street club worker and the stake animal seemed very unpromising. The objective situation was that when the worker first hove on the scene and began to invest time, energy, and resources in cultivating a relationship to the group, the stake animal welled to the surface and established a binding tie with the worker, while all the others in the group exploited this relationship. The other members of the gang were thus enabled to enjoy all the benefits of having a relationship with a street club worker without getting caught in the reciprocity of human relations which is the coin of the realm in street club work. While the worker was preoccupied with the stake animal the other members of the group did not feel they had been placed under any obligation to him, and thus he was in no position to place demands upon them for conforming behavior.

The occasions upon which this seeming neutralization of the street club worker's efforts were most readily observable were in situations of limited mobility. For example, we noticed that when the worker took the members of a group for a ride in a car, the stake animal in the group, if one was present, almost invariably occupied the front seat next to the worker. For the duration of the ride then, the worker's attention, except for his driving, was focused on the stake animal. The worker elicited an endless procession of problems; he advised, counseled, made suggestions, and only addressed the rest of the group in the car when absolute necessity required him to reduce the pandemonium. Similarly, when the street club worker was just "hanging around" with a group, by some process of spatial circulation and mutual choice, the worker was soon engaged in prolonged sessions of

one-to-one counseling with a stake animal instead of distributing his attention over the entire group.

Most of the street club worker's time spent with such a boy is taken up
with eliciting promises of reform, almost none of which are kept. At best a
stake animal is a short-run reformist and usually he is a classical backslider
and recidivist. In fact, some evidence seems to indicate that the amount of
time spent with stake animal boys is negatively related to the degree of
influence the worker holds over him, and it is not an unreasonable inference
that backsliding is the stake animal's very technique for preserving his
relationship to the worker.

It was our observation that, despite these repeated frustrations, the street
club worker's attraction to the stake animal remained strong. In fact, the
personal and humanitarian challenge to try to reform such boys, or at least
to do something for them, tended to override the supervisory pressures
placed on the worker to spread his time, energy, and resources over a larger
portion of the target population. In short, the worker's attachment to the
stake animal seemed to constitute as much of a problem to those supervising
the worker as the boy's behavior constituted a problem to the worker. More
important, from the standpoint of the effective use of manpower and
resources, the uneconomic concentration of effort on what seemed to be the
cases least amenable to change, when the objective of the action programs
was to have a mass effect, seemed to be a self-defeating enterprise. Such
was our state of mind when we were about to make some serious revisions
in our street club work program, but further research revealed that the
stake animal had some positive latent functions that made him a useful
animal indeed. In fact, we found that under certain conditions it was highly
profitable to maintain the relationship between the street club worker and
the stake animal in order to achieve a more widespread effect on our target
population.

Loud-Talking

The same research study which had indicated that there was a minimal,
if not a slightly negative, relationship between the degree of the street club
worker's effort and his influence over the stake animal type of boy produced
a further important but wholly unexpected finding. That finding was that
the relationship between the worker and the stake animal was serving not
only quite different functions than those that motivated the parties to the
interaction, but also quite different functions than those that had indicated
the futility of this relationship. In researching the nature of the worker's
influence over the boys with whom he associated, we were able to identify
a group of boys whose behavior had clearly been influenced but to whom

the worker had devoted relatively little direct attention. More frequently than not, these boys were members of a group which included a stake animal who had captured the major portion of a street club worker's attention, but they had remained peripheral to this central relationship. In other cases there were boys with whom the worker had been only minimally involved while he interacted frequently and intensely with the leadership or core members of the group. In either case, these peripheral members of the group demonstrated definite behavioral changes in the direction of the street club worker's goals.

Such unexpected successes were viewed with suspicion at first, and we actively entertained the hypothesis that this modification in behavior was the result of forces and influences quite independent of the worker. This did not, however, turn out to be the case, for the nature and direction of the change in these boys was clearly a reflection of the street club worker's example and exhortations, as expressed in his interaction with either a stake animal or a core member of the group. What seemed to be going on was that while the worker invested his time and energy in the stake animal, the other, more peripheral members of the group did not remain immune to the persuasions of the worker but, rather, benefited from the association primarily through observing and overhearing the worker.

We have used the term "loud-talking" to explain the technique and process by which these minimally involved boys, who were peripheral to some central relationship of intense interaction, were affected by the worker's attempts to influence others. The term loud-talking derives from prison argot and is defined in the *Dictionary of American Underworld Lingo*[1] as follows: "To inform upon a fellow convict by indirection, as to utter such information while within earshot of a guard or a known informer." The object of such loud-talking in prison is, obviously, to get some kind of a favorable response and action from the prison administration, such as getting the other prisoner punished or at least transferred. It is a technique employed by prisoners to use the machinery of the prison for their own ends without seeming responsible for the effect their actions have had upon either the prison administration or the person informed upon. The point, however, is that the loud-talker has produced what is, from his point of view, a desirable effect upon a situation he wanted to change. It is a very effective means of communication in that all those within earshot to whom the message is relevant get the full meaning even though they may remain anonymous and their reactions may be delayed.

Similarly, it appears that some of the youth group members not immediately involved in direct communication with the street club worker are

---

[1] Hyman E. Goldin, Frank O'Leary, and Morris Lipsius, *Dictionary of American Underworld Lingo* (New York: Twayne Publishers, Inc., 1950), p. 129.

able to "get the message" that he is trying to get across to a stake animal or a core member. On the other hand, the stake animal or core member, who is the direct object of the communication, is resistant. He is on the defensive and is internally organized to maintain what he conceives to be his personal integrity. The street club worker's example, counsel, and exhortations are perceived as an attack on the personal qualities of the stake animal by both the stake animal and the others present. The fact that the members peripheral to this intense interaction between the street club worker and the stake animal see it this way, however, is precisely what makes them vulnerable to the loud-talking that is going on. These other boys remain open listeners and observers, and are able to accept with greater equanimity that which is being said, insofar as it may have some application to their own situation. Their defenses are down; they do not feel personally threatened; someone else's problem behavior is the focus of attention and they are freer to reflect on the logic of the lesson that is being delivered.

The effectiveness of such indirect communication through loud-talking was manifested to some of our street club workers, and to us, by a number of empirical experiences. Several of our youth groups whose members had not been highly interactive with the worker, and had not appeared to be problem-laden on an individual level, nevertheless brought forth the fruits of such interaction even though discussions were carried on, for the most part, with stake animals. Such evidence was manifested in the form of unexpected constructive behavior and attitudes observed by the street club worker who, though pleasantly surprised at this turn of events, more frequently than not was unable to account for the degree of influence he had apparently had upon a group he felt he had been neglecting.

A dramatic example of the loud-talking effect is the case of a boy whom we will call Jojo. When he first came to our attention, Jojo was a member of a group called the Social Lords. The street club worker who had picked up this group did not consider it to be delinquent, although it had a few delinquent members and one all-around problem boy. In terms of status, Jojo was neither a leader nor a core member of the Social Lords, but stood somewhere in the middle ranks. Although reasonably active with the other members of the group, and accepted by them, his relationship to the street club worker was remote and superficial. The worker viewed Jojo as not seriously delinquent; while he was not entirely a model of good conduct, he was able to manage his life reasonably well. From almost every point of view he seemed to be a typical run-of-the-mill boy in our target population.

One day, after about eighteen months of such a peripheral relationship between the street club worker and Jojo, a remarkable thing happened. Jojo came into one of our outposts in the company of twelve boys who were previously unknown to the worker. He explained that he had organized these boys into a group and that he was their leader. He asked that the street club worker sponsor this new group just as the worker sponsored the Social Lords. The worker was surprised and bemused, for Jojo neither had occupied a leadership position in the Social Lords nor displayed the qualities that would be required to guide and control the new group. Although skeptical about Jojo's capacity for leadership, the street club worker agreed to sponsor the group whose continued existence he had every reason to doubt. It should be emphasized that the new group was not a splinter group of either the Social Lords or any other group then being worked with by any of our street club workers.

Over the next few weeks the new group took the name Iroquois as their own, held a series of meetings, and elected their officers. Jojo became president. He not only led the group well but assumed such a conventionally-oriented leadership role that the street club worker's guidance was hardly necessary. Jojo's means of handling the Iroquois, his personal mannerisms, preachments, and methods of social control were almost identical to those employed by the worker in his earlier relationship to the Social Lords. It took a considerable period of time for the street club worker to get over this almost total assumption of his role on the part of Jojo in relation to the Iroquois. The remarkable feature of this similarity in behavior was that Jojo had seemed to pay little attention to, or shown little interest in, the street club worker's earlier role with the Social Lords. Jojo had, apparently, acquired his learning by indirection, through simply being in the presence of the worker, rather than from any intimate and self-consciously directed interaction between them.

The practical lesson to be learned from these empirical experiences with stake animals and peripheral group members is the usefulness of loud-talking as a self-conscious and deliberate technique for influencing the behavior of others. Rather than abandoning stake animals as futile enterprises, or feeling guilty about a seeming overconcentration of time, energy, and resources on the leadership or core members of a group, street club workers should take full advantage of the opportunities that these interactional situations present. A perceptive street club worker who knows what he is about can, by generalizing his remarks, by raising the level of his voice, and by redirecting the relevance of his example and advice, reach a much larger audience and increase his effectiveness as an influence over a group with whom he is working. A station wagon, for example, can be viewed as a platform and an arena for his role-playing and pronouncements, and the stake animal can serve as a microphone or a sounding board for reaching an audience that would otherwise be lost to him. Almost any situation which was formerly reduced to private counseling with a stake animal may be used as an occasion for the rehearsal of a more general application to the problems that others may share, to a lesser degree, with the stake animal. In our search for effective street club work techniques we feel that loud-talking has a considerable potential. While we still view it as a heuristic device, for continued systematic study, it appears to have some eminently desirable qualities. It tends to maximize the worker's effectiveness as an influence with his current clients and, at the same time, seems to help him to achieve a mass impact over time. If further research tends to support our present impressions, then indirect communication as a technique of influence may make a more general contribution to the whole field of group dynamics.

Leadership Situations

The characteristic that the analysis of the stake animal and loud-talking, on the one hand, and of the leadership situations to be discussed, on the other, have in common is that both are based on erroneous initial perceptions. A series of interactions between the street club worker and the members of the youth group with whom he is working then ensue, based on this erroneous impression. As the drama between them is played out and subjected to scrutiny and analysis, the early judgmental conclusion, formed on the bases of these false perceptions, seems to indicate that the street club worker has gotten himself involved in a *cul de sac,* or is aggravating the very conditions he seeks to alleviate. Further observation and analysis, however, borne out by some empirical evidence, reveals the positive latent functions of manifest interactional situations between street club workers and their clients. In this process neither the street club worker nor the gang members (nor the researcher, for that matter, in the early stages of observation and analysis) are aware of what is going on, or of the ultimate consequences of their present activity.

When the street club worker first encounters a youth group he tends to react to it on the basis of its most obvious characteristics. Since his objective is to gain influence and control over the group, he will try to take advantage of the group structure that confronts him. More particularly, he will make a quick judgment about the leadership structure as he first finds it. There are, of course, many kinds of leaders and many styles of leadership. Leadership patterns among youth groups, as in the adult world, may be concentrated or diffuse, authoritarian or permissive, tyrannical or benign. We are concerned, here, with the kind of leader and leadership style that is associated with concentration of power, dictatorial methods, authoritarian personality, and tyrannical behavior. Such boys are found often enough on the streets of Chicago, but not nearly so often as the popular literature in the field would lead us to believe.

The street club worker contacting a youth group with such a leader tends to accept this leadership as the structure he must work through in order to influence the group. This leader is usually a tough boy whose leadership is clearly based on physical prowess and, in delinquent gangs, on criminal experience. He is a natural conservative and embodies the tradition of the group which he himself has fostered. He is the one to whom the other members of the group defer, and he enforces his will by the exercise of his veto power, backed up, if necessary, by his physical prowess. The uses of a leadership structure based on a veto power are clearly limited for the purposes of the street club worker. Whatever the worker may suggest by way of an activity for the group as a whole is simply negated by the leader who labels it as "too square," and thus manages to maintain what we have come to refer to as "leadership in the do-nothing situation." The street club worker soon learns that he was in error if he ever entertained the assumption that he could use the leader's veto power for constructive purposes. At the same time, do-nothing leaders tend to assiduously foster the myth of their omnicompetence, but prevent a testing of the myth by vetoing test situations in which the other members of the group would have a basis for judgment. Going here or there, or doing this or that, are beneath his dignity, "kid stuff," "too square," or "not cool." Under these circumstances the group as a whole tends to spend its time just "hanging around" in a restricted area; their conversation and interaction are limited to the narrow sphere of personal experiences and the surface phenomena of the local scene. Their situation can be summed up in the frequently overheard conversational gambit: "What's happening?" the reply: "Nothing."

Since the street club worker's interaction with the group is effectively checkmated by the veto power of a leader who maintains a do-nothing situation, the worker changes tactics. Perhaps the worker may even be taken in by the leader's bragging about how good he is and all the things he can do. In any case, the worker decides to cultivate the leader in order to make him a better leader. The worker's notion at this point of decision seems to be that if he can reform the dictator, the benefit to the group will be a benign despotism rather than sheer tyranny, and that this will constitute a more promising atmosphere inside of which to do constructive street club work. Thus the street club worker begins by exposing the leader, alone, to new experiences. He offers the leader a more privileged association, he shares more information with him, and extends him resources that he does not offer the others. If the do-nothing leader can be brought to respond to these overtures, no matter from what motives, a fateful process is set in motion. He is caught in a network of human reciprocity relations and is slowly maneuvered into a do-something situation.

It may be that, at the outset, the do-nothing leader is "going along with the program" out of the most cynical of motives—that is, to simply exploit the street club worker in all possible ways. To play this game, however, there has to be maintained a minimum relationship to give the appearance of cooperation, to mislead the worker, and to keep him "on the string," so to speak. In this stage of the relationship the do-nothing leader who is acting out of cynical motives pretends to respond positively to the preachments of the worker, and he gives voice to sentiments the worker would like to hear him express. There are promises not to get whiskey for the group next Saturday night, or vague and far-fetched plans about returning to school someday, or a half-expressed interest in vocational training or a job, none of which he entertains very seriously. If he is a good actor, he creates a sufficient impression upon the street club worker to make him act upon these phony sentiments by actively seeking the resources and procedures to respond to these falsely expressed needs. In other cases the street club worker is fully aware of the game that is being played but he hopes against hope that he can successfully entrap the do-nothing leader despite these elaborate charades. On the other hand, there are some do-nothing leaders who respond to the street club worker's cultivation processes out of more genuine motives. They view their special relationship to the street club worker as further recognition of their leadership capacity and, although they still maintain tight control over the status quo in their group, they tend to be more accepting of the opportunities that the street club worker offers to them on a personal basis.

It is our observation that, in the majority of such cases, as soon as the do-nothing leader is maneuvered into a do-something situation a process of status degradation sets in, for he almost invariably fails. If the street club worker gets him a job, he quits or gets himself fired. If the school authorities have been persuaded to take him back, he is soon cutting classes and gets expelled. If he is taken to a vocational school, he does not seem to have the motivation to pass the entrance exams. Although he may be a good street fighter, he is less good at sports and frequently refuses to participate. Such failures may more frequently reflect low motivation and disinterest in these kinds of pursuits than the absence of ability. Some do-nothing leaders display considerable ingenuity in pursuing their own concerns. In short, they may as often be unwilling as unable to perform. Nevertheless, as such experiences accumulate, the other members of the group begin to realize that their monolithic leader is a person who has failure experiences, and his supporting myth of omnicompetence begins to come apart at the seams. Although he does what he can to save face, neither his physical prowess nor his vehement denials about the significance of these failures can fully prevent the members of his group from having knowledge of what happened when his competence was brought to a test. In this respect, his veto power has effectively been neutralized.

As time passes, the perception of the leader as one who fails in do-something situations sets up a ferment in the group. Some of the lower status members, who had heretofore simply been intimidated, begin to challenge the do-nothing leader in a variety of ways. He is "put down" more often in the endless conversational game called "signifying." When the street club worker suggests an activity for the group, the leader's veto power is disputed. Other members of the group become more responsive to the street club worker because they *do* have some talent in do-something situations which they have, heretofore, not exercised or expressed. In short, the tough and delinquent leader has been subverted through the attempts of the street club worker to make him a better leader, by broadening his experience and exposing his failure to the group as an audience. At the same time, the stage has been set for allowing new leadership to emerge. On the other hand, we know of one case where leadership in a do-nothing situation successfully negotiated the change to leadership in a do-something situation. In that case, the theory that motivated the street club worker and led to the cultivation of the leader happened to have the consequences anticipated by the worker. That case resulted in a new, shared leadership situation in the group.

In either case, the new leadership that emerges from the subversion or modification of the do-nothing leadership pattern is more flexible, broader based, and more open to a wider learning experience. The group, therefore, becomes more receptive to forms of influence that can lead to conventional activities and these newer kinds of conformity can be more publicly affirmed than was previously possible.

The practical lesson to be learned from these empirical experiences with leadership in a do-nothing situation was, again, the usefulness of working with do-nothing leaders as a self-conscious and deliberate technique of either reaching or subverting them, and thus gaining access to the entire group. The way to do this was to appear to take their leadership seriously, particularly with respect to the real or pretended responses they made to the street club worker's early overtures. The object of this was to take advantage of the minimal set of reciprocal obligations the do-nothing leader was willing to assume, and through these, to gently maneuver him into do-something situations. He could then either grow with the new experience and thus change the nature of his relationship to his group, or he could fail and lay the basis for a change through the reaction of his group to his failure. An important element of this technique is to single out the leader and to preserve the rest of the group as an audience of potential critics. He must then be exposed to new learning situations or a series of new experiences in such a way that neither his veto power nor his physical prowess can prevent the judgment that his group forms about the quality of his performance.

A striking example of a do-nothing leader who was subverted through the sincere efforts of a street club worker to address his problems is a boy whom we will call B-jay. B-jay was the leader of a group called the

Reberls, who could always be found on "their corner." When the street club worker first tried to contact them, they remained suspicious and aloof. Persistent "hanging around" by the worker produced the comment from B-jay that the worker was probably "a fruit." The street club worker was not intimidated, but continued to come around and offer suggestions. B-jay told him to "get lost." Approaches to other members of the Reberls simply affirmed that B-jay was their spokesman. For several weeks B-jay parried the worker's efforts with remarks like, "The Reberls don't go swimming. This ain't no ball club. The Reberls wouldn't be found dead in the Boys Club." Nevertheless, B-jay accepted rides in the street club worker's station wagon. During the next few weeks, and after numerous car rides, it seemed to the worker that B-jay might be serious about his expressed desire "to have a job and get some money." The worker got him a job in a hotel but in three days he quit. He said the boss was "riding" him. A few days later B-jay was arrested for street fighting, but the worker's intervention at the police station helped to convert the case into a station adjustment. In the next few weeks two more job experiences ended in failure. The next job was out of town at a summer camp. After ten days B-jay was sent home because he "wouldn't work." The street club worker used these employment intervals to take the other Reberls on some trips through the city. When B-jay returned he vetoed these trips. A few days later he was arrested for strong-armed robbery and spent two weeks in custody. The street club worker went to court with him and B-jay received six months probation. Again the worker got him a job and this one was lost through being late and then absent. In disgust, B-jay decided to join the Army, but when the worker took him to the recruiting station, he did not pass the test.

Between B-jay's absences when at work or in custody, which the street club worker used to establish better relations with the group, and his failures, his leadership position began to be undermined. Some of the Reberls asked, "Where's all that money you were going to make and spend on us?" Or again, he would be asked, "When are you going to buy your own car?" Under such pressures, B-jay stopped vetoing the car rides offered to the Reberls by the street club worker. The worker used the car rides to propose an intra-group ball game at an early date. During the game it was established that B-jay was not a "star"; in fact, on several occasions he was "butterfingers." The street club worker next persuaded B-jay and the group to come into an outpost to plan a social. During that meeting the worker actively solicited the participation of all the Reberls present and they responded. A week later, at the social, B-jay and several others arrived with liquor on their breath, and B-jay tried to smuggle the bottle in. The worker confiscated the bottle on the grounds that drinking "would just cause trouble and break up the social," and he was supported by the sober members of the Reberls. B-jay left the affair in drunken anger and several of the remaining Reberls expressed the sentiment that this was "all for the best." Over the next few months several cycles of events of the type described took place. B-jay was not "kicked out" of the Reberls, but was reprimanded by some of the members who would not have raised objections six months earlier. He was degraded in status, but did not fall to the bottom. The Reberls exist today as a group with shared leadership, and the tenor of their behavior is somewhat improved over what it was a year ago. The more and less delinquent members of the group are now visible cliques inside the Reberls. A few weeks ago three of the more delinquent Reberls took part in an armed robbery during which one was killed and the other two were sent to the reformatory. Among the less delinquent members, one is in junior college and several are working fairly steadily. The street club worker related to this group is still actively working with them and their development is still under observation for research purposes.

What we have seen here is the history of a particular leader who worked from an extremely narrow base of physical prowess and delinquent behavior. He was provincial in every sense of the word—geographic, experiential, and attitudinal. When attempts were made to broaden his base by helping him to get employment and to lead his group in organized athletics or social events, he failed. Others in the group who had more capacity were enabled to emerge as leaders in their own right after the do-nothing leader had been debased in do-something situations. This made the group more accessible to the street club worker's influence and laid the groundwork for a higher potential of success in the future.

Conclusions

We believe that such concepts as the stake animal, loud-talking, and the manipulation of do-nothing leadership into do-something leadership situations transcends the field of street club work, which simply happens to have been the empirical experience arena from which they were derived. Stake animal-like individuals are apt to be found in the whole range of primary groups, from the demanding child in a family of several children to the imcompetent member of a work group under a foreman to the "sad sack" in an army platoon. Similarly, the technique of indirect communication, which we have called loud-talking, may have far broader application than the analogies to stake animals, indicated above. It may be a more effective form of communication in many situations where direct communication finds resistance in the receiver. Finally, do-nothing leadership may be found in a variety of human institutions and may well be subject to the kind of change process described above. At present we view the analyses we have made of these concepts as heuristic hypotheses, for which we have found some empirical evidence, but which require considerably more research for a more confident statement.

Part Three

SOME SOCIOLOGICAL CONTEXTS

Problem Youth
in a Small City

JOHN P. KOVAL
KENNETH POLK

There is the danger in any discipline that focusing on a restricted area of interest will result in an overly narrow understanding of the phenomena in question. Gang delinquency is primarily an urban, lower class problem that derives much of its flavor from its often squalid-seeming setting. But as a form of social deviance, it must also be placed in a larger context. This first paper of Part 3 provides one such context—the description of delinquency in the non-urban setting. Beyond serving this broad contextual purpose, the authors' description of their youth typology and dominant "themes" provides yet another anchoring point for the investigation of adolescent deviance.

JOHN P. KOVAL and KENNETH POLK, Lane County Youth Study Project, Eugene, Oregon.

The purpose of this paper[1] is to explore a range of youth problems as they exist in a small city setting. In order to encompass a variety of problems, a typology of problem youth is elaborated so that discussion can include more than simple delinquency. While the typology is not exhaustive (and excludes such major categories as mental instability and retardation), it is felt that necessary progress can be made in the understanding of hinterland youth problems with the presentation and explication of specific behavioral types. For in the recognition of discernible groups of problem youth, with their distinctively different complex of characteristics and problems, comes the realization of a need for differential approaches in programs of intervention.

The "hinterland" context within which the youth discussed in this paper reside and interact is referred to as descriptive of areas outside the major metropolitan centers of the United States. There are many different kinds of hinterlands. One is the rural farm type of area where the predominant economic structure is agricultural. A second type is the rural nonfarm communities, such as mining, fishing, and lumber towns, which have different ecological and social compositions than rural farm areas. A third type of hinterland community is the small city. Many areas which are "urban" or "metropolitan" by census definition are actually part of the hinterland. The small city is very different from the massive metropolitan areas in terms of its organization, and in the type and structure of the problems found within its boundaries. The present study was carried out in this part of the hinterland of the United States a—small city.

In recent years, a number of studies of rural or hinterland delinquency have been conducted.[2] The major conclusions to be drawn from these

---

1 This study is supported by a grant from the President's Committee on Juvenile Delinquency and Youth Crime, the grant being administered by U.S. Department of Health, Education and Welfare (HEW Grant No. 63001).

2 William T. Adams, "Delinquency Among Minorities in Rural Areas," paper read at the American Society of Criminology Meeting, Denver, Colorado, December 29, 1961; John P. Clark and Eugene P. Wenninger, "Socio-Economic Class and Area as Correlates of Illegal Behavior Among Juveniles," *American Sociological Review,* XXVII (December 1962), 826–35; Marshall B. Clinard, "The Process of Urbanization and Criminal Behavior," *American Journal of Sociology,* XLVIII (September 1942), 202–13; Marshall B. Clinard, "Rural Criminal Offenders," *American Journal of Sociology,* L (July 1944), 38–45; Robert A. Dentler and Lawrence J. Monroe, "Early Adolescent Theft," *American Sociological Review,* XXVI (October 1961), 733–43; Lamar T. Empey and Jerome Rabow, "The Provo Experiment in Delinquency Rehabilitation," *American Sociological Review,* XXVI (October 1961), 674–95; T. C. Esselstyn, "The Social Role of a County Sheriff," *Journal of Criminal Law, Criminology, and Police Science,* XLIV (August 1953), 177–84; Robert J. Havighurst *et al., Growing Up in River City* (New York: John Wiley & Sons, Inc., 1962); August B. Hollingshead, *Elmtown's Youth* (New York: John Wiley & Sons, Inc., 1949); Edward P. Hopper, *The Handling of Social Deviants in Two Rural Counties* (Springfield, Ill.: Illinois Youth Commission, 1961), mimeo; William P. Lentz, "Rural Urban Differentials and Juvenile Delinquency," *Journal of Criminal Law, Criminology, and Police Science,* XLVII (October 1956), 331–39; National Con-

studies are: 1) rural delinquency tends to be less serious than urban delinquency when we examine differences in the kinds of offenses committed; (2) rural delinquents are less "sophisticated" in terms of the methods they use to commit delinquent acts; (3) rural delinquency is not supported by a "criminal" culture organized around "professionalized" criminal activity; (4) rural delinquency does seem to be supported by a "troublemaking" culture that has some correspondence to what has been termed the "parent delinquent" subculture. A previous study in Lane County, Oregon, has shown that "troublesome" adolescents (including delinquents and dropouts) in this rural area are characterized by low economic position, alienation from school and community, involvement in a troublemaking subculture, and membership in disrupted families.[3]

The present study of youth in a small city in Lane County is more intensive. Six different types of adolescents are examined. "Problem" youth can be defined in a number of ways, two common foci of contemporary concern being delinquency and school withdrawal. The combination of these two yields three mutually exclusive problem types: *dropout delinquents, dropout non-delinquents,* and *in-school delinquents.* Teachers were approached to provide information on problem youth with the result that two additional types emerge: *teacher-nominated "behavior problems"* and *teacher-nominated potential dropouts.* These last categories are not always mutually exclusive—e.g., a potential dropout may be both a behavior problem *and* a delinquent. For classification purposes, if a youth has a delinquency record, he is classified as an in-school delinquent regardless of whether or not he was nominated as a behavior problem or a potential dropout. A person nominated as both a behavior problem and a potential dropout is classified as a behavior problem. The "normals" represent the residual groups of students who are in school, not delinquent, and not viewed by their teachers as either behavioral problems or potential dropouts. The operational definitions of these specific types come from information in the records of the juvenile authorities, the survey responses of high school youth and school withdrawees, and the academic records of in-school youth. Data for in-school youth were obtained from responses to a questionnaire submitted to nearly all youth in one high school of the small city. This yielded a total of 819 in-school males for analysis in this report. School records, court and police records, and teacher evaluations were used

---

ference on Prevention and Control of Juvenile Delinquency, *Report on Rural Aspects* (Washington: U.S. Government Printing Office, 1947); James E. Short and Ivan F. Nye, "Reported Behavior as a Criterion of Deviant Behavior," *Social Problems,* V (Winter 1957–58), 208–13.

[3] Kenneth Polk, *Rural Youth in Crisis* (Washington, D.C.: United States Department of Health, Education, and Welfare, in preparation).

to complete the information regarding these in-school youth. Information regarding out-of-school youth—i.e., dropouts—was obtained through interviews with a total of fifty-three males residing in Lane County. The interview schedule was constructed so that most items were identical to those in the in-school instrument. Initially an attempt was made to locate out-of-school youth by means of a random search of available rosters of youth of school age who were not in school. When this technique failed to produce adequate numbers of respondents, a supplementary "reputational" approach was used—i.e., known dropouts were asked the names of other individuals whom they knew to be dropouts. Caution should be used, therefore, in interpreting the findings here regarding dropouts. Because of the effects of in- and out-migration, it is always difficult to obtain an accurate accounting of the dropout population in a community at a given point in time. Our portrayal of this population is possibly distorted by selection of the more "visible" elements within this group.

Socio-Economic Theme

A theme of low socio-economic position runs through the responses of problem youth and is particularly pronounced in certain groups. School dropouts, whether they be delinquent or non-delinquent, show more consistent and dramatic patterns of low socio-economic position than any other group. Dropout delinquents, in particular, rank lowest in any measure reflecting the socio-economic theme which we have considered. The educational attainment of both parents is generally less than high school, nearly three-fourths rate their housing as less than excellent or good, and their fathers are almost entirely employed in blue collar occupations. They do not consider the potential for economic opportunity in the community as very promising and are totally oriented along blue collar occupational lines.

The educational attainment of parents of dropouts is also exceedingly low, but there appears to be a higher degree of economic success for these parents (in terms of proportions employed in white collar employment and the higher rating given to the housing conditions) in spite of the educational handicap they carry. Regardless, their offspring are another generation with a different set of factors operating in present day success themes. They are not too optimistic about their own possibilities of economic success in the community and receive confirmation of such feelings by reflecting upon their present occupational positions.

The economic profiles of potential behavioral problems and potential dropouts reflect similarly patterned sets of characteristics, with potential behavioral problem youth almost invariably ranking higher on all measures.

Significant and important differences exist between their fathers' educational backgrounds and the type of occupation expected by the adolescent in the future. Not only are more fathers of behavioral problem youth high school graduates, but a considerably higher proportion of these children expect to be involved in white collar employment.

In-school delinquents and normal adolescents of this hinterland community also show similarly patterned sets of economic characteristics with the same two important differences plus one other. Normal adolescents consistently rank higher than in-school delinquents on all items reflecting the economic theme. However, the educational attainment and occupational status of the in-school delinquent's father are indicative of important economic differences which exist between the two groups. Both of these, in turn, may play a part in the third major difference: a considerably higher proportion (60 vs. 45 per cent) of the normal adolescents expects later employment in white collar occupations than is the case with in-school delinquents.

Turning to an analysis of the variables within the economic domain, important differences appear in the operation of the items. The uniform high educational attainment of the mothers of the in-school groups, including the three problem populations, in comparison with the low educational attainment of the mothers in the two dropout populations, suggests that this variable is critical in the process of school withdrawal. Father's education, on the other hand, seems to operate more as part of the general cluster of socio-economic variables, showing the same pattern across the problem populations as does father's occupation, occupational aspiration, and self-rating of the individual's housing. Thus, while a theme of low socio-economic position seems to function in the profiles of these problem populations, this one variable, mother's education, seems to have specific impact on early school leaving.

Family Theme

Basic family structure, the patterns and extent of mutual interaction between parents and child, and parent-child authority relations constitute some components of this family theme which differentially characterize the problem type of adolescents presented here. Considerable variance in the basic family structure exists for the problem groups and persists in each of the other indicators.

Normal adolescents rank highest (80 per cent) in terms of coming from intact homes, spend more time at home as members of the family constellation, and rank high (with the exception of dropouts and dropout delinquents) in the amount of time spent with each parent. The parent-child relationship appears more apt to have communication built into it. High proportions of normal youth report that their parents almost always know where they are, and, additionally, over half consider their parents' disapproval hardest to take in comparison to teacher or peer disapproval.

Delinquent and non-delinquent dropouts demonstrate somewhat similar patterns for the family theme profile. Both groups rank lowest in the proportion that come from intact families. This appears to be compensated for by the fact that relatively high proportions of each group report frequent contact with one or the other parent, but relatively less time at home with the family unit. In keeping with the less frequent periods of time at home with the family, only half of the non-delinquent dropouts report their parents always know where they are, but nearly 60 per cent (higher than any other adolescent group) indicate their parents' disapproval is hardest to take. Other data suggest that the latter finding might not be so much a reflection of the choice of parents over peer groups, but more a reflection of the lack of any suitable alternative. That is, in many cases the non-delinquent dropouts appear to be *social isolates* and there are simply no competing social frames of reference when such a choice is to be made. Delinquent dropouts, on the other hand, report their parents generally do not know where they are all the time and that less than half (44 per cent) feel their parents' disapproval is harder to take than that of a teacher or peer.

Of the in-school populations, the behavioral problem youth exhibit a striking set of characteristics on the family theme profile. Family disruption is more common for this group than for normal youth, in-school delinquent youth, or potential dropouts. They spend relatively less time with either parent or at home with the family. There is less communication. Relatively little importance is attached to letting their parents know where they are and to incurring their parents' disapproval. In general, behavioral problem adolescents present a picture suggesting the least amount of responsibility toward parents and minimal contact and identification with parents or the nuclear family.

While more of the remaining two in-school groups (delinquents and potential dropouts) come from disrupted homes than do normal adolescents, both cluster together and follow the general pattern of familial characteristics set by the normals, with relatively less group involvement. In parental and family interaction patterns they report consistently lower amounts of interaction with parents and the family than do the normals. They (particularly the delinquents) communicate their whereabouts to a considerably lesser extent than do the normals and are less concerned about their parents' disapproval in comparison to disapproval from their peers or their teachers.

Subcultural Theme

There seems to be some evidence supporting a subcultural theme among problem youth in this area. Familiarity with and some degree of involvement in a deviant adolescent subculture seems evident for all of the populations of troublesome adolescents considered. While there are no "gangs" as the term is used to apply to the group behavior of metropolitan slum delinquents, data are found here which show a commonly held value and common patterns of behavior among delinquents and problem youth which are different from those of non-delinquents. They support the notion that there is an important subculture context for delinquency and other youth problems in the hinterland. It should be pointed out that this is a male subculture, and that delinquency in Lane County is predominantly a male phenomenon.

Delinquent school dropouts and in-school behavioral problem youth stand out as being most deeply enmeshed in a delinquent subculture (which is not to say that they either are or appear to be members of similar delinquent social systems). High proportions of each group are familiar with boys who have been in trouble with the police, who spend a good deal of time interacting with their friends, and who value "stirring up a little excitement" as status-conferring. The major distinction between these two groups and school dropouts and in-school delinquents is that while all of these groups know and have friendship patterns with other youth who have been in trouble, the school dropouts and in-school delinquents do not spend as much time interacting with these youth and do not place as high a value, as groups, on the importance of "stirring up a little excitement."

Potential dropouts and normal in-school adolescents (particularly the latter) appear somewhat cognizant of the delinquent subculture, but they interact along the fringe of its social boundaries. They are familiar with smaller proportions of youth who have been in trouble, vary considerably from the other four problem populations in the proportion of their friends who have been in trouble, interact less with other adolescents, and place less importance on the value of "stirring up a little excitement." This suggests the possibility that the so-called delinquent subculture may not be terribly different from, and in fact might be usefully viewed as an adaptation of the wider "adolescent subculture."

Isolation Theme

Isolation, defined here as the social structural condition of lack of involvement or interaction in a social system, can also be said to exist, to some degree, for each of the problem type adolescents. The most clear-cut case is visible in the instance of potential dropouts. Of the four in-school populations, there is little doubt that this group is most isolated. These youth have the lowest proportion of friends in school, belong to almost no school clubs or organizations, spend relatively little time in extracurricular or school-related activities, and are well aware of the fact that they are not "in" on things. Although they are isolated, it appears that neither overt aggression in the form of delinquency nor actual withdrawal from the system has been adopted as a "solution" to the isolation problem.

In-school delinquents, while spending more than a little time in extra-curricular and school-related activities, belong to relatively few school clubs or organizations and rate themselves moderately low as to how close they are to the center of things. School behavioral problem youth, on the other hand, have considerably fewer friends in school than do the normals, and are much less apt to belong to school clubs and organizations or to participate in extracurricular or school-related activities. Yet they report being near the center of things in almost the same proportion as do the normal adolescents. This would appear inconsistent on their part, and may reflect a defensive reaction more than objective reporting.

Out-of-school youth present relatively different pictures of school-community isolation profiles. Fairly high proportions of the non-delinquent dropouts report they spent some time in extracurricular and school-related activities. Smaller proportions than for the normals reported membership in school clubs and organizations and perceived themselves to be far from the center of things in school. Such reported high involvement in non-school community clubs or organizations is contradictory, since a considerably smaller proportion report actual membership in such organizations.

Delinquent dropout youth, by comparison, report negligible involvement or activity in school and extracurricular activities, indicate an awareness of being out of the center of things, and demonstrate a considerable lack of involvement or activity in organized behavior at the community level.

Alienation Theme

Alienation, viewed here as a perceptual disjunction in the relationship between self and other individuals or groups as demonstrated by a lack of affective social experience, is evident in the problem groups of in-school and out-of-school youth. Such alienation exists at the level of both school and community relations.

A generally extreme degree of variance from normal adolescents is found among behavioral problem adolescents, potential school dropouts, non-delinquent dropouts, and delinquent dropouts. In-school delinquents present a "middling" picture of neither so extreme a degree of alienation as these groups nor so strong an affective school or community identification as the normal adolescent population.

Anchorages for non-delinquent dropouts and dropout delinquents in their feelings of alienation from school appear most strong in their evaluation of the school as less than excellent and their perception of school as being dull and boring—institutional aspects of the school setting. Alienation from the community is strongly anchored in their evaluation of the community in general, police protection, and the public school system—again, institutional aspects of the community setting. Areas of school interpersonal relations, while still lower than those of the normal adolescents, are evaluated relatively high by each of these groups. Adults in the community (even in an abstract sense) are also evaluated high. Non-delinquent dropouts, however, are less inclined to feel their personal worth in the world today while delinquent dropouts lead one to conclude their personal image is positive and strong.

In-school potential dropouts also display definite alienative characteristics at the community and school levels, but internal variation does exist. The alienation anchorages tend to be comparatively stronger in the area of interpersonal relations and less pronounced in the area of institutional settings. The school and school system are rated comparatively high. In spite of an extremely low evaluation of police and community, it still rates higher than the two dropout groups, in one instance, and the two dropout groups and nominated behavioral problems, in another. In areas relating more directly to interpersonal contact or peer involvement (such as being "left out in the cold" in school affairs, thinking of school leadership less in terms of abilities or activities, or in feeling little attention is paid to children by adults), the nominated dropouts demonstrate a more extreme degree of alienation in comparison to the normals or to the other youth problem populations.

It should not be overlooked that there is no way of determining here the possibility of a halo effect on the school for non-school youth making school evaluations, or for a similar effect on the community on the part of in-school youth. That is, in reflecting back to the school of which they are no longer members, non-school youth may feel it really wasn't so bad after all. Problem in-school youth, who are less involved in the activities of an adult community, may be more favorably disposed toward it than those who are unsuccessfully competing in that world.

Teacher-nominated behavioral problems show strong and consistent patterns of alienation in a community, be it in an interpersonal or institutional setting, and marked degrees of alienation toward school and institutional level. Even though the members of this group have not been involved in any official delinquent behavior, they give distinct indications of alienation "across the board" that are more striking in intensity than any shown by the other in-school problem types.

The themes discussed above are descriptive of conditions that are extant for each of these groups. We have been concerned with pinpointing the specific *conditions* of problem populations so that logical modes of intervention aimed at curbing the problem can be implemented rather than sensitizing individuals to the *symptoms* of the problem so that "preventive" treatment may be applied. These conditions can be understood more completely if we examine the problem populations separately.

Potential Dropouts

Of the four in-school groups, teacher-nominated potential dropouts stand in an extreme position on any measure of the economic theme. Subjective and objective reports lead to the conclusion that this group occupies a definite economically disadvantaged position. Only in the area of mother's educational attainment do these youth compare favorably with normal adolescents. Here, incidentally, is a possible clue to the reason why they are potential and not *de facto* dropouts. For, while the father's educational attainment is exceedingly low, the mother's attainment is superior. This may possibly account for some of the holding power of education on the child. Additional credence is lent to this possibility when the comparative educational attainments of the two school dropout populations are considered. In this instance, *both* parents' educational attainment is low. One can propose, then, that if the parental educational background is lacking, the probability of support for their offspring's education is low. This is particularly true when other unfavorable economic factors are present in the family situation.

The family structure of potential dropouts is quite similar to that of the normals. Similar proportions spend time together with each parent, but they are at home with the family to a somewhat lesser extent. The lack of identification and communication with parents, however, suggests that the content and quality of parent and family interaction patterns are not the same for this group as they are for normal adolescents. These youth are less likely to report that their parents always know where they are and they express considerably less concern about being subject to their parents' disapproval.

Potential dropouts appear to be aware of some elements of a dissident adolescent group, possibly operate on its fringes, and are least likely of any group to share a "hell-raising" attitude. They report as few friends who have been in trouble with the police as do normals, and generally spend more time with their friends.

They appear isolated from the social structure of the school and from general adolescent behavior configurations, and only a little less so in the community at large. Such isolation is related to if not the producer of a general state of school and community alienation that is particularly deep-set in the area of interpersonal relations—both inter-adolescent and inter-adult. It is a passive alienation, however. It has not resulted in aggressive behavior, and tends more toward withdrawal than toward any form of aggressive reaction.

Nominated Behavioral Problems

Teacher-nominated behavioral problem youth, like the potential drop-outs, have a comparatively low economic profile. There is a good deal of variance in their parents' education, with the mother's education generally higher. They are more likely than a normal population to have a blue collar occupational background and to rate the economic opportunity in the community less favorably. Fewer expect white collar employment in the future.

Nearly one-third of these youth come from homes broken by separation, divorce, or death, and lack of contact or communication with either parent is more typical for this group than any other. There appears to be an absence of family unity, cohesion, and affective relations. These potential problem youth are generally remiss in keeping their parents in touch with their whereabouts and are not highly concerned about parental disapproval.

Every indication points to their knowledge of and involvement in dissident and delinquent patterns of behavior, although they have not been caught. The proportion from this group which reports knowing a number of boys in trouble with the police, having friends who have been in trouble with the police, and spending three or more evenings a week with these friends is nearly identical with the proportion among school delinquents and non-school delinquents. Only dropout delinquents evidence a higher proportion of members who value "hell-raising" activity as status-conferring.

Potential behavioral problems reportedly spend little time in extra-curricular or school activities; they belong to some school organizations although to a considerably lesser extent than do normal youth. Their friendship patterns involve fewer in-school and more dropout youth. These three factors—low school organizational involvement, low activity involvement, and in-school low peer relations—lead one to conclude that a relative degree of social isolation exists for this group. However, they do not see themselves as being removed from the center of things in school, as do some delinquents and potential dropouts. In fact, they rate themselves as close to the center of things in school as do normals. Participation in activity and non-school community clubs or organizations, however, is considerably lower for this group than for the normals.

This type of youth exhibits a pattern of general alienation from school and community which is more intense than that of any other in-school group. The community is rated low, school is considered dull and boring, and they usually will not go to a school activity if there is the opportunity to do something else with friends. At the same time, their self-image refuses to admit that they are "left out in the cold" (as was the case in their reacting to the question about being near the center of things in school), even though there appears to be little objective evidence that they are not. A general state of alienation also exists for community institutional setting and in their evaluation of the adult world.

This group appears most "out of joint" with the family, school, normal adolescent peers, and community, but in many instances seems to refuse to admit it. These potential problem youth report high degrees of involvement with delinquent youth and only the lack of formal police contact differentiates them from delinquents. Here is an alienated and apparently hostile group that gives every appearance of being more maladjusted socially than those who have been formally adjudicated for similar reasons.

In-School Delinquents

Officially adjudicated in-school delinquent youth from this small city area compare more favorably to normals on the economic theme than does any other problem adolescent type. At the same time, particularly important differences are evident for father's education and occupation and also for the proportion of school delinquents who expect future white collar employment—hard core items in the economic theme. Regardless of the comparability of items and the general similarities, however, a considerable degree of economic difference does exist between normal in-school youth and in-school delinquents.

Family structure is weaker and internal relations are less frequent for in-school delinquents than for the normal adolescent group. There are more instances of broken homes, less interaction with either parent, considerably less time spent at home in the evenings or spent in keeping parents posted of their whereabouts, and much less concern over parental disapproval. In some cases the difference between normals and delinquents is dramatic, and in all cases the indicators of family stability and homogeneity are consistently less favorable for the delinquent youth.

Knowing other delinquents, having them as friends, spending time with them, and valuing the ability to stir up a little excitement are fairly typical conditions for this group, but they actually report spending less time with their friends than do dropout delinquents or potential behavioral problems and fewer of them place as high a value on stirring up excitement. They possibly "act out" with other factors dominating their behavior.

Delinquents are generally more highly integrated into the school and community social system than are other problem groups, although less so than normal adolescents. Significantly, they belong to few in-school clubs or organizations and generally report being out of the center of things in regard to school activities. Their activity and participation in non-school clubs and organizations is again greater than most problem youth, though still considerably less than that of normals.

Linked with their comparative social isolation in the school and community is the additional condition of alienation. This is again demonstrably different from the existing state of normal adolescents. Quite consistently, it appears to be a less intense or less fluctuating phenomenon when compared to other problem youth.

Delinquent Dropouts

The most consistent and striking differences between dropout delinquents and the in-school problem and normal youth lie in the socio-economic domain. Uniformly, these out-of-school delinquent youth are at the "bottom of the heap," both in terms of parental position and in the position they see for themselves in the future. Concomitantly, there are important differences noted in other variable domains as well. This group is more likely than any other to come from "broken homes," they are the least inclined to spend time with their family, and it is this group that is most "out of touch" with their parents. Overall, there is consistent evidence of involvement in subcultural activities and a relatively high degree of alienation, especially with respect to the school.

Non-Delinquent Dropouts

In some respects the non-delinquent dropouts comprise one of the most important groups in this analysis. The comparison of this group with the delinquent dropouts, for example, shows that the two groups show similar economic status profiles. This suggests that the major impact of class here has to do with school adjustment rather than with delinquency and that, clearly, any explanatory theory of delinquency must include variables in addition to social class.

Comparison of the differences between the youth seem as a potential dropout (non-delinquent) and the non-delinquent dropout indicate that these two groups are quite different. The actual dropouts show a more depressed economic picture than do the potential dropouts. The critical factors here, however, are the family variables: the actual dropout group shows more family disruption, while the potential dropouts are nearly like the normals when it comes to the distribution of family characteristics.

Summary

This study of male youth in a small city has attempted to define a number of different types of problem youth and to examine factors related to such patterns. Responses of troublesome youth in this hinterland setting are characterized by themes of low economic position, subcultural involvement, disrupted family life, alienation, and isolation. The differential profiles observed for the different types of problem youth suggest that the distinctiveness of each group should be considered in the development of intervention strategy.

The findings here have suggested that there are similarities and differences between the various types of problem youth. Some of these findings may be of theoretical relevance. Among these groups, for example, when a crude control is exerted over school status, the economic status differential between delinquent and non-delinquent groups are not overwhelming. That is, a comparison of delinquent versus non-delinquent groups for the in-school and out-of-school populations shows small differences on the economic profiles, whereas enormous differences are observed in these same variables when the comparisons are made between in-school and out-of-school youth when delinquency is controlled. School maladjustment appears more important than economic status in the generation of delinquency. It may be, in fact, that the effect of economic status on delinquency is mediated through the process of school maladjustment.

Table 1

DIFFERENTIAL CHARACTERISTICS OF NORMAL AND PROBLEM MALE YOUTH IN A SMALL CITY

(Reported in Percentages)

Dimension	Normals (N = 665)	In-School Youth			Out-of-School Youth	
		In-School Delinquents (N = 93)	Potential Behavior Problems (N = 33)	Potential Dropouts (N = 28)	Dropouts (N = 26)	Delinquent Dropouts (N = 27)
Economic Theme						
Mothers with high school education	79	73	79	75	15	15
Fathers with high school education	74	59	48	39	12	04
Rate housing as excellent or very good	59	50	27	29	16	08
Fathers with white collar occupations	57	45	33	22	31	04
Rate economic opportunities as very good	32	23	27	21	08	07
Expect to have white collar occupations in the future	60	45	39	22	00	00
Family Theme						
Natural family intact	80	71	70	77	65	56
Spend more than 6 hours per week with father	26	22	15	25	38	26
Spend more than 6 hours per week with mother	27	25	18	32	54	48
Spend three or more evenings per week at home with family	83	70	57	75	58	47
Agree parents always know where they are	66	49	33	57	46	22
Agree parental disapproval hardest to take	50	44	36	32	58	44
Subcultural Theme						
Know 5 or more boys in trouble with the police	32	57	57	37	47	60
Know 5 or more girls in trouble with the police	06	19	09	19	20	23
Friends have been in trouble with the police	50	83	82	54	81	74
Spend three or more evenings per week with friends	20	35	48	37	36	48
Agree stirring up a little excitement is status-conferring	53	58	64	43	62	67

137

| | | In-School Youth | | | Out-of-School Youth | |
Dimension	Normals (N = 665)	In-School Delinquents (N = 93)	Potential Behavior Problems (N = 33)	Potential Dropouts (N = 28)	Dropouts (N = 26)	Delinquent Dropouts (N = 27)
Isolation—School						
Spend four or more hours in extracurricular activities	38	27	24	19	31	22
Spend two or more evenings in school-related activities	28	21	09	18	35	11
Belong to one or more in-school organizations	53	25	27	08	39	22
All or most friends are in high school	91	85	76	71	—	—
Perceive themselves as close or moderately close to "the center of things"	47	31	45	11	39	33
Isolation—Community						
No dropout friends	62	37	24	29	08	18
Belong to one or more non-school organizations	59	40	33	39	30	18
Spend one or more evenings per week in clubs or activities	48	41	30	44	39	08
Alienation—School						
Rate high school excellent	56	42	27	43	19	07
Disagree they are "left out in the cold"	53	46	48	39	49	48
Would go to rally	41	24	09	22	—	—
Agree being leader in activities/athletics status-conferring	80	65	60	57	73	66
Disagree school is dull and boring	70	56	36	36	39	33
Alienation—Community						
Rate community excellent	41	26	18	11	00	07
Rate police protection very good	34	32	15	21	19	18
Rate public school system very good	54	42	27	32	19	18
Disagree that adults don't pay much attention to kids until they get into trouble	62	54	36	29	54	51
Disagree that one person doesn't count much	65	60	36	50	47	69

Family Integration
and Police Contact

WILLIAM R. LARSON
BARBARA G. MYERHOFF

One of the most common themes—and recurring problems
—running through the history of delinquency theory and
research is the place of the family in the causal chain.
Everyone agrees on the importance of the family in the
socialization process, but few agree on how family systems
may feed the development of deviance, nor on how one
should measure or conceptualize the salient elements of the
family system. William R. Larson and Barbara G. Myerhoff
attempt here another scheme for both conceptualizing and
measuring family integration, and provide validating data
which give at least partial support to the utility of their
approach. More refined criterion measures are needed,
however, before the full value of their scheme can be
assessed.

WILLIAM R. LARSON and BARBARA G. MYERHOFF, Youth Studies
Center, University of Southern California.

Three major tasks are undertaken in the present paper: 1. the identification and transcendance of some methodological traditions which the authors regard as unfortunate in studies of the relationships between family disturbances and antisocial behavior of children; 2. the development of two indices of family integration and the relationship of these indices to undesirable social behavior on the part of children; 3. the presentation of a paradigm of four types of family organization and the relationship of these types to two kinds of undesirable social behavior on the part of children.

Perhaps more than most areas of sociological inquiry, delinquency research is carved by deep ruts and well traveled paths which often draw investigators away from other potentially more fruitful approaches. Three closely related methodological traditions in studies of the relationship between attributes of family life and antisocial juvenile behavior are of particular concern to us.

The first of these may be called the "broken home" cliché, which refers to studies of the effects on children of a missing parent—for example, working mothers, absent fathers, and female-dominated households. A glance at the literature on this subject reveals a seemingly inexhaustible concern about this situation shared by laymen, social scientists, and workers in action intervention programs.[1] Such studies are likely to postulate simple, direct, causal relationships between two relatively complex and abstract conditions (broken homes and delinquency). Although this procedure is not logically erroneous, it is frequently misleading. Both conditions may be thought of as outcome criteria of prior processes and the connection between them must be supplied by vague and tenuous inferences. The part played by intervening or mediating variables is largely overlooked. A more desirable procedure would be one in which delinquency is first related to more simple and unidimensional components or indices of family organization, and only after that, to more abstract, complex conditions.

The second tradition we have called the "phenomenological oversight." It occurs as a result of investigators' neglect of the meaning of broken homes to the actors in the situation. This often comes about in spite of the fact that it is a commonplace observation that a family may remain intact though riddled with strife. The mere presence or absence of a parent does not reveal what Shaw and McKay[2] have called "the conflicts, tensions, and

---

1 See, for example, Section V, "Social Values and Social Structure: Theoretical Analyses," pp. 211–318, and Section VI, "The Family Setting," pp. 319–52, in Marvin Wolfgang, Leonard Savitz, and Norman Johnston, eds., *The Sociology of Crime and Delinquency* (New York: John Wiley & Sons, Inc., 1962); James H. S. Bossard and Eleanor S. Boll, *Family Situations* (Philadelphia: University of Pennsylvania Press, 1943); Sheldon and Eleanor Glueck, *Unraveling Juvenile Delinquency* (Cambridge, Mass.: Harvard University Press, 1950).

2 Clifford R. Shaw and Henry D. McKay, *Social Factors in Juvenile Delinquency* (Washington, D.C.: National Commission of Law Observance and Enforcement, Report No. 13, Vol. II, 1931), 275–76.

attitudes which contribute to family disorganization" and which may cause children to become delinquent irrespective of external and visible family disruptions. Indeed, social scientists are demonstrating a growing concern with the damaging and pathological bonds which may tie a family together as tightly as or more tightly than positive forces.[3]

The concept of the "psychologically broken home" suggested by Wolfgang, Savitz, and Johnston[4] represents an attempt to overcome the common neglect of the *meaning* of a family's life to its members, and thus goes beyond consideration of only visible, crude outcome measures of family disruption, such as parental presence or absence. While such measures are by no means without value, they cannot serve as substitutes for phenomenological indicators of family disturbance.

The third tradition may be called the "psychology is deep and sociology is broad" fallacy. This tradition rests on the assumption that sociology perforce deals with relatively numerous, general, and crude variables, and psychology with fewer, less generalizable, and more precise variables. It is too often the case that after completing a survey-like description of the phenomena in question, the sociologist turns his findings over to the psychologist, implying, as it were, that greater precision is not within the purview of sociology. A preferable alternative open to him is to tighten his focus on his subject matter while continuing to ask *sociological* questions and attempting to develop more precise and refined measures of intra-organizational attributes. Certainly there is no logical reason why intra-organizational variables cannot be as specific, deep, and sharply defined as are intra-personal variables.

Let us now turn to our second task, the development of finer indices of family integration which, we feel, is a step away from the three traditions we have identified. (What other unfortunate traditions we may now be establishing is a matter to be reckoned with by others.)

The indices we have developed are based on data gathered in the course of an ongoing study of family socialization of adolescent boys.[5] The sample consisted of 150 adolescent boys, their mothers and fathers in a southern California city. One of the major foci of the study is the identification of various types of family organizations and their relationships to two kinds of outcome criteria—undesirable social behavior on the part of the son 1. in school and 2. in the community. It should be kept in mind that this

---

[3] See, for example, "Family and Personality," in Norman W. Bell and Ezra F. Vogel, eds., *A Modern Introduction to the Family* (New York: Free Press of Glencoe, Inc., 1960), Part IV, pp. 499–649.

[4] Wolfgang, Savitz, and Johnston, *op. cit.*, p. 319.

[5] The study referred to is entitled "Critical Factors in Adolescence: Intra-Family Relations and Differential School Adjustment," and is supported by U.S. Office of Education (Grant No. 1353).

process results in the development of only *one* index of integration, pertaining to the child. School behavior has been appraised on the basis of teachers' and deans' evaluations, sociometric tests, grades, and school records. For the analysis presented in the present paper, only two categories of school adjustment are employed—successful and unsuccessful. The latter category includes both underachieving and aggressive boys. Community behavior has been defined by the presence or absence of police contacts. A "contact" here means an arrest on record.

The data used as the basis of these indices represent a fraction of the total information gathered during four-hour interviews with the boys and their families. Further, only fifty of the 150 families in the sample have been considered in this preliminary and exploratory paper—twenty-five families whose sons have had police contacts and twenty-five whose sons have not had such contacts. That part of the interview used to develop these indices involved questions pertaining to the family's goals and values for the son, and questions pertaining to the family's perceptions of serious problems concerning the son.

Each member of the family was presented with 110 specific items describing presumably socially desirable behaviors and attitudes referring to the son, and was first asked to rate the importance of each item on a seven point scale. The results of this inquiry comprise the first index of family integration: the extent of agreement between family members as to relative importance of certain values, goals, and beliefs pertaining to the son's activities and feelings. This technique provides an external indicator of family integration—that is, one which is determined by *outsiders*. The second index was obtained by asking each of the family members to designate which of the items constituted serious problems to anyone in the family. The extent of the seriousness of these problems was rated by family members to a seven point scale. This measure is a phenomenological one, for it taps the member's own evaluations of the extent of family disturbance concerning particularly items. For example, mothers, fathers, and sons were asked to rate the extent to which they felt it was important that the son obey even those laws which most people ignored. They were then asked to rate the extent to which they felt this issue comprised a serious problem in their family. The same technique was applied to an additional 109 items concerning the son's behaviors and feelings.

The indices of family integration so obtained are but two of a great many parameters of family organization. They serve as a useful point of departure for characterizing the differential ability of various families to successfully socialize children. The indices, we feel, overcome the three methodological objections raised earlier. First, they are simple, unidimensional components of family organization which can be related directly to outcome criteria without requiring elaborate inferences as to intervening mechanisms. Thus, they avoid the "broken home" cliché. Second, the phenomenological oversight is remedied by the employment of a perceptual measurement of family disturbance—namely, the frequency with which serious problems occurred. Finally, the emphasis on an organizational variable, such as the extent of agreement in the family, allows for greater depth than is usually characteristic of such studies, and achieves it without shifting the focus from group to individual attributes. This emphasis makes it possible for us to ask the question, "What kinds of family *organizations,* defined by these two parameters, are most likely to produce children who engage in antisocial behavior?" rather than "What kinds of *individuals* are found in families whose children are engaged in antisocial behavior?" The question so put is precise and thoroughly sociological. A paper by Professor Hughes illustrates the thinking involved here—that the "structural" and the "psychological" perspectives are in need of further study as to their utility when considered in combination.[6]

In working toward answers to the question as to what kinds of family organizations are associated with antisocial children, it can be seen that a paradigm of four ideal family types is implicit in this research. A family may be high on the extent of agreement on expectations and goals (the importance attributed to the items) and low on the number of perceived problems designated. Such a family might be regarded as *maximally integrated;* all the members agree on which of the son's behaviors and attitudes are highly important and feel that few difficulties accrue in these areas.

At the other extreme, a family may agree but little on the importance of the items and may identify a very large number of serious problems. This family can be called *minimally integrated,* for members do not share common values and expectations, and they experience much discomfort and distress concerning aspects of the son's behaviors and attitudes. Further, a family may have a very high level of agreement as to the importance of various items and may indicate numerous serious problems concerning the items. In this type of family, the members seem to share common values and expectations but cannot seem to work out satisfactory ways of implementing them. There is a suggestion in this situation of a distressed and worried group of people whose anxieties are not mitigated by the fact that everyone agrees on what is desirable. This type of family we have called *oversocialized.*

---

[6] Everett C. Hughes, "The Structural and Psychological Perspectives: Mutually Exclusive or Integrative?" paper presented at the Society for the Study of Social Problems meetings in Los Angeles, August, 1963.

Finally, a family may be characterized by very little agreement among members and very few problems which they describe as serious. This might mean that the family members share few common definitions but are not distressed about this state of affairs and do not regard their family life as troubled. We have labeled such a family *anomic,* because of the normlessness suggested by a situation in which members do not see eye to eye but do not particularly care.

With these four types in mind, it is now possible to hypothesize their various relationships to the outcome criteria—the absence of antisocial behavior in the school and the community.

Common sense alone would lead one to the first two hypotheses regarding both extreme types of family organizations, the maximally and the minimally integrated. It was hypothesized that 1. maximally integrated families will be more likely than not to produce children who *will not* engage in antisocial behavior in school and in the community, and 2. minimally integrated families will be more likely than not to produce children who *will* engage in antisocial behavior in school and in the community. The outcomes of children in the remaining two types of families are not immediately apparent and it is necessary to speculate on the basis of findings and observations of others rather on the basis of common sense alone. It has been stated by Wrong[7] and Bronfenbrenner[8] that oversocialized people are more likely than others to be anxious, dependent, and conforming. This would lead one to the third hypothesis, that 3. children from oversocialized families would not be as likely to engage in antisocial behavior in the community (no police contacts), nor as likely to be successful in school, because the school criteria included grades, demonstration of leadership, independence, and initiative.

Finally, concerning the anomic family, we base our suppositions regarding the connection between normlessness and antisocial behavior on the relationships indicated in such compilations of delinquency research as that of Moles, Lippitt, and Withey.[9] In many of the works they cite, the condition of normlessness figures prominently in the etiology of antisocial behavior. Empirical evidence of this relationship can be found in A. W. McEachern's[10] study of adolescents on probation. Therefore, it was hypothe-

---

[7] Dennis Wrong, "The Oversocialized View of Man," *American Sociological Review,* XXVI (April 1961), 183–93.

[8] Urie Bronfenbrenner, "The Changing American Child: A Speculative Analysis," *Journal of Social Issues,* XVII (1961), 6–17.

[9] Oliver Moles, Ronald Lippitt, and Stephen Withey, *A Speculative Review of Research and Theory in Delinquency* (Ann Arbor, Mich.: Institute for Social Research, University of Michigan, Document Series No. 2, September 1959).

[10] A. W. McEachern *et. al., Views of Authority: Probationers and Probation Officers* (Los Angeles: Youth Studies Center, University of Southern California, 1962).

sized that 4. children from anomic families will be more likely to engage in antisocial behavior in the community. There is no reason or evidence to suppose, however, that they will be more or less likely to have difficulty at school.

Table 1

HYPOTHESIZED RELATIONS BETWEEN PROBLEM INDICES AND OUTCOME CRITERIA

Family Type	Disagreement	[Criteria as Hypothesized] Problem Perception	Police Contact	School Adjustment
Integrated	Low	Low	No	Successful
Oversocialized	Low	High	No	Unsuccessful
Anomic	High	Low	Yes	Successful
Disintegrated	High	High	Yes	Unsuccessful

Table 1 shows the hypothesized relations between the two indices, disagreement and problem perception, as well as the relationship between these indices and the school and community outcome criteria.

Ideally, in the development of sets of independent variables which one wants to relate in some patterned way to dependent criteria, one strives for measures which are themselves uncorrelated, but which bear strong relationship to the chosen criteria. In this case, the two measures approach this ideal, in that a very low chi-square (.38, 1 df, corrected for continuity) was found with both measures as dichotomized.

To evaluate the data as to their conformity with the hypotheses, the following procedures were carried out.

The composite measures of school adjustment, developed in previous research by Fred J. Shanley and his staff at the Youth Studies Center,[11] were used to define two groups—those making successful and unsuccessful adjustments.

Police contact information was also dichotomized, separating those with no record of arrest from those with one or more. The range of arrests in this latter group was from one to eleven.

The family variables were dichotomized on the basis of scores above and below the median score for each variable. High problem families, then, are those in which the number of perceived problems exceeds the median number perceived by the total group of fifty families. The division of families on the disagreement variables was done in the same manner.

---

[11] Fred J. Shanley *et. al., Comparative Study of Factors Influencing the School Adjustment of Adolescents—A Preliminary Report* (Los Angeles: Research Paper No. 2, Youth Studies Center, University of Southern California, 1961).

With the score dichotomized, the frequency of families within each category is as shown in Table 2. The probability of obtaining cell differences by chance has been determined by a binomial test of the differences between relevant cells as predicted. A 50/50 or chance model was used, reflecting the null hypothesis of "no difference" between frequencies.

Table 2

POLICE AND SCHOOL SUCCESS CRITERIA AS RELATED TO FAMILY TYPE

	Police Criterion		School Criterion	
Family Type	Contact	No Contact	Not Successful	Successful
Integrated	3	16	1	18
		p = .016		p < .001
Oversocialized	6	1	7	0
		p = .05	p = .008	
Anomic	6	5	7	4
	p > .10			p > .10
Disintegrated	10	3	9	4
	p = .035		p = .087	

In the body of the table the underlined numbers indicate the location of hypothesized high frequencies. These frequencies should be compared with the adjacent value. Of eight relations, five attain statistical significance at or beyond the .10 level in the direction predicted; two are equivocal, and there is one statistically significant reversal. It can be seen that for the integrated and disintegrated family types, the model predicted the distributions accurately for both school and police criteria. Such success was not obtained for the other two types, however. Although the school criterion shows the expected relation for the oversocialized family (seven not successful, zero successful), the police criterion shows a reversal of the direction anticipated (six with contact, one without).

The data for the anomic family show little difference on the police criterion, although the direction of difference is as predicted. A reversal from expectation is seen for the school criterion. Neither of the divisions for the anomic family represent significant departures from an even split using a binomial test.

All in all, the conceptual scheme presented here would seem to be moderately successful, particularly considering limitations accruing as a result of the extremely small sample used. Although the literature and previous findings do not allow clear-cut bases for predictions for the anomic and oversocialized families, the model presented here distinguishes well between the more often discussed integrated and disintegrated families.

More importantly, even the small amount of data presented here can serve as a basis for further speculation and study. A considerable amount of refinement is needed in the measurement of the criteria used. Antisocial behavior should be measured in more discriminating units than mere presence or absence of police contact or arrest data. On the basis of the anomic family type, one could speculate, for example, that the boy who is anxious, dependent, and given to overconformity could easily be led into illegal activities by more dominant boys, particularly in gang-ridden neighborhoods. Sutherland, and more lately Cloward and Ohlin,[12] have discussed this very situation, although in somewhat different terms.

In our future work with these data, we hope to make the kinds of additions mentioned above, as well as to extend the analysis to the other one hundred families in our sample. At the same time, we will more fully specify the relations between the two variables, disagreement and problem perception, and will develop a model according to principles of axiomatic theory. Using this model and the enlarged sample, we hope to continue to explore the fertile conceptual area of the family as a social organization. Only by such investigation will the differential effects of the family as a socializing agent become more fully understood.

---

[12] Richard A. Cloward and Lloyd E. Ohlin, *Delinquency and Opportunity* (New York: Free Press of Glencoe, Inc., 1960).

Factors Related to Disposition in Juvenile Police Contacts

A. W. McEACHERN

RIVA BAUZER

Reference has been made several times in this volume to the conceptual and methodological complexity of delinquency measurement. One of the most commonly discussed problems has to do with the "distance" from the behavioral act to the measured criterion. This distance can be made up of such steps as detection, arrest, referral, court appearance, and final disposition. At each step an official judgment occurs which determines whether or not the offender will pass on to the next step. This paper reports data on factors affecting or related to one set of judgments at one step of the adjudication process. While it appears from the analysis that the nature of the offense is the overriding determinant of the judger's decision, perusal of the authors' tables reveals that *many* other variables also play a part. This demonstration of the complexity of the problem is both overwhelming and challenging.

A. W. McEACHERN, Youth Studies Center, University of Southern California; and RIVA BAUZER, Escola Brasileira de Administracao Publica, Rio de Janeiro, Brazil.

It is a commonplace observation that police tend to respond differentially to different ethnic and socio-economic groups, although some contend that police are concerned with the individual needs of juveniles with whom they come in contact, and therefore make dispositions in response to characteristics of the juveniles. Most police, in conversation at least, maintain that their job is to respond to the crimes rather than to the individuals who commit crimes. An earlier analysis of the offenses committed by over one hundred probationers in the Santa Monica area suggested that police disposition of recorded offenses was a function almost exclusively of the offenses, and did not depend on such characteristics as sex, age, residential status, number of the offense in the youngster's delinquent history, or whether or not he was on probation at the time he committed the offense. These findings surprised almost everyone to whom they were described except police, but they were questioned on the grounds that they provided no information about police response to different ethnic groups. The data and analyses presented in the accompanying tables were obtained and carried out in part to answer this objection to the earlier analysis, and in part to provide data on the basis of which one criterion of delinquency could be empirically defined and justified.

In California a youngster who commits or participates in a crime may or may not be contacted by the police. We have no information about delinquent activities in which police (or some other agent of society) do not contact the youngster. If there is a juvenile-police contact, a record may or may not be made of the event. We have no information about contacts for which no record is made or kept. If a record is made, the police may leave it at that, "counseling and releasing" the youngster, or they may request the probation department to submit a petition to the juvenile court. Such a request is the only formal (and legal) alternative to "counseling and releasing" available to law enforcement agencies in handling juveniles. Implicit in such a request is the suggestion that the youngster requires either sanctioning, or help, according to the legal provisions of the state. In other words, youngsters who are referred to the probation department with a request for a petition are being given the only legal "sanction" that police may use.

What factors determine whether or not police request petitions? Do they respond differently to boys than to girls? Are Negroes, Mexican-Americans, or "Angloes" more likely to have petitions requested? Do police give different treatment to youngsters from intact homes in which both parents are living than to those in some other family situation? To answer questions like these, two bodies of data were used. One is based on a random sample of 1,010 records drawn from the Central Juvenile Index maintained by the Los Angeles County Sheriff's Department. This sample provided information about 1,915 incidents, of which 1,117 were delinquent incidents. (The remaining 798 incidents were minor traffic violations, dependency referrals, and uncodeable incidents; they were excluded from this analysis.) The other body of data is based on a record of all juvenile-police contacts in Santa Monica from 1940 to 1960. This record provided information about 7,946 delinquent incidents. Some of the information available in the Central Juvenile Index is not available in the Santa Monica Records (for example, ethnic identification), and vice versa (for example, the identification of the investigating officer). For this reason, as well as because the Central Juvenile Index is current while the Santa Monica data are historical, the two bodies of data provide complementary rather than substantiating evidence with respect to each other.

The first, most difficult, and probably most controversial step in the analysis of these data was the classification of the specific offenses recorded into a smaller number of categories. Table 1 presents the classification used throughout the subsequent analyses. Three criteria were used in assigning an offense to one of the seven categories: first, whether it was a "juvenile" offense (an offense with which adults could not be charged) or an adult offense; second, the proportion of petitions requested for that offense, which was used as an index of the "seriousness" of the offense; and third, in the case of relatively infrequently occurring offenses, (forgery and forcible rape, for example) its logical similarity to other offenses in that category.

Tables 2 through 11 present distributions and analyses from the Central Juvenile Index data. In Table 2 are the results of a number of zero order analyses between characteristics of the juvenile, of the incident itself, whether or not a petition was requested, and what the recorded offense was. The nature of the relationships described by these chi-squares is available in the marginals in subsequent tables. Not surprisingly with N's of this magnitude, almost everything is significantly related to whether or not a petition was requested. The one exception, "Race," is perhaps the only surprising finding in the table. The proportions of petitions requested for the three ethnic categories used in this analysis are .28 for Negroes, .27 for Mexican-Americans, and .26 for "Angloes." (These figures and the N's on which they are based can be found in the marginals of Table 5. The proportions and categories on which the other chi-squares are based are presented in Tables 3 through 11.) This finding with respect to the proportion of petitions requested for different ethnic groups does *not* mean that there is no differential treatment of these groups by individual police officers or by different police departments. It does mean that there are no *systematic and consistent* differences in requests for petitions throughout the county.

The general conclusion suggested by an examination of the chi-squares in Table 2 is that there are a number of characteristics of individuals which are related to whether or not police request petitions, over and above the offense that was committed. Sex, age, number of the offense in the youngster's delinquent history, whether or not he comes from an intact family, whether or not he is on probation, and the year in which he was born all apparently have some influence on the police disposition. To balance these findings, the nature of the offense, the police department, and the year in which the incident occurred are also all very significantly related to whether or not a petition is requested.

If different kinds of youngsters commit different kinds of offenses (as boys and girls tend to do), then differences in the proportions of petitions requested may be accounted for by the kind of offense rather than the kind of youngster. The analyses and distributions presented in Tables 3 through 11 were designed to test this hypothesis. In the case of girls and boys (Table 3) this notion is borne out. When the effects of the different kinds of offenses boys and girls commit are controlled, there is no significant difference in the proportions of petitions requested for boys and for girls, although there is a significant interaction effect. Boys are less likely to have petitions requested for juvenile offenses and more likely to have them requested for the more serious adult offenses.

Similar analyses were carried out for the remaining characteristics of youngsters and incidents. In every case, the relationship between the nature of the offense and whether or not a petition was requested remained highly significant, holding constant the effect of the characteristic, and there was a highly significant interaction effect. When offense is held constant, however, the effects of family status, as well as of sex, are eliminated. The effects of the number of the offense and probation status are considerably reduced, the effect of age remains about the same, and that of year of birth is considerably increased, as is that of year of incident. Since these two time variables are confounded in this analysis (the presence of a record in the Central Juvenile Index is controlled by year of birth), it is difficult to separate their effects, although an examination of the changes in proportions of petitions requested by the Santa Monica police over a twenty-year period (Table 17) suggests that the year in which the incident occurred has more effect than the year in which the youngster was born. Finally, the differences among police departments remain highly significant when offenses are held constant.

Clearly, these data and analyses provide no simple answer to the initial question of this paper: petitions are requested in part as a function of characteristics of the individual and in part as a function of the incident itself (the offense, the year, and the jurisdiction).

An examination of Tables 12 through 18, in which distributions from the Santa Monica data are presented, suggests a similar conclusion. Age, sex, number of the offense, and family status are characteristics to which police apparently respond in requesting or not requesting petitions. Perhaps of greater interest, however, are the differences in proportions of petitions requested during different time periods, and by different investigating officers. In the period from 1940 to 1944, only 19 per cent of the delinquent incidents recorded resulted in requests for petitions. From 1955 to 1960, 43 per cent resulted in requests for petitions; this trend holds fairly well for each offense category, so that it cannot be attributed exclusively to youngsters committing more of the serious offenses in the later years. Incidentally, it is interesting that the total number of delinquent incidents recorded during the four time periods changed very little. In Santa Monica, at any rate, it is possible to conclude that the steadily increasing juvenile court population is attributable to changes in police response rather than to increasing or more serious juvenile delinquency.

The effect individual police officers have is displayed in Table 16. Investigating officers were classified according to the proportion of incidents with which they were concerned on which they requested petitions. It is apparent that no matter what the offense, some officers are more likely to request petitions than others, and this trend is consistent for each offense category.

These data and analyses suggest that police do respond to characteristics of individuals, but that their dispositions are just as much a function of who the police are as of what the delinquent is like. Two of the most important characteristics of individuals, sex and ethnicity, were found to have relatively little relationship to whether or not a petition was requested. Others were related, but none so markedly as the nature of the offense, or the police department (in the case of the Central Juvenile Index data), or the police officer (in the case of the Santa Monica data). The marked changes over time demonstrated with the Santa Monica police data point up the fact that delinquency cannot be sensibly described as isolated acts of bad individuals, but must be thought of as interactions between deviant individuals and agents of the society which defines their deviance. Changes in society, changes in its agents, or changes in the deviant individuals will all result in changes in delinquency, one way or the other.

Table 1

CLASSIFICATION OF OFFENSES, NUMBER OCCURRING (N), AND PROPORTION OF THIS NUMBER ON WHICH PETITIONS REQUESTED (P)

Juvenile Offenses (1–3)	CJI N	CJI p	SM N	SM p
(1) Less Serious				
Disorderly conduct	33	.09	244	.20
Runaway	68	.07	838	.11
Curfew violation	107	.07	492	.12
Other school violations	48	.00	—	—
Improper companions	1	.00	—	—
	257	.07	1574	.13
(2) ± Serious				
Association with narcotics	9	.44	37	.35
Truancy	24	.33	18	.06
Transient	9	.22	12	.92
Violation of liquor laws	63	.19	479	.07
Probation violation	2	.50	31	.23
	107	.25	577	.11
(3) Most Serious				
Incorrigible	43	.77	174	.68
Illegitimate sex relations	23	.74	354	.51
Rape (1–01)	—	—	40	.50
Other sex delinquency	8	.62	86	.26
	74	.74	654	.53

Adult Offenses (4–7)	CJI N	CJI p	SM N	SM p
(4) Less Serious				
Other specific Violation	30	.17	310	.09
Vagrancy	21	.14	97	.16
Arson	10	.10	53	.36
Malicious mischief	91	.06	297	.09
All other theft	46	.06	190	.23
Weapons	22	.00	44	.09
	220	.08	813	.15
(5) ± Serious				
Robbery	14	.43	82	.66
Assault and battery	27	.41	166	.37
Burglary	122	.36	916	.49
Petty theft	185	.25	1939	.15
Forgery	2	1.00	21	.76
Hit and run	5	.60	14	.43
Drunk driving	4	.25	21	1.00
	359	.28	3160	.28
(6) More Serious				
Auto theft, joy riding	80	.61	1027	.49
(7) Most Serious				
Aggravated assault	18	.72	7	.71
Possession and use of narcotics	12	.67	26	.46
Grand theft	3	1.00	103	.45
Forcible rape	1	1.00	5	1.00
	34	.74	141	.48

Table 2

RELATIONS BETWEEN PERSON AND INCIDENT CHARAC-
TERISTICS AND REQUESTS FOR PETITION AND OFFENSE,
CJI

Characteristics of Persons	Petition Request			Offense		
	X^2	df	p	X^2	df	p
1. Sex	5.23	1	.025	130.30	6	.001
2. Age	32.07	6	.001	122.00	36	.001
3. Race	.52	2	.500	50.82	12	.001
4. Number of the entry	57.42	6	.001	79.54	36	.001
5. Father-mother	9.44	1	.005	8.60	6	.250
6. Probation status	50.83	1	.001	17.28	6	.010
7. Year of birth	12.59	7	.050	45.32	42	.250
Characteristics of Incident						
8. Offense	265.89	6	.001			
9. Referring agency	213.22	4	.001	143.43	24	.001
10. Year of incident	46.43	6	.001	79.10	36	.001

Table 3

PROPORTION OF PETITIONS REQUESTED FOR DIFFERENT
OFFENSES AND SEX, CJI†

Offense	Male*	Female*
1	.05 (195)	.10 (62)
2	.23 (81)	.35 (17)
3	.65 (31)	.81 (43)
4	.08 (197)	.11 (18)
5	.30 (319)	.18 (39)
6	.62 (76)	.50 (4)
7	.71 (31)	1.00 (3)
Total	.25 (930)	.33 (186)

X^2 off. = 153.66 X^2 tot. = 280.60
6 df   13 df
prob. < .001   prob. < .001
X^2 sex = 1.02 X^2 int. = 125.92
1 df   6 df
prob. < .500   prob. < .001

* In each column, the first figure represents a proportion whereas the figure in parentheses represents the number of cases. This system will be observed in all the following
tables.
† William F. Dossett, *Extension of Chi-Square as a Nonparametric Method in the Analysis of
Experimental Data* (Santa Barbara: Tempo, General Electric Company, May 1961). All
subsequent chi-square analyses follow the procedure outlined in this reference.

Table 4*

PROPORTION OF PETITIONS REQUESTED FOR DIFFERENT OFFENSES AND AGE, CJI

				Age			
Offense	*5–10*	*11–12*	*13*	*14*	*15*	*16*	*17–18*
1	.07 (15)	0 (16)	.02 (41)	.04 (44)	.09 (54)	.04 (54)	.16 (32)
2	0 (3)	0 (1)	.12 (8)	.38 (13)	.32 (22)	.26 (27)	.19 (21)
3	0 (1)	.86 (7)	.78 (9)	.75 (12)	.61 (18)	.69 (16)	1.00 (10)
4	.07 (29)	0 (36)	.17 (30)	.06 (36)	.02 (40)	.21 (29)	.07 (14)
5	0 (33)	.19 (48)	.29 (63)	.26 (68)	.30 (77)	.41 (39)	.63 (30)
6	0 (0)	.50 (2)	.60 (5)	.54 (28)	.63 (19)	.65 (17)	.78 (9)
7	0 (2)	0 (1)	.50 (4)	.83 (6)	.80 (10)	1.00 (7)	.75 (4)
Total	.04 (83)	.14 (111)	.23 (160)	.27 (207)	.28 (240)	.32 (189)	.41 (120)

X^2 off. = 121.49   6 df   prob. < .001
X^2 age = 31.42   6 df   prob. < .001
X^2 tot. = 343.88   48 df   prob. < .001
X^2 int. = 186.97   36 df   prob. < .001

* See Table 3 notes.

Table 5*

PROPORTION OF PETITIONS REQUESTED FOR DIFFERENT OFFENSES AND ETHNIC GROUP

	Ethnic Group						
Offense	*White*	*Negro*	*Mexican*				
1	.06 (175)	.07 (43)	.08 (36)				
2	.26 (70)	0 (5)	.30 (23)				
3	.78 (58)	.78 (9)	.50 (6)	X^2 off.	= 116.86	6 df	prob. < .001
4	.07 (158)	.07 (28)	.15 (26)	X^2 race	= 1.79	2 df	prob. < .500
5	.27 (233)	.35 (86)	.26 (39)	X^2 tot.	= 283.05	20 df	prob. < .001
6	.60 (60)	.80 (5)	.60 (15)	X^2 int.	= 164.40	12 df	prob. < .001
7	.88 (16)	.67 (9)	.36 (9)				
Total	.26 (770)	.28 (181)	.27 (154)				

* See Table 3 notes.

Table 6*

PROPORTION OF PETITIONS REQUESTED FOR DIFFERENT OFFENSES AND FATHER-MOTHER ENTRY, CJI

	Father-Mother Entry					
	Father-Mother Intact					
Offense	*F-M*	*Other*				
1	.06 (173)	.07 (84)				
2	.22 (68)	.33 (30)	X^2 off.	= 240.57	6 df	prob. < .001
3	.78 (45)	.71 (28)	X^2 F-M	= 2.31	1 df	prob. < .250
4	.07 (162)	.09 (53)	X^2 tot.	= 285.23	13 df	prob. < .001
5	.24 (234)	.38 (125)	X^2 int.	= 42.36	6 df	prob. < .001
6	.61 (50)	.62 (24)				
7	.68 (22)	.83 (12)				
Total	.23 (760)	.32 (356)				

* See Table 3 notes.

Table 7*

PROPORTION OF PETITIONS REQUESTED FOR DIFFERENT OFFENSES AND NUMBER OF ENTRY, CJI

			Number of Entry on Record				
Offense	*1*	*2*	*3*	*4*	*5–6*	*7–10*	*11–18*
1	.02 (108)	.08 (53)	.21 (28)	.12 (25)	.05 (19)	0 (21)	0 (3)
2	.22 (32)	.25 (16)	.40 (10)	.22 (9)	.33 (15)	.20 (10)	.17 (6)
3	.78 (37)	.77 (13)	.83 (6)	.71 (7)	.67 (3)	.50 (6)	.50 (2)
4	.08 (119)	0 (38)	.19 (16)	.09 (11)	.14 (14)	.08 (12)	.20 (5)
5	.12 (168)	.25 (69)	.48 (44)	.50 (28)	.54 (28)	.77 (13)	.78 (9)
6	.45 (29)	.56 (18)	.87 (15)	.62 (8)	.80 (5)	.80 (5)	0 (0)
7	.67 (12)	.75 (8)	1.00 (4)	.50 (2)	1.00 (5)	.33 (3)	0 (0)
Total	.17 (505)	.24 (215)	.46 (123)	.34 (90)	.38 (89)	.30 (70)	.40 (25)

X^2 off. = 138.54   6 df   prob. < .001
X^2 no. ent. = 23.79   6 df   prob. < .001
X^2 tot. = 376.58   48 df   prob. < .001
X^2 int. = 214.24   36 df   prob. < .001

* See Table 3 notes.

Table 8*

PROPORTION OF PETITIONS REQUESTED FOR DIFFERENT OFFENSES AND PROBATION STATUS, CJI

	Probation Status		
	Not on	*On*	
Offense	*Probation*	*Probation*	
1	.05 (213)	.11 (44)	
2	.20 (81)	.53 (17)	X^2 off. = 54.01 6 df prob. < .001
3	.72 (57)	.82 (17)	X^2 prob. = 20.07 1 df prob. < .001
4	.07 (192)	.13 (23)	X^2 tot. = 319.26 13 df prob. < .001
5	.24 (309)	.62 (50)	X^2 int. = 245.18 6 df prob. < .001
6	.56 (63)	.82 (17)	
7	.70 (23)	.82 (11)	
Total	.22 (938)	.47 (179)	

* See Table 3 notes.

Table 9*

PROPORTION OF PETITIONS REQUESTED FOR DIFFERENT
OFFENSES AND YEAR OF BIRTH, CJI

					Year of Birth				
Offense	1943–44	1945	1946	1497	1948	1949	1950	1951–58
1	0 (5)	.06 (65)	.06 (89)	.08 (49)	.19 (16)	0 (21)	0 (3)	0 (8)
2	0 (2)	.20 (49)	.36 (22)	.27 (15)	.50 (4)	0 (0)	0 (1)	0 (2)
3	1.00 (1)	.78 (18)	.68 (25)	.69 (13)	.86 (7)	.75 (4)	.80 (5)	.14 (7)
4	0 (2)	.10 (58)	.06 (49)	.05 (42)	.07 (28)	.16 (19)	0 (8)	.05 (20)
5	.75 (4)	.35 (105)	.24 (90)	.23 (60)	.29 (38)	.41 (27)	.33 (15)	0 (0)
6	0 (0)	.68 (31)	.61 (23)	.60 (15)	.33 (6)	.75 (4)	0 (1)	0 (0)
7	0 (0)	.90 (10)	.78 (9)	.67 (9)	1.00 (3)	0 (1)	0 (2)	0 (0)
Total	.29 (14)	.30 (336)	.25 (307)	.24 (203)	.28 (102)	.26 (76)	.26 (35)	.05 (37)

X^2 off. = 77.98   6 df   prob. < .001

X^2 yr. of birth = 50.03   7 df   prob. < .001

X^2 tot. = 313.07   55 df   prob. < .001

X^2 int. = 185.07   42 df   prob. < .001

* See Table 3 notes.

Table 10*

PROPORTION OF PETITIONS REQUESTED FOR DIFFERENT
OFFENSES AND REFERRING AGENCY, CJI

			Referring Agency		
Offense	LAPD	Sh. LA	Larger Cities	Smaller Cities	All Others
1	.05 (62)	0 (52)	.04 (50)	.03 (32)	.16 (61)
2	.22 (18)	.16 (19)	0 (20)	.07 (15)	.65 (26)
3	.72 (19)	.25 (8)	.71 (7)	.75 (8)	.88 (33)
4	.13 (38)	.03 (60)	.07 (57)	.04 (56)	1.00 (4)
5	.28 (103)	.12 (87)	.22 (69)	.23 (61)	.92 (39)
6	.58 (24)	.54 (11)	.25 (16)	.64 (11)	1.00 (18)
7	.75 (12)	.20 (5)	.50 (2)	.50 (2)	1.00 (13)
Total	.28 (275)	.10 (242)	.14 (221)	.17 (185)	.65 (194)

X^2 off. = 162.02   6 df   prob. < .001

X^2 ref. ag. = 114.37   4 df   prob. < .001

X^2 tot. = 450.20   34 df   prob. < .001

X^2 int. = 173.81   24 df   prob. < .001

* See Table 3 notes.

Table 11*

PROPORTION OF PETITIONS REQUESTED FOR DIFFERENT OFFENSES AND YEAR OF INCIDENT, CJI

Offense	*1953–56*	*1957–58*	*1959*	*1960*	*1961*	*1962*	*1963*
				Year of Incident			
1	0 (4)	1.00 (10)	0 (26)	.02 (46)	.04 (57)	.10 (99)	.14 (14)
2	0 (0)	0 (3)	.25 (8)	.33 (15)	.24 (31)	.24 (29)	.44 (9)
3	0 (0)	1.00 (1)	.83 (6)	.46 (13)	.77 (13)	.76 (34)	1.00 (6)
4	0 (11)	.07 (28)	0 (29)	.06 (33)	.15 (41)	.12 (58)	0 (14)
5	0 (11)	.13 (31)	.14 (49)	.20 (66)	.32 (73)	.42 (110)	.56 (18)
6	0 (0)	1.00 (1)	.50 (6)	.70 (20)	.55 (20)	.52 (27)	1.00 (6)
7	0 (0)	.50 (2)	.50 (2)	.67 (9)	.75 (4)	.83 (12)	.80 (5)
Total	0 (26)	.13 (76)	.14 (126)	.23 (207)	.26 (239)	.33 (369)	.44 (72)

X^2 off. $= 120.91$　　6 df　　prob. $< .001$

X^2 yr. of in. $= 131.26$　　6 df　　prob. $< .001$

X^2 tot. $= 331.06$　　48 df　　prob. $< .001$

X^2 int. $= 78.88$　　36 df　　prob. $< .001$

* See Table 3 notes.

Table 12*

PROPORTION OF PETITIONS REQUESTED FOR DIFFERENT OFFENSES AND SEX, SM

Offense	*Male*	*Female*
1	.13 (1064)	.12 (510)
2	.12 (457)	.08 (126)
3	.55 (313)	.50 (341)
4	.16 (733)	.06 (79)
5	.30 (2809)	.14 (351)
6	.52 (928)	.15 (98)
7	.29 (133)	.21 (8)
Total	.29 (6431)	.21 (1513)

* See Table 3 notes.

Table 13*

PROPORTION OF PETITIONS REQUESTED FOR DIFFERENT OFFENSES AND AGE, SM

Offense	*0–10*	*11–12*	*13*	*14*	*15*	*16*	*17–21*
				Age			
1	.18 (59)	.11 (91)	.13 (162)	.14 (247)	.14 (331)	.12 (367)	.13 (316)
2	.33 (12)	.29 (17)	.13 (15)	.18 (34)	.11 (108)	.10 (165)	.09 (225)
3	.22 (40)	.50 (40)	.68 (56)	.57 (130)	.60 (44)	.51 (130)	.43 (114)
4	.17 (63)	.50 (40)	.11 (80)	.07 (118)	.18 (125)	.16 (189)	.21 (181)
5	.19 (263)	.19 (404)	.24 (394)	.28 (495)	.29 (573)	.34 (553)	.39 (477)
6	.00 (1)	.58 (19)	.54 (72)	.56 (197)	.50 (288)	.48 (262)	.37 (186)
7	.50 (4)	.40 (10)	.41 (17)	.43 (14)	.46 (22)	.55 (31)	.51 (43)
Total	.19 (442)	.21 (637)	.26 (796)	.30 (1235)	.31 (1591)	.29 (1697)	.27 (1542)

* See Table 3 notes.

Table 14*

PROPORTION OF PETITIONS REQUESTED FOR DIFFERENT
OFFENSES AND FATHER-MOTHER ENTRY, SM

Offense	Father-Mother Intact	Other
1	.14 (613)	.14 (522)
2	.10 (238)	.17 (165)
3	.56 (214)	.74 (225)
4	.18 (337)	.20 (245)
5	.29 (1267)	.36 (998)
6	.50 (428)	.52 (360)
7	.43 (54)	.49 (75)
Total	.28 (3151)	.35 (1688)

* See Table 3 notes.

Table 15*

PROPORTION OF PETITIONS REQUESTED FOR DIFFERENT
OFFENSES AND NUMBER OF ENTRY, SM

Offense	Number of Entry 1	2	3	4	5–6	7–10	11–16
1	.09 (1241)	.31 (210)	.30 (80)	.35 (26)	.39 (18)	.00 (5)	.67 (3)
2	.09 (455)	.14 (71)	.30 (27)	.44 (9)	.40 (10)	.20 (5)	—
3	.46 (475)	.62 (112)	.85 (41)	.71 (14)	.83 (6)	1.00 (5)	1.00 (1)
4	.11 (659)	.25 (89)	.32 (31)	.31 (13)	.69 (13)	.75 (8)	—
5	.22 (2405)	.42 (428)	.54 (155)	.58 (89)	.70 (60)	.74 (23)	.40 (5)
6	.78 (771)	.58 (143)	.71 (59)	.48 (23)	.79 (19)	1.00 (10)	1.00 (2)
7	.43 (104)	.58 (19)	.67 (9)	.80 (5)	.75 (4)	—	—
Total	.22 (6110)	.40 (1063)	.52 (402)	.52 (174)	.65 (130)	.65 (130)	.63 (11)

* See Table 3 notes.

Table 16

PROPORTION OF PETITIONS REQUESTED FOR DIFFERENT
OFFENSES AND INVESTIGATORS, SM

Offense	1	2	3	4	5
1	.06 (420)	.15 (403)	.17 (222)	.19 (26)	—
2	.07 (168)	.10 (316)	.21 (84)	.25 (8)	—
3	.37 (99)	.46 (387)	.74 (136)	.80 (30)	1.00 (1)
4	.06 (265)	.20 (368)	.18 (164)	.43 (14)	—
5	.18 (913)	.29 (1512)	.39 (597)	.47 (127)	.88 (8)
6	.29 (260)	.44 (436)	.72 (257)	.66 (65)	1.00 (5)
7	.39 (33)	.47 (68)	.54 (35)	.80 (5)	—
Total	.16 (2158)	.27 (3990)	.41 (1495)	.52 (275)	.93 (14)

		Range of Proportion of Petitions Requested
I group*	39 investigators (26 = .000)	.000–.199
II group	22 investigators	.200–.399
III group	6 investigators	.400–.499
IV group	6 investigators	.500–.699
V group	5 investigators	.700–1.00

* See reference note, Table 3.

Table 17*

PROPORTION OF PETITIONS REQUESTED FOR DIFFERENT OFFENSES AND YEAR OF INCIDENT, SM

	Year of Incident			
Offense	*1940–44*	*1945–49*	*1950–54*	*1955–60*
1	.11 (422)	.10 (425)	.17 (489)	.13 (238)
2	.07 (163)	.11 (173)	.09 (107)	.19 (134)
3	.27 (203)	.42 (134)	.64 (132)	.78 (185)
4	.05 (220)	.19 (205)	.22 (303)	.19 (185)
5	.18 (875)	.25 (854)	.33 (645)	.40 (786)
6	.42 (227)	.30 (206)	.40 (237)	.70 (357)
7	.67 (12)	.40 (68)	.52 (25)	.56 (36)
Total	.19 (2122)	.22 (2065)	.20 (1838)	.43 (1921)

* See Table 3 notes.

Table 18*

PROPORTION OF PETITIONS REQUESTED FOR DIFFERENT OFFENSES AND RESIDENCE, SM

	Residence		
Offense	*SM*	*Venice*	*Others*
1	.17 (698)	.16 (168)	.08 (708)
2	.17 (227)	.05 (63)	.08 (287)
3	.57 (478)	.51 (49)	.36 (127)
4	.17 (479)	.20 (46)	.11 (290)
5	.31 (1854)	.47 (431)	.24 (875)
6	.57 (480)	.34 (119)	.44 (418)
7	.54 (69)	.40 (15)	.44 (57)
Total	.33 (4295)	.25 (891)	.21 (2762)

* See Table 3 notes.

A Theoretical Orientation
for Police Studies

EUGENE P. WENNINGER
JOHN P. CLARK

As indicated in the previous paper, police response to deviant acts is part and parcel of the very concept of delinquency. If police response were automatic, unvarying from place to place and time to time, then one major source of variance would be eliminated. But of course this is not the case. Police officers are human beings acting as the instruments of a highly complex, varying, and sometimes inconsistent system of social norms and values. No less than that of the offender, the behavior of the police officer can only be properly understood within its several contexts. The authors of the following paper have suggested two important socially derived dimensions that may shape and even determine the nature of police responses to deviant acts. The model serves their purpose well.

EUGENE P. WENNINGER, Kent State University, and JOHN P. CLARK, University of Illinois.

The role of municipal police looms large in any concern for delinquency and its participants. It has been pointed out many times that a meager change in the activities of local law enforcement can result in the creation of "crime waves" of proportions sufficient to cause national concern. Yet there has been remarkably little systematic investigation of the manner in which municipal police help define the limits and consequences of delinquency or other types of deviant behavior. There is even less known about the characteristics of the interaction between the police and the public they have sworn to serve. Almost totally neglected in empirical research is the measurement of how the character of the interrelationship between police forces and the communities in which they operate colors or determines the nature of deviant behavior in those communities.

This paper is a brief discussion of some sociological perspectives on municipal police departments that may be of value in suggesting theoretical frameworks for research on the police.[1] Two perspectives are presented below. The first is that of value maintenance.[2] Of concern here is the social cohesion of a community. From this perspective we view the police as an ancillary aid to the value maintaining processes and as a *symbolic* agency of social control.

The second perspective is that of goal attainment.[3] The political institution is of primary interest here, particularly government as the structure devised by society to effect ends in its name.[4] In this perspective, we study the police as the enforcement arm of government—that is, as an *instrumental* agency of social control.

Empirically, of course, the two perspectives are not mutually exclusive. We are analytically separating them for the purpose of suggesting research orientations. Both perspectives utilize the same sociological processes, essentially those of socialization and institutionalization. The end product of the joint operation of these processes is, in the majority of cases, social structures

---

[1] Much of the inspiration for this paper is provided by Talcott Parsons' discussion of functional and structural categories for the analysis of a social system. For an introduction to Parsons' most recent elaborations on these categories, see Talcott Parsons *et al., Theories of Society* (New York: Free Press of Glencoe, Inc., 1961), Vol. I, "An Outline of the Social System," 30–79, and "The Point of View of the Author," the final chapter in Max Black, ed., *The Social Theories of Talcott Parsons* (Englewood Cliffs, N.J.: Prentice-Hall, Inc., 1961). Another major source of inspiration is Robert K. Merton's discussion of "pairs of values not simultaneously realizable." See his epilogue to Robert K. Merton and Robert A. Nisbet, eds., *Contemporary Social Problems* (New York: Harcourt, Brace & World, Inc., 1961), pp. 731–37.

[2] Parsons, *Theories of Society*, pp. 38–39. We are taking value maintenance to be a special case of the over-all functional imperative of pattern maintenance.

[3] *Ibid.,* p. 39.

[4] Cf. Parsons, *Theories of Society*, pp. 47, 51. We are indebted to Parsons for noting the relationship between political organization and the functional imperative of goal attainment. The application of this relationship developed in this paper is our responsibility.

which operate more-or-less routinely. Members of the structure do what they are expected to do in a relatively non-conscious manner.

A theoretical assumption upon which much of the following is based is that goal attainment and value maintenance cannot be equally stressed during the same period of time within the same social structure.[5] To the extent that one is being emphasized, the other is not. The usual state of society or social structure in this view is one where institutionalized members support customary value systems in an essentially non-conscious manner. The support is cybernetic in effect—self-reinforcing. An awareness of alternative patterns to those customary at a given time arises in problematic situations. These alternatives can become goals, and to the extent that members of a structure support them in opposition to the prevailing patterns, goal attainment becomes paramount. Goal attainment to us suggests a *conscious* transformation of one steady state of a structure to another.[6] To the extent that the transformation is successful, value maintenance reasserts itself, the level of awareness or of conscious concern with the structure drops, and a dynamic equilibrium is reestablished.

Value Maintenance and the Police

In this perspective the police operate as part of the background or social milieu affecting all members of a society. This milieu is "given" from the moment of entrance of a member into the society and is consciously or unconsciously taken into account in most social behavior.

Social control is largely built into the system by means of mechanisms reinforcing the prevailing values. The value maintaining society operates on custom; its members have internalized the norms and values associated with it and the allocation of rewards and punishments serves to reinforce these

---

[5] This assumption is based upon much the same distinction that Scheler makes between "the carrying out together of fully conscious spontaneous actions which are by intention objectively referred," and "those activities which are not carried out 'spontaneously,' but which 'carry themselves out,' such as automatic or semi-automatic psycho-physical activities." In the former category Scheler includes law, education, art, science, and government; in the latter, myth, folk-language, folk-song, folk-religion, custom, and tradition. See Paul Schlipp, "The 'Formal Problems' of Scheler's Sociology of Knowledge," *Philosophical Review*, XXXVI (March 1927), 101–15, and Howard Becker and Helmut Dahlke, "Max Scheler's Sociology of Knowledge," *Philosophy and Phenomenological Research*, II (March 1942), 310–22.

[6] We are defining a social structure as a "steady state" to the extent that its form persists even though its members are continually being replaced and removed by metabolic events. See Wolfgang Kohler, "Directions of Processes in Living Systems," in Philip G. Frank, ed., *The Validation of Scientific Theories* (New York: Crowell-Collier & Macmillan, Inc., 1961), p. 138.

normative patterns. Such a society is self-regulating, in the sense that Nadel implies:

> Taking the whole society to be the relevant system, any "output" of the intended kind—any conduct in accordance with the social norm—is partly returned as "input," that is, as information sustaining further action of that character. . . . Controls both follow from the value system and demonstrate it, since the punishments and rewards bestowed by societies are normally public acts.[7]

We might wonder why even the "symbolic" influence of the police would be needed in such a society. The reason, of course, is that humans are somewhat recalcitrant.[8] Socialization and institutionalization are not perfect or all-pervasive processes, and rarely is the social "insulation" of the society sufficient to keep it free from new ideas. There may also be a basic obsolescence factor operating inter-generationally that disrupts perfect acceptance of the status quo.[9]

The processes of socialization and institutionalization work more to the benefit of value maintenance than of goal attainment since they are inherently long run in effect, and the attainment of specific goals is usually of relatively short term duration.

Summarizing this first perspective, socialization and institutionalization are basic social processes contributing to the maintenance of the normative patterns within a given society. Feedback between value systems and public allocation of sanctions is the chief support of these processes. Since the conduct of the members of a given society is not completely determined by these processes, there remains a relatively wide latitude of behavior open to the members which prompts the need for constraints and guides to conduct. The police perform one function in the framework of this perspective. To the extent that their presence is felt through their constant visibility, they serve as reminders and symbols of societal expectations. In this role they represent passive, potential, and symbolic force.

Goal Attainment and the Police

Motivation of the members of a society to contribute to its "well-being" is the major function of the political system.[10] In the first perspective we

---

7 Siegfried F. Nadel, "Social Control and Self-Regulation," *Social Forces,* **XXXI** (March 1953), 272–73.

8 Cf. Morris R. Cohen, *Reason and Law* (New York: Crowell-Collier & Macmillan, Inc., 1961), pp. 93–94.

9 C. A. O. Van Nieuwenhuijze, *Society as Process: Essays in Social Science Method* ('s Gravenhage: Mouton & Co., 1962), pp. 111–13.

10 Parsons, *op. cit.,* pp. 39, 47, 51.

pointed out that no society is entirely self-regulating; while custom produces a high degree of stability, the normative system has to be continually created and justified to and by the members of the society. While this is obviously true when the attainment of new norms is desired, it also may hold for old norms. When behavior is most customary and values most accepted, they may be peculiarly vulnerable to violation, for by this time the original purpose and justifications for the norms and values may have been forgotten. In such situations justifications have to be re-created if the norms are to continue to be viable.

In the absence of legitimate justification, force may be utilized. In most societies legitimate use of force resides in the hands of government. Naked force is not well accepted by those governed, and so governments usually mask force or remove its immediate presence through the use of rules, regulations, sanctions, and laws.

Law is more highly dependent upon force than is custom. Both custom and law serve to integrate a society, though law can serve as a disintegrative instrument as well. Custom most commonly serves maintenance of the status quo since it implies internalization with its implications of non-conscious behavior. Law also may contribute to the maintenance of the status quo, but in a qualitatively different manner. There is always an awareness by the members of a society that the law is being consciously used to attain given ends and that it has potential physical force to sustain it.[11] Hence, the important characteristic of law for us is not its utility as an instrument of integration, but its utility as an instrument of goal attainment.[12]

From the goal attainment perspective law serves the "self-conscious" society. That is, it serves the society which no longer runs on the self-reinforcing dynamics of custom, but which has become aware of alternatives to the patterns of behavior delimited by custom. Attempts to implement alternatives may involve the use of law as a means of breaking the hold of

---

[11] See Kingsley Davis, *Human Society* (New York: The Macmillan Company, 1949), pp. 66–70.

[12] Merton discusses this same difference in outlook in terms of "prescriptive" and "proscriptive" controls. Robert K. Merton, *Social Theory and Social Structure* (New York: The Free Press of Glencoe, Inc., 1957), p. 133. Also see Ephraim H. Mizruchi and Robert Perrucci, "Norm Qualities and Differential Effects of Deviant Behavior: An Exploratory Analysis," *American Sociological Review*, XXVII (June 1962), 391–99. The proscriptive and prescriptive dimensions of norms that they utilize in their study are applicable here. An emphasis on goal attainment should produce a corresponding emphasis upon proscriptive norms, while value maintenance in its most effective form is accomplished through internalization of norms and values which are in the main prescriptive.

Parsons sees the legal order as the primary integrative structure in a social system, and states that problems focusing on integration of systems make up the central core of sociological theory. See *Theories of Society,* pp. 40–41. To us concentration on legal integration makes a rather one-sided approach to sociological theory.

custom upon those segments of the society affected.[13] To the extent that the enforcement of law is successful in motivating members along desired lines, the legally induced behavior patterns become part of the background of action and are considered customary.

Therefore, law can serve two masters, sociologically speaking. On the one hand, as an instrument of government it can serve the task of goal attainment. On the other hand, allied with custom, it can serve in maintaining the values of the larger community.[14] The relation of police to law enforcement and hence to goal attainment is an active one. From this perspective the police function as an agent of government in an "instrumental" capacity.

The difference in the functions of law and custom in goal attainment and value maintenance, respectively, is a major source of deviant behavior. This type of deviant behavior is in many ways similar to the type Merton has labeled "nonconforming."[15] It also meets Cohen's definition of deviant behavior as "behavior which violates institutionalized expectations,"[16] and is, in one sense, a lack of integration of societal norms and values with the personality systems of individuals. This lack may be due to factors ranging from non-exposure to a normative structure to outright rejection of it.

An act which turns out to be defined as deviant may not be intended as such by the actor. Thus the definition of behavior as deviant may be objective (deviant from the standpoint of others witnessing the act) and/or subjective (deviant from the standpoint of the persons performing the act). A point so often overlooked is that a given individual is deviant, in the nonconforming sense, only from the viewpoint of the members of a given structure at a particular time who believe for one reason or another that: 1. the norms of that structure apply to the individual in question; 2. the individual is not conforming to these norms; and 3. the individual cannot

---

[13] Cf. Richard T. LaPiere, *A Theory of Social Control* (New York: McGraw-Hill Book Company, 1954), pp. 316–18.

[14] This duality has long been recognized. Davis discussed it in terms of "customary law" versus "enacted law." The former category includes "everything between sheer folkways and fully developed law." Enacted law comes into being "with the development of large-scale political organization, extensive specialization, and writing." (Davis, *op. cit.,* pp. 64–70.) LaPiere uses the concept "representative law" in much the same manner as Davis' "customary law." Representative law "expresses the sentiments, values, normative standards of conduct, and the like which are more or less common to the various status and other groupings within a large formal or informal community...." (LaPiere, *op. cit.,* pp. 318–20.)

[15] Merton and Nisbet, *Contemporary Social Problems,* p. 725.

[16] Albert K. Cohen, "The Study of Social Disorganization and Deviant Behavior," in Robert K. Merton *et al., Sociology Today* (New York: Basic Books, Inc., 1959), p. 462.

justify his behavior through appealing to other, higher ranking norms held by both parties.[17]

If the integration of social norms and personality systems is not accomplished by the dynamics of the social structure concerned—that is, by the functioning of the processes of socialization and institutionalization—and if maintenance of the given social structure is deemed essential by the community, then other techniques of integration will be resorted to. The application of force, as a mediating agency as well as a coercive one, becomes intensified, and dependence upon law supplements dependence upon custom.

Nonconforming deviant behavior can be defined with reference to the expectations of the community or to the expectations of that segment of the society which has created a normative structure through the legislation of laws. Either way, being labeled as a deviate is a function of the failure to meet the relative expectations of the persons or groups doing the labeling.[18]

A Typology of Nonconforming Deviant Behavior[19]

In view of the preceding, it would seem logical that the nature of police activity would be deeply colored by the nature of the deviant act and its value maintenance or goal attainment implications. That is, the police reaction to acts that deviate merely from community custom probably will differ qualitatively from the reaction to those acts that violate legal structures. The cross-association of the adherence or non-adherence to

---

[17] For an elaboration of ways of neutralizing one set of norms by another, see Gresham Sykes and David Matza, "Techniques of Neutralization: A Theory of Delinquency," *American Sociological Review,* XXII (December 1957), 664–70.

[18] Cf. Muzafer Sherif, "Conformity-Deviation, Norms and Group Relations," in I. A. Berg and B. M. Bass, eds., *Conformity and Deviation* (New York: Harper & Row, Publishers, 1961), pp. 159–99, for a similar emphasis upon relative expectations.

[19] The development of this typology has been influenced by several previous writings in this area. Ross suggested a distinction between the "ethical" and the "political" supports of social order in a manner that directly parallels the major theme of this paper. See Edward A. Ross, *Social Control* (New York: The Macmillan Company, 1910), pp. 411–12. Sorokin has made a distinction between "law-norms" and "moral-norms": the first backed by authority and the second not. See Charles P. Loomis and Zona K. Loomis, *Modern Social Theories* (Princeton, N.J.: D. Van Nostrand Co., Inc., 1961), p. 450. Cloward and Ohlin discuss a distinction between "norms" and "moral values," stating that discrepancy between those two makes for an unstable social structure unless the members of the structure can discount, de-emphasize, or neutralize the moral issues. See Richard A. Cloward and Lloyd E. Ohlin, *Delinquency and Opportunity* (New York: Free Press of Glencoe, Inc., 1960), pp. 18–19.

customary and legal expectations by members of a given community gives us four types of behavior, three of which are deviant by definition. As mentioned earlier, the adherence or non-adherence to expectations may be on a conscious or non-conscious level.

		LEGAL EXPECTATIONS	
		Adherence	*Non-adherence*
CUSTOMARY	*Adherence*	Conforming Behavior	Politically Deviant Behavior
EXPECTATIONS	*Non-adherence*	Communally Deviant Behavior	Societally Deviant Behavior

FIGURE 1 : TYPOLOGY OF CONFORMING AND DEVIANT BEHAVIOR

Conforming behavior results from the adherence by a given individual or group to behavior that is in accord with both customary and legal expectations. As long as both sets of expectations agree, either in regard to change or to keeping the status quo, conformity is no problem. In addition, in cases of disagreement there is obviously no way of assigning the deviant label when conflicting sets of expectations do confront each other in one and the same situation. Only when individuals are placed in situations where they are forced to choose between one set or the other does conformity become problematic. Once a choice is made, the individual immediately shifts into one of the three categories of deviant behavior. If the choice cannot be made, the effective functioning of the individual or group within that society may come to a halt.[20]

Conforming behavior is perceived by all parties as both customary and lawful. In such a situation neither the government nor the community expect the police to perform anything other than the reinforcing or "symbolic" role. Such behavior does not involve police action directly.

The *communal deviate* adheres to legal expectations but not to customary ones. Here the government defines the behavior as conforming but the community labels it deviant. To the extent that the police identify with government, sanctions will not be applied to control this kind of behavior.

---

[20] At present, the best examples which occur to us of these types of behavior come from the field of race relations. On a structural level, an illustration of the problems that can be created by attempts to conform to differing legal and customary expectations can be seen in the dilemma of a Southern university when the first Negro decides to enroll. In a very real sense, the administration of such a university is "damned if they do and damned if they don't." Structural disintegration may result from inabilities to cope with the situation, to reconcile the opposed expectations. For an excellent illustration of an individual's attempt to reconcile what in his experience are conflicting sets of expectations, see Norman Podhoretz, "My Negro Problem—and Ours," *Commentary*, XXXV (February 1963), 93–101.

However, to the extent that the police identify with the community, "unofficial" action may be taken against the "deviate" in spite of the government.[21]

Such "extra-legal" action on the part of policemen may include those practices sometimes referred to as "scare techniques," "harassment," "personal justice," and formal arrest for "nuisance offenses" such as vagrancy, loitering, littering the streets, and so on, when they are imposed as legal "substitutes" for the real complaint which is not legally valid.

Failure to respond to communal demands jeopardizes the established relationships or rapport that an officer may have with various members of the community. The officer himself who is not likely to be identified entirely with the law or with community custom is likely to be ambivalent about his actions, regardless of what he does in the handling of such situations.

The reverse of the communally deviant pattern is that of the *political deviate*. The community perceives his behavior as customary, but the government sees it as unlawful. In such a situation the government would expect instrumental action by the police. But the community, for whom this behavior is customary, would not desire police action. Again, as in the case of the communal deviate, the action taken by the police would be a function of their personal convictions and their relationship with one side or the other. The nature of any actual police action in such a case would probably be determined by attributes other than the sheer morality or legality of the issue. Such facts as ethnic and community origins of policemen, reciprocity obligations, economic conditions, and alternative dispositions available would be likely to influence the decision. The community may resent or actively resist legal police action in such cases.[22]

Thus, there may be considerable pressure brought to bear on individual police officers at least to mitigate the imposition of the law (via encouragement to issue warnings only, charge with nuisance offenses, deliver juveniles to their families, and so on) and even to ignore the offense altogether. Police officers assigned to areas to which they are most culturally identified would likely be most "efficient" in mediating between custom and law, though perhaps they would be also most vulnerable to pressure and therefore less "successful" from the point of view of attaining the goals of government.

---

[21] Political informers also epitomize this "communal" type of deviate, especially in societies with sharp cleavages between government and governed, such as "occupied" countries. Overzealous bureaucrats also fall into this category in some cases.

[22] The classic example of behavior judged as "politically" deviate is the purchase of alcoholic beverages during Prohibition. A more recent example might be participating in charitable lotteries, such as bingo games conducted in communities even where state laws prohibit such games of chance. Lynching and other forms of vigilante action also come under this type. In another area, we might mention violations of government acreage restrictions. Numerous other examples come to mind.

The last type of deviant behavior in this typology stems from non-adherence to either law or custom. This *societal deviate* represents a serious lack of institutionalization in certain behavior areas from the standpoint of both the society and the community evaluating him.[23] Since the behavior is defined not only as a violation of the norms and values of the community but also as illegal, both government and community will expect the police to take action against the offender. The police can unambiguously do so. Offenses falling into this category are the "traditional" and usually the more serious types of misbehaviors such as murder, sex offenses, burglary, and so on. Police officers find considerably more public support for their efforts in dealing with these kinds of offenders and can proceed with their work with greater confidence[24] than in cases of other types mentioned above.

The above discussion provides a framework within which to evaluate both the quality and quantity of police activity. For example, the commonly accepted notion that police and others enforce the law differentially by such criteria as social class and ethnic group becomes more clearly understood. It would be our judgment that "custom" generally takes precedence over "legality" both for policemen in their decisions to act and for citizens in their decisions to request, accept, or cooperate with police action. A highly "professional" department might not be as willing to honor local customs over legal requirements. To the extent that customary and legal expectations are the same, the work of the police will be more symbolic than instrumental.[25]

The police function in both an active and a passive manner with regard to social control. We have been suggesting that it is fruitful to separate these functions analytically—to associate the symbolic, passive function with maintenance of custom, customary law, and the normative system of the community or other social structure. The instrumental, active function has been associated with goal attainment, thus involving enacted law, regulatory norms, and government.

The labels "active" and "passive" are not meant to be applied to the rate of activity of the police per se; they refer to the expectations of the community and of the government with regard to the police function as expressed above. In other words, a particular department may be constantly checking complaints, patrolling, and performing similar duties, and yet be

---

23 For examples in the area of race relations again, communally deviant behavior is manifested in the behavior of the young Negro college students in the South who initiated the "sit-ins," and also in the person of James Meredith. A Southern white racial liberal, judged from the standpoint of Southern customs, also becomes a communal deviate. In contrast, politically deviant behavior is illustrated by the White Citizens Council of the South, with their rejection of the Supreme Court decision and acceptance of Southern customs. Societally deviate behavior, at the moment, is found in the Black Muslim movement, which tends to reject both customary and legal expectations in the United States regarding racial issues.
24 "The Relations Between the Police and the Public" (London: Social Survey Central Office of Information, Her Majesty's Stationery Office, 1962).
25 Cf. Ross, *op. cit.*

defined by the community as essentially "passive" since their function is perceived as more symbolic than instrumental.

Some data already in the sociological literature on police reinforce this idea of a symbolic-instrumental continuum. Goldman, in a study of rates of referrals to court of juveniles in various kinds of communities, found an inverse relationship between rates of police-juvenile contact and rates of referral.[26] As his community types progressed from cultural homogeneity to greater degrees of cultural heterogeneity, the rates of contact decreased and court referrals increased. These findings can perhaps be explained through application of the symbolic-instrumental continuum to the action of the police in the four cities studied. Goldman's "Manor Heights" had the highest contact rate and the lowest court referral rate of any community studied. Manor Heights was a very homogeneous upper class suburb. The police had the cooperation of the citizens of the community as well as of the municipal government, as evidenced by the higher rate of citizen complaints in this community than in the others. The police responded to citizen cooperation by restoring the great majority of the juvenile offenders to their homes, thus reinforcing the customary process of socialization. With their knowledge of community expectations relatively well defined, the police could be said to be acting in a symbolic capacity.

As the type of community moved in the direction of greater cultural diversity, the rates of contact decreased and the rates of court referrals increased. This might be explained as a function of loss of citizen cooperation as the duties of the police became more instrumental and as segments of the community experienced enforced regulation. In other words, as the customary and legal expectations became further separated, the quantity of instrumental police action increased.

If the symbolic-instrumental continuum holds, we would expect that it would take fewer police per unit of population to perform the symbolic function than to perform the instrumental function. It is well known that the ratio of the police to population increases as we go from rural to urban areas.[27] It is not known as yet whether differences in the ratios between urban areas of comparable population would roughly correspond to differences in the degree of cultural heterogeneity. Our orientation suggests this should be the case. It also suggests that the concentration of police should be higher in areas of highly probable politically deviant behavior than in areas

---

[26] Nathan Goldman, *Differential Selection of Juvenile Offenders for Court Appearance* (Unpublished doctoral dissertation, University of Chicago, 1950). This same phenomenon has been observed by Professor Lyle W. Shannon, Chairman, Department of Sociology, University of Iowa, in his comparative studies of Racine and Madison, Wisconsin. (Information received through private correspondence.)

[27] The median number of police per 1,000 population is 1.37 for cities in the range 10,000 to 25,000 and rises to 2.68 for cities over 500,000 population. See *Municipal Yearbook* for 1962. Also, the Federal Bureau of Investigation, *Crime in the United States: Uniform Crime Reports, 1962* (U.S. Department of Justice, Washington 25, D.C.), pp. 108–9.

of high communal or societal deviant rates. Some evidence for this latter statement is provided by what we already know about such phenomena as "police states."

Even from this very brief discourse on the nature of the police role in social control, several research possibilities present themselves. 1. Throughout the paper the unknown quantity of police officers' orientation toward customary behavior versus the legal standards remains more or less unanswered. Although some preliminary factors have been identified in previous research,[28] the further specification of the manner in which the police are differentially committed to take action against deviates under varying conditions is sorely needed. 2. The police are only part of the social control complex of the community. What are the reciprocal consequences the police and other agencies have upon each other in regard to whether they primarily play a symbolic or an instrumental role in the community? Data cited above suggest that the more homogeneous the community, the lower the juvenile court rates but the higher the "contact" rates. One might speculate that other non-penal agencies in the community would be utilized relatively more in the handling of deviates than in a heterogeneous community.[29] 3. From the standpoint of the individual police officer, the closer to the "instrumental" end of the continuum his duties lie, the greater the probability of ambivalence concerning the enforcement of the law. Having been born and reared in his home community, he probably has personal and social entanglements with that community. In what manner does his heritage affect his police work? Some police departments recruit only from the local community, some select from "outsiders." Both procedures have supporting rationales. A study involving police departments that use both procedures or a comparison of otherwise similar departments that differ only in their hiring procedures should provide insights into the effects of the concerns of this paper upon police work. 4. If there is anything to the continuum, we should expect to find differences in outlook among individual police officers corresponding to these different functions. Some very tentative evidence supporting this hypothesis has been gathered in the police study currently being conducted by the authors. It is our feeling that those officers glorifying the "personal" relations of the "beat" policeman personify the symbolic outlook, while those supporting the more recent trend toward routinization of the policeman-public relationship personify the instrumental outlook.

---

[28] See, for example, Wayne R. LaFave, "The Police Non-enforcement of the Law," Parts I and II, *Wisconsin Law Review,* I (January 1962), 104–37 and II (March), 179–239. Also William A. Westley, *The Police: A Sociological Study of Law, Custom, and Morality* (Unpublished doctoral dissertation, University of Chicago, 1951).

[29] The second author is now engaged in studies that should shed some light on this specific topic.

Part Four

ACTION PROGRAMS

Gang-Related Services
of Mobilization for Youth

MARYLYN BIBB

Mobilization for Youth is a massive program located on New York's lower East Side. Based on the theoretical framework provided by Cloward and Ohlin, it was the first major program funded in part by the President's Committee on Juvenile Delinquency and Youth Crime. As such, it has been observed, investigated, copied, attacked, and admired. As an attempt to translate social science into direct action, Mobilization is a fascinating, imaginative, comprehensive, and perhaps unrealistic demonstration. In this article, Marylyn Bibb gives a brief overview of the program with special emphasis on youth services. Gang intervention is not the central focus in this large program, with the result that the paper provides us with yet another context for gang matters.

MARYLYN BIBB, Chief of Group Work and Community Organization, Mobilization for Youth, New York.

Delinquency prevention and control programs are based on certain assumptions, explicit or implicit, as to why delinquency exists in the first place. We are aware that little is known empirically about the origins of juvenile delinquency and yet the juvenile delinquency field abounds in theories of causation. Solutions that are proposed for this social problem, of course, depend upon what one's assumptions are regarding the causes.

Mobilization for Youth is a complex, multi-disciplined, time limited, action-research project put forward as one possible answer to the need for a broad systematic attack on the problem of juvenile delinquency. It is unique in being the first of sixteen planned projects to take place throughout the country with financial support from the President's Committee on Juvenile Delinquency.

The purpose of this report is to describe those aspects of the MFY program relevant to intervention with gang youth. The theoretical foundations of our program will be discussed only briefly. For a more complete coverage of the theory and the assumptions on which it is based, the reader is referred to the MFY Proposal and the book by Cloward and Ohlin entitled *Delinquency and Opportunity*.[1]

Mobilization for Youth takes the position that there is no single theory or program which can comprehensively deal with a problem which we believe to be part of a complex social system. The opportunity theory, as developed by Cloward and Ohlin, draws on concepts initiated by Durkheim, Merton, Shaw, McKay, and Sutherland, and is based on certain assumptions which lead up to a program involving an *integrated* approach to the environmental system which in our view produces delinquency. To summarize these assumptions, it is our belief that delinquent behavior is engendered because *opportunities for conformity are limited*—that the desire to meet social expectations itself becomes the source of delinquent behavior if the possibility of doing so is limited or nonexistent. If we wish to reduce the incidence of delinquent behavior or rehabilitate those already so engaged, we must provide the social and psychological resources that make conformity possible.

What is the "environmental system" of which we speak? Our best evidence indicates that delinquent behavior appears highest in the economically depressed sectors—the slums of urban areas. Slums and their problems, we believe, produce a highly complex and interrelated style of life in such a community. We see delinquency and youth crime as aspects of this lifestyle. The most important pressure, in our view, toward delinquent behavior in youth arises from the inconsistency present between their aspirations—social and economic—and their opportunities to achieve these aspirations within legitimate means.

---

[1] Richard A. Cloward and Lloyd E. Ohlin, *Delinquency and Opportunity* (New York: Free Press of Glencoe, Inc., 1961).

176

In this light, then, deviance into delinquent behavior is seen as a social adjustment mechanism. The slum youth, if his opportunity to achieve a conventional pattern of adjustment is closed, must and will take whatever other alternative path may be open to him—and such an alternative may be delinquency.

With this as background, Mobilization for Youth feels that its program must direct itself to *changing the pattern of poverty*—both because poverty multiplies opportunity for deviant adjustment and because the culture of poverty produces the massive self-defeating attitudes so prevalent in slum youth. In other words, our job must be to enable the slum youth to develop means by which he can control and affect his environment, and thus his life chances.

Given this view, it is clear that we would de-emphasize those traditional forms of intervention which locate pathology in the individual and plan services accordingly, and we would emphasize those forms which speak to the failure of the social order.

From this flows one of Mobilization's most important goals—*the promotion of social change*. How could one presume that any meaningful opportunities for social necessities would be available to deprived groups without emphasizing our legitimate responsibilities to work toward major change in the political, economic, and social policies which regulate access to these opportunities in our society? Throughout the program, there falls to us as workers a large responsibility to encourage opportunities for collective social action.

Roy Sorenson in his presentation to the Joint Conference of Children and Youth[2] emphasizes the point that alienation from the adult society is one of American youth's focal problems. Our task is to direct the expression of alienation *against the social structure* which is its cause and to discourage its expression in delinquent acts.

To locate the Mobilization for Youth program in time and space, here are some brief vital statistics:

1. Our funding sources are four-fold:
   a. President's Committee on Juvenile Delinquency and Youth Crime
   b. National Institute of Mental Health
   c. Ford Foundation
   d. City of New York
2. Two years of research preceded our action phase, which began September, 1962.
3. Our research-action laboratory area comprises some sixty-seven blocks on New

---

[2] "Youth's Need for Challenge and Place In American Society," an address to the opening session of the Joint Conference on Children and Youth, April 10, 1962, Washington, D. C.

York City's Lower East Side—an area with a long and colorful tradition presenting the assets, the problems, and the weaknesses of a complex, high density, low income, urban community.

4. Although this is a racially and ethnically heterogeneous area, our target population includes in the main the especially deprived minorities of Puerto Rican and Negro people, who, combined, represent roughly 35 per cent of the approximately 107,000 people in the area.

As a social experiment with a particular point of view in the area of delinquency prevention and control, we work with existing institutions, agencies, groups, and individuals of all ages on various problems related to this goal. For that reason, the entire program of Mobilization for Youth has relevance to the question of work with gang youth. Here, then, is an overview of the Mobilization program.

Mobilization operates four service divisions:

1. World of Work
2. World of Education
3. Services to Individuals and Families
4. Group Work and Community Organization

In addition, a training division provides resources to all service areas. The following description will be limited to the four service divisions.

The Mobilization Program

WORLD OF WORK

No one will dispute that ours is a money-oriented culture, with gainful employment as the socially acceptable means of attaining its monetary rewards. Further, occupation, as any social scientist will attest, is the chief determinent of social status. But our country today faces a grave national problem of youth unemployment. We all know the shocking statistics, just as we know that lower class youth comprise a disproportionately large number of these unemployed. Mobilization places great emphasis on its youth employment program.

Major objectives of our World of Work include: (1) creation of new employment opportunities, (2) publicizing existing opportunities and routes to the achievement of these opportunities, and (3) making youth more employable.

Toward the achievement of these objectives, an extensive subsidized work and on-the-job training program has been developed in conjunction with a comprehensive vocational guidance program for all unemployed out of school youth—boys and girls, sixteen to twenty-one years of age—residing in the Mobilization area.

WORLD OF EDUCATION

Education is the principal means by which our youth achieve occupational mobility, and yet the slum school imposes severe educational inequalities on the slum child. Cognizant of this fact, Mobilization spends a substantial part of its funds toward the following educational objectives:

1. increasing the school's responsiveness to lower class life;
2. reducing teacher turnover;
3. bringing parents into contact with the school so that educational efforts may be supported in the home;
4. developing curriculum material and methods consistent with lower class culture;
5. providing extra tutorial help to grade school students in order to arrest the pattern of failure which starts in the primary grades.

This last objective is embodied in our Homework Helper program. In this program high school youth are paid to help the grade school youngster. This additional income often helps the tutor stay in school while giving such youth recognition and status for educational achievement. The grade school pupil reaps the advantages of a relationship with a role model much closer to him in age and interests than his regular day teacher.

INDIVIDUAL AND FAMILY SERVICES

How does this program help the inner-city slum resident and his family cope with the many complexities of the urban industrial establishment? All Mobilization programs are concerned with individual functioning, but here description will be confined to the unit known as Individual and Family Services, a program especially designed to aid in arresting self-defeating modes of behavior.

Four Neighborhood Service Centers have been opened throughout the area to administer concrete, coordinated, highly visible social services without the customary bureaucratic stumbling blocks. Under the single roof of a modest though attractive store front setting, resources are available to help persons coping with problems including welfare eligibility requirements, baby sitting, improvement of homemaking skills, family problems, and many others. Skilled staff are prepared to give on the spot help, as well as to provide information about and help in attaining other needed community resources.

Our assumption is that efforts directed at reorganizing an individual's personality system are useless if the environment of which he is a part continues to evoke the same debilitating response. Because of this, our efforts must first be directed to improvement of his social conditions as a prior condition to the effective use of any therapeutic process.

We use the term "social broker services" for the work done by the case workers in the Neighborhood Service Centers. Their task is to provide immediate, concrete supportive service primarily to "walk ins" from the neighborhood.

SPECIALIZED SERVICES TO GROUPS

Very often group services and recreational programs provide the one link between the conventional world and the already deviant youth.

Among the mandates under which MFY operates is one that states our intent to use approaches to the problem of juvenile delinquency that can be replicated. As a time limited project, we are fully aware that whatever of value is learned must be continued in the community by both public and private agencies. Because of this concern for the permanence of any innovations in program, several of our programs have been contracted to existing institutions.

Mobilization has four programs designed to offer services to children and youth. Only one of these, the Coffee House program, is directly operated.

Two of the other programs are concerned with the populations from eight to twelve whom we define as potentially delinquent. Their objective is to provide exciting and meaningful recreational, educational, and vocationally geared activities. One of these programs, the *Adventure Corps,* uses leadership recruited from the community—particularly and preferably youth who themselves have been through the gang structure and have made their way out, yet retained "rep" in the eyes of the younger children. Fifteen squads of twenty-five children each are planned throughout the Mobilization community. The program is designed around a quasi-military form, in response to the desire for adventure and discipline. To avoid an overmilitaristic emphasis, program content and award recognition are based on the quality of social, educational, and cultural participation.

The Pre-Adolescent Project, like the Adventure Corps, is a small group program for predelinquent boys and girls from eight to twelve. The aim is prevention. Such programs are based in community centers with the objective of gradually moving these children into the regular on-going programs of the agency as they achieve a more positive identification with their community life.

The Detached Work Program in its general outlines would be very familiar to the reader. Here our program attempts to go beyond the traditional stress on relationship as the instrument for dissuading gang members from antisocial behavior. In essence, simply because of the availability of the umbrella services of the total MFY program, a detached worker acts as the "bridge" relating the street gang to the major institutional orders impinging upon it—schools, law enforcement agencies, employers, courts, and so on. The immediacy of service provided through the World of Work, World of Education, and Services to Individuals and Families offers the worker the needed supports to help youth "make it."

The Coffee House Program is designed especially to serve youth in gang groups, though not to the exclusion of other youth. Essentially, its membership is drawn from the same membership covered by the Detached Worker Program. A sponsoring council made up of the leadership of the various gangs who have been invited to participate are the responsible agents for the maintenance and operation of such shops. By its very structure, which is not confined to a single group, the Coffee House can address itself to the creative rather than to the antisocial actions of youth.

Three store front cultural centers are conceived of as having the outward aspects of a Coffee House; by offering an attractive new facility that can be expressive of the socially acceptable interests of lower class youth, they attempt to provide an alternative to illegitimate patterns. Contact with skilled adults ("informed bartenders") in such a natural setting provides these youth with access to other needed Mobilization services in the educational, medical, vocational, and psychiatric areas.

COMMUNITY ORGANIZATION—OR ORGANIZING THE UNAFFILIATED

We equate unaffiliation with powerlessness, and lack of power plays a crucial role in the inability of the slum community to help itself. With all the services being brought to bear on the slum community as just outlined, we believe this is not enough. Something must be done to help the adult community achieve adequate institutional connections, because it is through these connections that adults can play a role in affecting necessary community change. Participation, then, is the key here.

Enabling the lower class residents of the inner-city slum to function *as a part of the structure* of the community encourages the provision of additional necessary services, offers a structure for the redress of grievances with public and private institutions, develops leadership and organizational skills, and provides youth of the community with some optimistic evidence of what the future might hold.

Organizing the unaffiliated becomes crucial when viewed in the perspective of our frame of reference, which sees poverty as the problem, and power, in the hands of those suffering the consequences of poverty, as the solution. Here are two brief examples. One thousand additional registered voters in a slum district will affect the schools, the police, the welfare organizations, the job market in *that* district more permanently and dramatically than *any* service program. Or again, helping a slum family deal with the large bureaucratic public agency or private slumlord can help *that* family, but a true tenants' organization can change the housing practice of an entire community.

Nor is the effort to help the community achieve *collective social action* on its problems confined to the adults. The youth, of course, can be provided with a different role model as he sees significant adults actively engaged in community concerns, but we believe that youth must be heard, too.

To this end, a Community Action for Youth program is being developed that will encourage attention to social issues among young people, help them develop specific action programs, and provide them with material aids to further their efforts. To channel the anger directed at social injustice *away* from self-defeating deviant behavior and into constructive avenues of collective social action becomes one of our central tasks.

The Chicago YMCA Detached Workers: Current Status of an Action Program

CHARLES N. COOPER

The earlier papers by Tennyson and by Rivera and Short employed data collected from the Chicago YMCA detached worker program. In the present paper, the author describes this program in some detail. While he claims that the program is a-theoretic and strictly pragmatic, the careful reader will discern that this is a surface impression only. Some of the underlying conceptual guidelines are described on the last pages. No action program is truly a-theoretic, merely more or less explicitly and planfully theoretical. Special attention should be paid to the experimental spirit which runs throughout the program as described. The "consultant" approach seems particularly promising.

CHARLES N. COOPER, Assistant Director, Program for Detached Workers.

Introduction[1]

A little over seven years ago, in March 1956, the YMCA of Metropolitan Chicago assigned one man to the streets in a Youth Gangs Pilot Project, which later became the Program for Detached Workers. The Y Board of Managers supported this effort as part of a general commitment to maintain services in the inner-city. Other financial assistance has come from the National Institute of Mental Health, the Ford Foundation, and the Community Fund.

Neither at its beginning nor at any time during its development has the Program for Detached Workers been a rationally designed project with a specified theoretical basis. It has always been and remains a highly pragmatic, experimental, and, we believe, realistic undertaking which incorporates much of the milieu of the youths and the areas with which it is involved.

The daily conduct of the program is in our own patois, which includes a heavy base of street language, with a liberal sprinkling of sociological and political terminology. An example might be: "Dig, baby, you can't capture that heavy stud if you keep threatening his status," from the director to a worker. The reply from the worker might be: "I'm hip, but every time I try and do him some solids with the local power structure he middles me."

The absence of a preordained, specific aim and a structured content for the program, combined with the controlled, gradual growth in staff, is viewed as an advantage enjoyed by few other social service projects. The reasons for this viewpoint and the way these features have been worked out will be discussed in the material that follows.

An important feature, which we believe to some extent justifies the operational freedom of the program, is that for three years (September 1959–1962) we had an intensive involvement with a basic research project. The Youth Studies Program, Department of Sociology, University of Chicago, Dr. James F. Short, Jr., Director, had both sociological and psychological aspects. The results of this research are currently being published. Other research is continuing in special areas of interest. It is expected that in the future considerable analysis will be given to how the program conducted itself at the time of the research project, and to what extent this was in accord with the basic behavioral science findings. Also, some of the instruments of the Youth Studies Program will be used during the coming year in an attempt to measure the impact of our program.

[1] Acknowledgement is hereby gladly given to James F. Short, Jr., Washington State University, and to Fred D. Hubbard, Director, Program for Detached Workers, for the contributions and criticisms they have offered to the ideas herein, and to Mrs. Joyce Klein and our office staff for the work involved in getting them on paper.

Although at various points reference is made to gangs, it should be noted that the particular form of collective behavior (both the nature of the collectivity and the types of behavior) indicated reflects the past experience rather than the current service population of the majority of detached workers. At no time has the program observed the sort of formal and inflexibly delinquent organization implied in the popular press. Originally each detached worker was assigned to a single group. This developed into each worker being assigned to several groups, including new and latent old cliques. Now, in an increasing number of instances, detached workers can be described as offering service to unaffiliated inner-city youth populations and utilizing available peer group leadership as staff assistants to perform key organizational and operational roles. This development is integrally related to the shift toward positive, preventive activities which is discussed below.

Staff Organization and Management

The current staff of the program consists of sixteen full-time professional men and sixty-three part-time men and youths. The members of the administrative and support staff, all but one of whom began as detached workers, include a director, an assistant director, an employment coordinator, a programming coordinator, and two field supervisors. Ten detached workers complete the professional staff at present. The part-time staff is comprised of indigenous youths and a few adults who began as a special "Youth Consultant Project" and have become an integral part of the program. Local adults, known as "part-time sponsors," are paid fifty dollars a month and are used by detached workers either for specialized duties or to keep tabs on fringe groups. At present seven others are volunteering their services.

More intriguing, and for some reason more controversial, is the utilization of youths from the groups to which workers are allocated. Youths with leadership position or potential who cooperate with the worker are made "Field Assistants" at ten dollars a month or "Consultants" at twenty dollars. They may be promoted to "Senior Consultants" at thirty dollars after a year.

The major youth position is that of the consultant. (The field assistant is the entry position and has more limited functions.) Consultants have a multitude of duties assigned by detached workers. They are expected to attempt to control delinquency as well as they can, but especially to control behavior while their group is engaged in program activities. They have specific duties in planning and carrying out legitimate activities. The manpower of a worker's "staff" has on several occasions been used quite successfully to operate programs (which will be discussed later) for large numbers of youngsters in a neighborhood.

Perhaps the greatest limitation on these functions is the ability, energy, and circumstance of the individual detached worker. He remains the key element in the selection, training, and management of these youths. Fortunately, this aspect of the program is currently undergoing research, so that eventually we will have to rely less upon speculation as to its effects. The staff generally agrees that we do not *have* to pay the youths since they have been assisting us to some extent all along. However, it is recognized that the money is a considerable factor in legitimation of these roles from the boys' point of view.

The effect of the role on the consultants appears to be heightened by their joint, centralized functions. These include operation of program-wide activities such as tournaments, with special emphasis on their monthly meetings downtown and the newspaper they publish. The paper visually resembles a tabloid offset-printed with type and pictures. From thirty to sixty articles each month are written by the consultants and their friends, including some girls and local adults. A yearly four-day trip to New York City is one of the fringe benefits for consultants which has the side effect of developing considerable rapport among them.

There are safeguards built into this project which have two primary aims: to ensure that these are legitimate roles, and to guard against their being seen by the boys as a "profession." As to the former, the consultants have ratified a rule that anybody who is arrested is automatically suspended, to be reinstated if released as innocent and to be "busted" (fired) if guilty. (Often, the latter are allowed back into the role after a probationary period.) Also, anyone claiming to be a "YMCA social worker" to avoid the law is automatically busted. The concern that youths do not unrealistically attempt a career of "gang leading" is incorporated in the requirement that all consultants either be working or in school full time. In addition, it is made clear that this is a position that terminates in two years.

At present there are six senior consultants, twelve consultants, and thirty-eight field assistants in the project.

The Groups and Their Members

It may be surprising that little has been said to this point about what "our" gangs and their "members" are like. We do have some assumptions: all gangs are different, few gang members are emotionally disturbed, gangs usually are not formal organizations, gang leaders can be worked with, gangs will accept legitimate activities. The detached worker is expected to determine, in a somewhat informal but nevertheless empirical fashion, what "his" gang is like and, pragmatically, how best he can work with it. From this comes the addage: "Each worker best knows his group." For more information we must wait until the data are in from the research project. To give some idea of the range of our experience during the past seven years, the statistics in Table 1 are cited.

Table 1

GROUPS SERVICED BY THE PROGRAM

	Total	*Negro*	*White*	*Latin*
Number of groups (all male)	63	39	20	4
Size range	7–92	15–92	7–63	13–40
Age range	11–25	11–24	13–25	13–24
Average length of service (months)	19	24	11	17

During the research project the core age was roughly between seventeen and nineteen. There are currently thirty-two groups considered "in the program"; four years ago, with eight detached workers, there were only eleven groups. The expansion of the program has been due to an extension of service over a wider age range, rather than to a shift from older to younger groups. The program remains firmly convinced of the necessity for working with the sixteen-to-twenty-year-old groups. It has found that the leadership in these groups serves as a powerful role model, reference, and at times active leadership for younger boys.

The Detached Worker and His Program: Control

Although each detached worker operates in his own manner, there are some general guidelines that have been developed over the years. There are only two absolute commandments: 1. *the worker must take action,* even if it is only to leave the scene of a situation he cannot alleviate rather than stay and legitimate it by his presence; and 2. *the worker must not allow himself to be put in a compromising position*—the trick bag—or to be "middled" between two opposing forces, such as "his" boys and the police. The worker is urged to utilize the structure of the program to "lay off" information, pressure, or blame for actions which he rightfully must take. He is told to "put the heat" on the program, its director, the boys, or any other place rather than jeopardize his effectiveness as a worker.

Direct attacks on delinquency by the detached worker vary considerably with the situation. Examples of some of the ways in which some of the detached workers would handle things follow.

In areas of subculturally approved activities that have been referred to as "private behavior," the program's main emphasis has been on the way in which these activities are conducted, the behavior that accompanies them, and their consequences.

As far as smoking is concerned, we attempt to place no limitations "so long as it has a brand name on it" (as a marijuana cigarette, of course, does not).

Drinking is not permitted at any program activity, in the worker's car, or in his presence except when he must be there for control purposes. Workers may check out private parties where their boys are drinking, but they do not *attend* them. The attitude toward sanctions upon drinking will vary from worker to worker, but with older youths will often take the form of emphasis on social, in-the-home, well behaved drinking—if it must be done—rather than the cheap bottle of wine on the corner or in the alley. Detached workers have cooperated with the police in identifying establishments which sell liquor to minors.

Influence on sex behavior is easily the weakest aspect of the program. One of our aphorisms is that "you can't outprogram them broads." Because this is probably the most compromising activity, workers are urged to be circumspect in attempts to deal with it.

It should be understood that we are not arguing that the above activities are not often harmful to adolescents (or to adults, for that matter). We have found, however, that detached workers who attempt to prohibit these activities by moralizing can lose their rapport with the group, and thereby their effectiveness in stopping serious crimes which threaten life and property.

Another area of delinquency is the spontaneous attacks upon persons and property by small numbers of boys. This category includes arguments and fights with the local winos or passers-by, wrecking abandoned cars or buildings, and stealing merchandise from delivery trucks. The detached worker's control over these is pretty much limited to the times when he is present, or when one of the youths—perhaps a consultant—is willing and able to act as his representative. Perhaps some of this sort of behavior can also be alleviated by the alternative uses of time that the worker's program provides, and especially by the commitment and involvement of these youths to the worker and his program—which hopefully will lessen their tendency to participate in any negative situations that arise.

Crimes for profit—primarily strong-arm robberies for the youths with which we are involved—seem related to some extent to the flow of legitimate income in a group. Jobs for individual youths may or may not completely stop these crimes, but they do lessen the possibility. One of the complicating factors is that a boy who is employed may go along with one of his partners who wants to "make up" because he has no job. Furthermore, job income does not supply all the desired goods and services, even with the extension of credit (which is often abused and can itself lead to an illegal attempt to "get straight").

Here again the detached worker can seldom have a direct influence, but the jobs he provides and the changes he makes in group attitudes and expectations—particularly regarding consideration of the consequences—may have a considerable effect. If a worker learns of a planned crime sufficiently in advance and is unable to dissuade the participants, he informs them that he must relay this information to the police, and then does so.

The area in which the detached worker is expected to wield the most influence and control is the alleviation and prevention of major subcultural group activities—primarily gang fighting, and in several instances, drug use (mainly barbiturate and amphetamine pills). Here he works through the leadership of the group, invoking the commitments (including those of the consultant role) he has obtained from them and cashing in on the favors he has done for them. The worker actively participates in the decision-making process of the group, constantly pointing out the negative consequences and immediate positive alternatives available to them. Whenever the worker feels he is losing the argument, he tells the group that he does not approve of this planned action and must call the police. If this does not disperse the group, he then calls the police and informs them of the impending hostilities. The program has never seen an instance in which this action seriously impaired its relationship with a group.

Most of the above discussion applies to gang fighting. With retreatist, pill using groups, the approach has been more hesitant and unsure. In the two or three groups in which this pattern existed, the worker has attempted first of all to prevent new youths from coming into the group, secondly to weaken the group support for drug use, thirdly to separate out individual members of the group, and continually during this process to cooperate with the police in stopping the source of supply. This is done informally if it is an underworld source, but more directly if it is something like pills coming from a disreputable druggist.

In staff meetings the program has worked out two formal control policies. One concerns the use of the worker's station wagon. It prohibits the carrying of contraband and illegal behavior of youths in or around the wagon. The other policy, in force for three years, directs the worker who knows that a firearm is being carried on the street either to confiscate the weapon or to report it to the police. The program has experienced no difficulty because of these policies.

The program has increasingly become involved in secondary, preventive activities (which will be discussed below) in community areas where it is not required to devote all of its energies to essentially negative control. The aim remains the lessening of delinquency, but the methodology shifts to include more far-reaching causality.

The Detached Worker and His Program: Prevention

Since the beginning of the program, workers have found other things to do with their boys besides hanging around on the corners and "keeping their game up tight" (in this case "their game" being control of conflict). These have included organizing athletic teams, which at first play in local leagues. Later program-wide tournaments in softball, basketball, and pool were organized, with the intent of increasing mobility and lessening fear of other areas of the city, in addition to whatever might be learned from participation in an organized, rule-bound activity in which punctuality was emphasized. Through the years the program has also utilized a tremendous number of free tickets to spectator events—professional and college athletics, jazz and popular music, even indoor polo. (It is assumed that with the urging of a worker a group will go anywhere—once.) Tours and camping trips also have been utilized. "Socials" (dances) are inevitable.

A worker is challenged by the program to consider the needs of the group and the status of his relationship to it in deciding whether to become involved and how he is to conduct an activity. In other words, the worker is expected to have a reason for whatever he does—a reason based on a realistic appraisal of his current situation and consistent with some appropriate goal. It should be observed that these are just generalities; they might be followed to the letter with no appreciable results if the worker was wrong in his estimation of the group's needs, his situation, or the appropriateness of a goal. The worker must then be shown where the plan went wrong and urged to try anew.

About a year ago the program embarked upon a "new dimension" in programming. It came about indirectly through the urging of workers to develop significant roles for their field assistants and consultants. The critical features of this development are the use of these youths as a staff in operating activities not only for their own group but for much larger numbers of youngsters from the entire neighborhood. Activities in this realm again have included athletic leagues, social dancing and roller skating, bid whist and pool tournaments, talent shows, and anything a worker and his staff could dream up and pull off.

The consultant meetings downtown have served as a powerful impetus, with consultants eager to report on their findings and eager to urge their workers to action when they had nothing to report. In addition to the sense of accomplishment these activities have given the groups involved, they also have served to lessen the animosity between gang and non-gang youngsters and the alienation of gangs from legitimate adults in the community. Again, two conditions affecting the development of this type of program are the energy and ability of the worker and the peacefulness of the community in which he is located. Large, community-wide programs have proven to be unwise where gang strife is rampant. What is more, the managerial tasks involved in these undertakings call for new or much more highly developed skills than does a program of control and limited activities.

Two more series program activities which have been attempted are a youth employment service and a school dropout prevention project. The full-time employment coordinator spends two days each week in the field, making contacts for job openings, and three days interviewing and counseling applicants referred by our workers. In a little less than three years about 400 jobs have been held by 250 boys out of 450 boys referred by workers. The most striking fact of this operation is that about 78 per cent of the jobs obtained have been lost, with "fired," "quit," and "laid off" accounting for roughly equal proportions. Although this is to be expected, since any population of youths in this age range runs through a series of jobs, it puts considerable strain on the efforts of such a project to develop an expanding number of jobs for an increasing number of youths. Most of the jobs have been in regular unskilled and semi-skilled industrial and merchandising positions, with a mean starting wage of $1.50 per hour. The average length of employment was three months, and the most frequently given reason for loss of job was absenteeism. We also suspect that interpersonal relations on the job and the outward pull of "his partners on the corner" are contributing factors. A special research project is investigating this much more systematically, however.

A school dropout prevention project has been attempted for the past two years. The aim is simply to raise the high school completion rate of younger groups whose members are still in school above that of the older groups with 65–99 per cent dropouts. The means utilized were changing group norms toward school attendance and improving individual expectations, motivation, and performance. The methods included offering a series of activities to designated "school project groups," providing individual counseling, offering short term rewards for school attendance and performance, and bringing in volunteer college tutors in an effort to improve performance. Although final analysis will not be made until all of the participants should have been graduated from high school, some informal findings are at hand. The most notable change is in the peer group attitude toward schooling and the greater expectation to graduate. Performance lags behind this, but we anticipate considerably fewer dropouts. Well run tutoring sessions are quite popular with the youths and seem to be rewarding to the tutors. The administrative strain, however, that obtaining and keeping school records and managing tutoring sessions put on a detached worker has caused the program to question the wisdom of its involvement. These efforts seem to provide enough work to call for a major special project, rather than our sideline attempts.

Analysis and Conclusion

As might be gathered from all of the above, the program has at no time been a stable, specific "treatment" developed from one theoretical point of view. It has rather been constantly changing and hopefully dynamic, shifting its emphasis to whatever it feels is currently appropriate. A wide range of theoretical disciplines are reflected in its approach, but the ones that the program has chosen to make explicit *may* have caused it to differ considerably from superficially similar projects.

Much of what the program does is produced by the individual worker, on his own, in response to a particular situation. The *management* of the program attempts to see that the worker is aware of all the ramifications of the situation, the alternative lines of action, and the implications and probable consequences of these alternatives. At the same time, we are quite conscious of the fact that much depends upon the reflexes and determination of the individual worker, since we can't be out there in the streets with him.

There are three theoretical aspects of the program's approach that seem most important.

The first is the subculture. The program believes that in order for a worker to show results he must be able to deal effectively *within* whatever subculture is involved. This is important, as it affects both his personal relationship with the boys and his ability to manipulate rather than be manipulated *by* the subculture.

The second is informal small group process, with a leaning toward *sociological* social psychology. The emphasis here is on the worker's direct influence on the group, and especially on his indirect influence through key members of the group. The aim is not to attempt a change in individual youths through group pressures, but instead to utilize youths in leadership positions to change group norms and expectations. The program does not claim to be able to change individual behavior, although attempts at this are made. The primary effort is devoted to changing that behavior which is group-oriented. Workers have generally been much more successful in intervening in interpersonal, group decision processes than in intrapersonal decision processes.

The third theoretical emphasis is that of opportunity structure. This involves us in a struggle not only to provide activities and status which will be seen as immediately desirable by the youths in the program, but also to develop involvement in opportunities which will be recognized as significant by the general community—specifically, schooling and jobs. The pressures of the current technological revolution, in addition to those of the century old Emancipation, are strongly felt by the program. While we are intensely aware of these problems, we have not yet seen what we consider a realistic approach of the magnitude necessary for their solution. We do know that the scope of such an attempt is well beyond our project.

Perhaps the best summary of what we are trying to do could be expressed as the development of an alternative system, or subculture, if you will, which might be called The Program. Hopefully, it is seen as an alternative set consisting of legitimate activities, school, job, and eventually family—rather than delinquency, fighting, hospital or morgue, crime, jail or prison—or than wine, junk, street corners, alleys, and oblivion. Despite the obvious preferability of the set which we are attempting to provide, those familiar with the persistence of delinquent subcultures will understand our amazement at how often we can get agreement "to go along with the program" for its own sake.

To conclude, we are aware that our program owes much to the current and past efforts and knowledge of others in Chicago and elsewhere. Indeed, we are startled by the number of times we run across something we had believed to be new, only to find it is being rediscovered. Hopefully the research contributions of the Youth Studies Program and the continuing support of the YMCA will preserve what has been of value in our experience and allow us to continue to experiment in this fascinating field.

The Nature, Variety, and Patterning of Street Club Work in an Urban Setting[1]

NATHAN S. CAPLAN, DENNIS J. DESHAIES
GERALD D. SUTTLES, HANS W. MATTICK

Most detached worker programs stress the notion that the worker himself is the indispensable element in effecting change. It is through his personal relationships with the gang members that all influence is channeled. While this point of view may in fact be challenged, it certainly behooves us to know something of the process through which this relationship develops. The authors of this paper take a stride in this direction with interesting results. It appears that differentials in worker "style" are a function of the *affective* component of the worker-member relationship, and that this relationship provides the worker's major, if not only, conceptual guideline. The authors employ the phrase "despite training and experience" and thereby emphasize the dependence of the workers on common sense, rather than on professional tenets.

NATHAN S. CAPLAN, DENNIS J. DESHAIES, GERALD D. SUTTLES, and HANS W. MATTICK, Chicago Youth Development Project, Institute for Social Research, University of Michigan and Chicago Boys Club.

---

[1] Detailed statistical appendices, omitted from the final version of this paper, may be obtained by writing directly to the authors.

T he research staff of the Chicago Youth Development Project (CYDP) has utilized a variety of approaches in studying street club work. Those studies which have been shown to hold the most promise at a pilot level of investigation have now been incorporated into a program of research designed to define and clarify some of the fundamental processes involved in street club work. It is our purpose in the present paper to out-line this program of studies and to illustrate one of these approaches in detail by presenting data from a recent study.

There are many aspects of street club work. The choice of any particular aspect for investigation depends largely upon the purpose of the investiga-tion. Our initial purpose in studying street work stemmed from an interest in determining the nature of the CYDP action program as an independent or treatment variable. The primary responsibility of the CYDP research staff is to evaluate the effects of the action program. A fundamental prerequisite for the proper evaluation of a social change program is, of course, the identification of the treatment variables actually employed to alter some behavioral characteristics in a chosen target population. Unless these treat-ment variables can be properly determined or described, the interpretation of the effects cannot be legitimately attributed to those aspects of the program which are presumed to be responsible. Such effects may be the consequence of incidental or peripheral factors, especially in a program designed to bring about change in a natural social setting where variability from a number of intervening sources could seriously affect the degree of correspondence between the prescribed program and its implementation.

Our second purpose in pursuing research along these lines grew out of a desire to intelligently and systematically interpret target population changes in relation to the operating causes—that is, in relation to their responsible agents. In particular, we hope to interpret the accomplishments of the action program meaningfully by explicating the connecting links between the worker's efforts and their effects upon the target population. Such research involves a detailed examination of street club work with a view to obtaining findings of immediate relevance to on-going program activities. In the discussion to follow, attention will be concentrated upon those aspects of our research program which appear to hold the most potential for providing feedback information to make street club work a more profitable enterprise.

Four separate sets of studies in our research program focus on street club work: (1) Activities Analysis, (2) Behavioral Innovations, (3) Crucial Determinants, and (4) Factor Relations.

The essential feature of the activities analysis study is a system for coding and categorizing the range and frequency of street worker activities over a given time period. The data for this study are gathered from each worker's daily activity reports, and augmented by interviews with each worker and, when possible, by nonparticipant observation.

From the research point of view, the activities analysis study is designed to provide a large body of descriptive data which can be used to clarify the nature of street work at a rather low level of generalization. It is research in its simplest form, the research approach and procedures being necessarily subordinate to the limitations in the available data. Nevertheless, we are making attempts to check the validity of such data and to refine the workers' reporting procedures so as to increase the usefulness of this approach.

The behavioral innovations studies involve a combination of insights from field observations and supplementary, ad hoc research to clarify and test these conceptualizations as they evolve. The presentation by Mattick[2] contains examples of this type of research. Such innovations as "loud-talking," "stake animals," and subverting "do-nothing leadership" relate to tangible problems at a rather concrete level. They are also useful in the immediate sense because their meaning and implications are obvious and easily communicated to the workers.

The crucial determinant study represents an attempt to isolate and describe the particular practices of street club workers that lead to the successful handling of situations that have important relevance to the goals of the action program. This research will center upon the determination of two crucial components of the action worker's activities: 1. *situations* which are crucial in the sense that they represent problems which workers must satisfactorily resolve if the program is to be successful; and 2. the worker's *behaviors* that are responsible for the satisfactory handling of these crucial situations. Further, it is, of course, the configuration of the man and his particular pattern of behavior under specific circumstances, rather than techniques per se, that leads to success in crucial situations. Therefore, we are interested not only in validating street work techniques, but also in identifying the individual talents essential for success.

The factor relations studies consist of a series of investigations designed to provide a basis for making inferences about street work practices at a rather high level of generalization. The feedback of findings from such studies is slow, the translation of data difficult, and the applicability of the findings not always immediately evident. Such an approach to the isolation and measuring of the fundamental components of street club work may, however, eventually enable the researcher to provide the worker with information at the broadest level of practical usefulness.

In summary, then, the research program of the CYDP, insofar as it relates to street club work, has four major components: 1. activities analysis; 2. behavioral innovations; 3. crucial determinants; and, 4. factor relations. A study illustrating the last component, factor relations, will now be pre-

---

2 Hans W. Mattick and Nathan S. Caplan, "Stake Animals, Loud-Talking, and Leadership in Do-Nothing and Do-Something Situations," this volume.

sented in some detail. It is one of a series of studies designed to gain some understanding of the interrelatedness and significance of several variables associated with the adaptation of the street club worker to his target population. The scope of inquiry was limited to the worker's judgment on a series of variables as they are involved in his particular mode of street work.

At the time of this study the action program had been in operation for eighteen months and was being carried out in three traditionally high delinquency, inner-city areas of Chicago, each approximately one square mile in size. The CYDP target population was defined as all boys aged ten to nineteen residing within these three areas. Those members of the target population who were actually being worked with by the CYDP street club workers will be referred to as "contact" boys in the discussion to follow. At the time of the present investigation we were able to identify 645 such boys. Thirty-eight per cent of these boys were known to have official delinquency histories. This percentage of official delinquencies was at least double that for all boys of comparable age living in these areas. Therefore, the CYDP contacts can be considered the more delinquent

Table 1

CYDP TARGET AREAS AND WORKER ASSIGNMENTS

Target Areas		Area I	Worker Assignment	
Total Population		31,391	Workers	Time on Project
White	5,819		I	18 months
Negro	25,375		II	16 months
Other	197		III	18 months
Boys (10–19)	2,260			
Contacts	286			
Target Areas		Area II	Worker Assignment	
Total Population		40,710	Workers	Time on Project
White	31,695			
Negro	7,971		IV	15 months
Other	1,044		V	9 months
Boys (10–19)	2,727			
Contacts	138			
Target Areas		Area III	Worker Assignment	
Total Population		39,121	Workers	Time on Project
White	21,313			
Negro	17,735		VI	15 months
Other	73		VII	15 months
Boys (10–19)	3,560			
Contacts	221			

segment within the target population. Table 1 identifies the workers and provides a brief demographic description of these areas.

The data used in this study were obtained by a procedure which required each street club worker to make a series of scale point judgments for his contact boys along some general dimensions. The dimensions in question were arrived at by a variety of procedures. Most of them were obtained from the workers in discussions about what distinctions they considered to be important in their own work. Others were determined directly from the aims of the action program. Once these dimensions or criteria were spelled out to the worker he was presented with a deck of 5×8 cards containing the names of each of his contact boys. He was asked to sort the cards into stacks ranging from "most" to "least" insofar as he was able to distinguish between stacks and cases along the particular dimension in question. In most instances these dimensions were not defined any further than to provide the worker with a general description of the nature of each variable under study, such as, "the amount of time spent with them," "the degree of influence you have over them," and so on. No restrictions were placed upon the spread or the number of different stacks into which the worker chose to separate his contact cards. Further, no attempt was made to aid the worker in structuring the limits of the dimensions or the selection of choice points determining the empirical divisions between the stacks of contact card rankings. At the completion of each sort, the worker was interviewed intensively in order to secure a full description of the total scale dimension as he saw it and, also, the basis for his discriminations resulting in the isolation of scale segments represented by the division between stacks of contact cards.

This sorting procedure was carried out for a number of variables. For a variety of reasons, however, not all sorts yielded sufficient data for statistical treatment. The present discussions will, therefore, be limited to worker judgments on variables where the application of statistical techniques was possible; briefly, those variables are:

1. Stage of contact—that is, the degree of program progress
2. Level of influence over the boy by the worker
3. Time spent with the boy by the worker
4. "Tightness" between the worker and the boy—that is, mutual confidence and trust
5. Level of success
6. Level at which a boy is liked by the worker
7. Level at which worker is liked by the boy
8. Prestige level of the boy among his peers
9. Delinquency level in terms of delinquent activity known to worker
10. Level of official legal involvement

11. Time boy has been known to the worker and
12. The boy's age

Some of these variables will be discussed later in greater detail.

In the first phase of analysis, the data derived from the workers' scale point estimates for each contact boy on the variety of variables were handled separately for each of the seven workers so as to determine a configuration of variable interrelations by worker. Kendall's[3] tau beta was used to express the interrelationship between variables. The statistic ZA, derived by Somers,[4] was used as a test of significance. For convenience of discussion, the data will not be treated in detail at this time. However, two general comments must be made. First, the intercomparison of different variables among all workers produced surprisingly low correlations. Even among variables on which one would normally expect high intercorrelations on a priori grounds —for example, tightness, influence, success, and contact—the tau seldom exceeded .60. Unless we have failed to consider some of the more relevant and critical variables associated with the system of interaction between the worker and his contact boys, it would therefore seem plausible to assume that the development and outcome of such interaction must involve a number of only modestly related variables, none of which can be considered to play a dominant role.[5]

Secondly, a number of variables produced similar intercorrelations across workers. These are presented in Table 2.

Those variables that held up across workers as being interrelated at a significant level were 1. stage of contact, 2. influence over boy, 3. tightness with boy, 4. success with boy, 5. liking for boy, and 6. liking by boy.

These findings are important both in their own right and as a prerequisite for formulating future research. The fact that some variables relate similarly across workers would indicate that it is highly probable that the workers adopt a common conceptual framework about the aspects of street club work associated with these variables. It is fortunate that the particular cluster of variables represented in Table 2 includes some which are central to our interest—contact, influence, success, and so on. We are now in the process of applying a series of both inferential and descriptive analytical

---

[3] D. G. Kendall, *Rank Correlation Methods* (New York: Hafner Publishing Co., Inc., 1962), pp. 45–48.

[4] R. H. Somers, "Testing Hypotheses of Order Correlation in the Population," Technical Report, No. 11, NSF–G–17438 (Ann Arbor, Mich.: University of Michigan), mimeographed.

[5] Various sources of evidence support the contention that these low interrelations are not the consequence of the particular methodology or system of analysis employed. The data presented here were obtained from scales which indicated a high degree of reliability.

Table 2

UNIFORM INTERCORRELATIONS ACROSS WORKERS*

Variables	1	2	3	4	5	6	7
		.56	.52	.43	.36	.38	.47
1. Contact	—	(.43–.71)	(.28–.64)	(.20–.60)	(.27–.47)	(.33–.44)	(.22–.85)
			.58	.52	.48	.42	.48
2. Influence		—	(.50–.73)	(.24–.70)	(.28–.59)	(.26–.64)	(.26–.66)
				.57	.51	.48	.61
3. Tightness			–	(.48–.72)	(.17–.65)	(.42–.57)	(.33–.79)
					.57	.39	.46
4. Success				—	(.52–.63)	(.27–.48)	(.31–.64)
						.44	.53
5. Liking for boy					—	(.21–.56)	(.43–.56)
							.41
6. Liking by boy						—	(.27–.63)
7. Time Spent with boy							—

* Top figure represents the mean tau_b. Lower figure represents the range. $P(ZA > X)$ < .05 for all tau's, using a one tail test of significance.

schemes to these data in order to generate a model which will explain antecedant-consequent relations involved among all six variables in the table, as well as the other variables in the matrix not included in the table.

One interesting feature of these attempts to generate a model has been the performance of certain variables. When "liking for boy" is included in the various permutations and combinations of the remaining variables, most arguments which would otherwise produce a satisfactory model break down.... It now appears that how well a boy is liked sometimes is a precondition for the worker's judgment of the boy on some other variable, and at other times may be the consequence of such a judgment. On the basis of present information, it appears that we can account for some of the variance by delineating two types of workers in this regard: 1. those workers who view themselves as having a particular service to perform and who will exercise preference for boys whom they perceive to be in need of their service, irrespective of whether they like the boy or not; and 2. workers who concentrate their attention largely upon those boys whom they like with relatively little regard for their need or amenability to change. Among the first type of workers, liking for the boy tends to develop as a consequence of the boy's conforming to the worker's aspirations for him; among workers of the second type, the same variable serves primarily as a criterion for determining the contact population and may also bias the workers' judgments on variables such as influence, success, and so on.

The tentative implication that can be drawn from these preliminary findings is that a high rating on "liking for boy" in the initial phase of contact may have a "halo effect" upon some workers' judgment and result in a prolonged expenditure of program resources along lines which are not always in the best interest of the program. The foregoing is only one of a number of analytic inferences that are presently being drawn from these data, but it serves to illustrate how generalizations from the findings of such research may be brought to bear directly upon the improvement of street work practices.

In addition to the analytic operations already described, the data across workers were transformed along a common scale for each variable on which uniformities could be observed among the criteria offered by each worker as a basis for ranking. This procedure revealed that, in the case of some variables, no special incongruity would result from the simple transformations necessary to convert individual worker judgments to equivalence positions along a single scale so as to accurately represent variation from worker to worker. . . .

In the study outlined here we have relied entirely upon street workers' representations of certain interactive effects in their work with contact boys as the data source. The weight of the evidence from this study clearly reveals some basic coherence in the way most workers customarily regard some rather crucial aspects of their work. Certain judgments occur at predictable times and have predictable effects upon future judgments.

We are presently involved in procedures to refine the relationships which we have already established. We are gathering data on additional variables which we now feel may play a role in determining some important consequences of street club work. Further, we hope to establish behavioral correlates for those variables. Even though we presently have less than a perfect understanding of the way workers conceive of and go about their task, nevertheless, it appears evident that despite training and experience, the common conceptual framework reported by the workers studied, with the exception of worker No. 1, is built largely upon a series of common sense expectations that would apply to almost any interpersonal relationships. This is to say that, by and large, the workers bring to their task a conception of interpersonal relations that is formed by their experience, and hence is somewhat more sophisticated than that of the public at large. Nevertheless, their conception of interpersonal relations is not yet systematic and rationalized. While, on the one hand, street club workers may share many of the role characteristics of teachers, foremen, or policemen, their roles do not yet have a technical vocabulary and a corresponding set of practices that would distinguish them from such informal roles as parent, friend, and neighbor.

The street club worker, like many persons intimately involved in complex social relations, is hardly responsible for the fact that his role lacks clear definition, a technical vocabulary, and a well established set of corresponding practices. One need only think of the politician, the public administrator, the union organizer, and the religious leader—all of whom find themselves in somewhat similar situation. The fact is that the behavioral disciplines, and the possible contributions that they can make in these spheres of human activity, have found limited acceptance there. Furthermore, the translation of the findings of the social sciences into an application in the fields of human action have been limited by the very complexity of social situations. Therefore, street club workers, like others who must operate in the realm of interpersonal relations, are inevitably thrown back upon the precedents of their own profession or, simply, upon common sense. The value of having a research project accompany this process is that it can actively intervene to evaluate specific instances where the workers either follow common sense practices or engage in new innovations. Hopefully, it is out of this constant interchange between action and research that the street club worker can eventually adopt a more standardized and technically certain approach to his job.

The Response of Chronic Juvenile Delinquents to a Program of Close Supervision

LAURENCE L. FROST
MORTON COOPER
WALTER J. KEPHART

The program described in this selection is more rehabilitative than preventive, as these terms are normally employed. Heavily psychological in orientation, it demonstrates in at least one setting the feasibility of community-based rehabilitation programs for juvenile offenders. The evaluative design and data are not totally convincing, and yet they are provocatively explored by the authors. One very interesting point implicit in the treatment is the possibility of developing an offender typology based on the youngsters reactions to the program—a pragmatic development through the back door, as it were.

LAURENCE L. FROST, MORTON COOPER, and WALTER J. KEPHART, Juvenile Court of the District of Columbia.

The Youth Guidance Project of the Juvenile Court of the District of Columbia has directed its attention and efforts toward the chronic delinquent. By chronic delinquent, we mean those boys who had been in trouble several times and who continued to get into trouble despite the "tender loving care" of the probation services of the Juvenile Court. It was hoped that a group of these boys could be worked with, not so much to find causes of delinquency or reasons for recidivism, as to start with a boy who was severely damaged in terms of his being able to live at peace in his community, and to see what could be done in a relatively short time to help him to a way of life somewhat more in tune with the community at large.

The Youth Guidance Project was begun in the fall of 1960, supported by a grant from the Eugene and Agnes E. Meyer Foundation of Washington. Two essential elements are behind the project. First is the project itself and the actual physical offerings it makes to the boys enrolled in it. Second is the supervision that it organizes for the boys, extending over a twenty-four hour period, seven days a week.

The project, its classrooms, gymnasium, and office, is in a vocational high school located near the center of the District of Columbia in an area quite well known for its high rate of delinquency. The boys report to this building immediately after their day in school, between 3:30 and 4:00 P.M. In the succeeding two hours they participate in various activities: remedial school work, mainly remedial reading; arts and crafts; gymnasium sports and exercises; individual counseling; and group therapy. During the course of a week each boy participates in each of these activities several times— except group therapy, which is scheduled for once each week. The remedial work, arts and crafts, and gymnasium are taught or supervised by teachers on contract from the District of Columbia Public Schools. The counseling is done by one of the two social workers who constitute the full time professional staff of the project. The group therapy is carried on by the staff of the Juvenile Court Clinic. The boys report to the project as soon as possible after their day ends in their several schools; since they don't have time to stop for an after-school snack, and because most of them couldn't afford to buy a snack anyway, they are given a candy bar at the project. They are supplied with gym clothes and shoes where needed and, of course, with all necessary equipment.

With boys of this sort, close supervision for the full twenty-four hours is a necessity. While they are in the project, this is accomplished in two ways: first by close coordination and cooperation with the schools the boys attend, and second by frequent visits by the project social worker to the boy's home anytime of the day or night or on weekends.

The school system of the District of Columbia has been interested in this project from its inception and has been very cooperative. In coordinating with the schools, one of the staff members of the project visited the boy's school soon after the boy was sent to the project. The principal, assistant principal, and the boy's section teacher were told of the boy's court-required attendance at the project, and the program was carefully outlined to them. They were asked to send weekly reports of the boy's attendance, effort, and citizenship on forms supplied by the project to facilitate this reporting. This initial meeting was followed by frequent phone calls and personal visits to the school. As a result of all this, a pretty clear, first-hand picture was formed of the relationship that existed between the boy, his school, and his teachers. Since the schools were aware of the boy's special status with regard to the court and the community, they supervised him closely. The boys were fully aware of this close liaison and seemed to recognize that the school's supervision went beyond that usually exercised over its pupils.

Home visits were made on a very flexible schedule; they were generally more frequent in the early weeks of a boy's stay in the project and tapered off somewhat toward the end. The visits occurred at irregular intervals and only rarely by appointment. The social worker who made the visits talked with whomever he could in the home—parents, siblings, other relatives—to gather a fairly clear picture of the family unit and its inner workings. The home and neighborhood, of course, came under scrutiny as well. If the boy was not at home, the worker was as apt as not to go where he said he would be to see if he was, in fact, there. Frequently when the worker would go there the boy would not be home, but he was asked always to tell someone where he was going to be. If he were not at home the person to whom the worker talked to at the time would tell the social worker, and the social worker would go to the place where the boy said he was going to be. Usually he found him. The frequent home visits seemed to engender close cooperation between some of the families and the project and helped the family in their supervision of the boy.

The population of the Youth Guidance Project consisted of boys whose delinquent activities had actually earned them commitment to the training school. In the case of the District of Columbia, this was the Department of Public Welfare or the National Training School for Boys. In fact, the judges of the court had actually committed these boys, but had suspended the execution of the commitment if the boy participated in the project for a period of three months. During this three month period, the boys lived in their own homes and attended their regular schools. If a boy attended the project regularly for three months and got into no further trouble in school, community, or home, he was returned to court, his suspended commitment was vacated, and he was placed once again in the less precarious status of probation. If, however, at any time during his three month period he got into further trouble, he was returned at once to court and the previously imposed commitment was instituted. The boys were told this many, many times. They were told this by the judge in the courtroom on the occasion of the initial sentencing. It was repeated time and again by the social workers, by everyone who had contact with the boys: "Stay out of trouble. Once in trouble, away you go to training school."

In a little over two and one-half years, 170 boys were referred to the project. Sixty-eight per cent of that number, 115 boys, completed the program, were returned to court, and placed on probation. Fifty-five boys, nearly one-third, were sent on to training schools from the project. Of the 115 boys returned to probation, twenty-nine eventually were in more trouble and were committed. A boy referred to the project, then, has slightly better than two chances out of three of completing it, and after having completed it, has three chances out of four of staying out of trouble. Those who have remained out of trouble have done so for an average of fifteen months with a range of three to thirty-three months.

Prior to being sent to the project, the majority of these boys were problems in their schools. Over 80 per cent of them were occasional or persistent truants; over 80 per cent of them put forth only poor, if indeed any, academic effort. Data in their school records indicated that fully two-thirds of them were not good citizens in school. Generally, these were boys who avoided school in spirit if not in body. When physically present, they expended little effort in learning and much in actively disrupting the classroom. Most of them were overage in grade; they had been held back from one to three or four years.

After entering the project, 6 per cent persisted as truants and they were soon sent on to the training school. The remainder attended school faithfully. By their teachers' evaluations, 70 per cent gave average or better than average effort to their school work and 75 per cent were graded average or better in school citizenship. By and large, these boys returned to school and behaved in school after they got back. In the project, then, their school behavior—both academic and citizenship—improved markedly.

The responses of these boys to the project are best discussed in light of the boys themselves. All were delinquents with from one to thirteen complaints filed with the court, and nearly three-quarters had been involved in at least one felony-type activity. Their average age was nearly fifteen years and most had lived continuously with one or the other of his parents during this time, though frequently it was the grandparents or other relatives who assumed most responsibility for his supervision, at least in his younger years. Most of the boys were retarded at least one year academically, and one in five was in a special class as a result of behavior problems. As a group their personalities, as pictured by the Rorschach, were shallow and immature with no good evidence of the ability to form either close or warm interpersonal relationships. They seemed prone to react quickly and thoughtlessly and to lack the ability to recover from this precipitousness. There were, of course, individual differences among the boys. However, those who worked most closely with them were more impressed with their basic similarities than any differences between them.

The boys' responses to this project fall into three categories: those who failed to complete the project because of further law violations; those who completed the project but subsequently got into further trouble; and those who completed the project and who have been in no further trouble.

It is hardest, of course, to get to know the fifty-five boys in the first group —those who failed while still in the project. Part of this was due to their short stay and part due to the fact that these particular boys were generally quiet, reserved youngsters. The word "reserved" is used advisedly. They did not avail themselves of what they full well knew was truly a last chance to avoid placement in a residential training school. They seem to have been basically hostile boys who chose to avoid contact with their peer group, whether in or out of the project, and who placed barriers between themselves and adults, including their families and the staff of the project. Some of them left the impression that at the time, at least, they were incapable of forming any object relationship. Neurotic or perhaps psychotic problems were involved, but their short stay and their general lack of communication made more accurate diagnoses difficult to determine.

From their histories or from the little they would talk, it was possible to see that some devastating family problems were represented in this group. One boy's mother was shot and killed by his father and it was the boy who was first to his mother's side. His behavior began to deteriorate from that point and, after several law violations, he was sent to the project where he had a "hostile, resentful attitude" which was "barely kept under control." The psychiatric report said, in part, ". . . he is not psychotic. He seems still to be trying to absorb the enormous psychological shock of the murder of his mother and the . . . loss of his father to the mental hospital. . . . Much of his energy is spent in trying to keep this overwhelming subject out of his mind. When it is under control he is capable of behaving in a lethargic but rather cooperative fashion, and when it is nearer the surface he becomes somewhat detached and unable to be aware of, much less interested in complying with, the ordinary demands of life. . . ." Another law violation, while the boy was in the project, resulted in his being sent to the training school.

This is an example in which extreme violence is involved, but other children in this group of early failures were as efficiently, if not as abruptly, shut off from their families. In some, the psychological distance between son and parents was so wide that it was not possible for either child or parents to use the project as a bridge between them.

In the second group, the boys' response to the close supervision is more clearly seen. The second group consisted of those twenty-nine boys who survived their stay in the project only to fall back into trouble within days or in some cases weeks or months after dismissal from the project.

In some respects, the surveillance organized by the project served the function of a closed institution. Being given the rules and seeing themselves checked on at frequent intervals, they responded very much as though they were in fact in an institution. Being in a quasi-institution, they behaved; upon release, they resumed their old patterns of behavior. This group of boys settled rather comfortably into the situation. Decisions were made for them, they had a legitimate excuse when tempted by their erstwhile fellows, and yet they suffered no real deprivations. When they returned to the relative freedom of probation, they were thrown back again into a decision-making role and, in their decisions, they were too easily influenced by their fellows in the delinquent subculture.

Generally, upon admission to the project, these boys adjusted quite promptly. They were cheerful, responsive, and very superficial. They started attending school regularly and stopped being behavior problems while they were there. Their parents knew where they were at all times and things seemed to be going well. Shortly after leaving the project, however, it was as though it had never existed. They re-entered, just as enthusiastically, their old life.

Another facet of this second group concerned the seeming emergence of dependency feelings which in some way or other were better satisfied by the project than they had been at home. Many of these boys had no home in the psychological sense of the word. They lived some place with a group of other children and one or two adults—usually only one. Daily, overtly and covertly, it would be exhibited to them that they were not particularly wanted. One boy said, "My mother told me, she say, 'You get into trouble again and I ain't gonna come get you out. You can just stay locked up. I all through with you and your meddling ways.' And she meant it too, 'cause when I got locked up this last time, she didn't come see me." There was no closeness, no love, no feeling of being wanted in that home, yet this was a youngster who still needed to be dependent in some ways. The project fulfilled this need for him. There he found honest, consistent, non-threatening adults who had time for him, who listened to his talk, who tried to help him with his school work. When he left the project, even though he came back frequently to visit, he began to lose the dependency satisfaction, and he certainly didn't gain any of it at home. Eventually he got into more trouble and was committed.

Many of the boys told the same story of outright verbal rejection by their mothers, and it was obvious that this had deep meaning for them, but that they had no way of meeting or adjusting to this crisis. They could, however, relate at least superficially to the project, to some of their peers, or to one or more of the staff—which the first group who broke out of the project could not do.

The third group consisted of the eighty-six boys who completed their stay in the project, who were returned to probation, and who have been in no further trouble for the period of, in some cases, nearly three years. This is a very heterogeneous group. One boy in it was quite psychotic, others quite neurotic, others typical though perhaps overly mature adolescents. While in the project, their behavior ranged from being so benign as to be unnoticed and now forgotten to being continuously troublesome in school or home, but not troublesome enough to warrant removal from the home or the community. Some of these boys continued to visit the project with some regularity for periods of nearly a year, while others never returned after the moment of their release.

Certainly these boys came from homes and families fully as deprived as those in the other two groups. Closer looks show the presence of some qualities that seemed to have been lacking in other families. It can probably be best summed up by saying that these boys were better accepted in their homes; they had feelings or realizations of being, if not actually wanted, at least not actively rejected. One boy said: "Yeah, my mother say she not going to help me out anymore if I got into any more trouble, but I know she don't mean it. And when I got into more trouble she come to help me out." One boy, in this same discussion, came from what seemed to be an extremely rejecting and psychologically divided home. He was, however, shocked at the revelation of another boy (the one quoted earlier,) whose mother said she would not come to help him out and didn't. Further investigation revealed that this boy felt much more warmth in the home than was immediately apparent to the project observers.

First, this feeling of not being actively rejected at home seemed to be a crucial factor in the boys' response to the supervision provided by the project. These boys could point to positive aspects of the project: "It gave me some place to go after school," they would say. What they did not go on to say was that it "gave me some place where I could do something that was constructive and not just pass the time." Second, they learned to improve their sports skills, made objects in arts and crafts with which they adorned their homes, and acquired greater confidence in their ability to learn. Some of them could say that they had found someone—and by this they meant adults—who would take time with them and for them and who seemed to attempt to understand them. Couples facing a multitude of problems, only one of which is a delinquent son, cannot always be adequate, complete, and understanding parents. Teachers are not always able to be sympathetic or understanding with a non-motivated and trouble-making student. The staff of the project seemed to have been able to fill in on at least some occasions and to meet the needs that were not fulfilled by the boys' parents or teachers. Third, this group of boys could point to direct avenues of assistance that the project provided—such as showing them how to apply for a job—or perhaps something as nebulous as the fact that there are in life some things that are better than hanging around on the street. One boy said: "It showed me somebody cared enough for me to help me keep out of trouble, and it showed me I had heart enough to keep out of trouble myself since I left it." This boy in fact is going to be our first high school graduate. He is doing very well. Instead of flunking, he is passing. He has been "hooked" by school and he thinks it is "the greatest since cokes."

Reactions such as these are most apt to be made by persons who have not been actively rejected by their families.

It is not to be believed that the Youth Guidance Project, or any other such program, can change a chronic delinquent into a law-abiding citizen in three months; nor, of course, was that the aim of the project. Such a program does provide boys with constructive after-school activities, with understanding adults who try to be helpful and who help the boy to help himself. It also provides a boy with the clear-cut responsibility for his own decision making. On a very simple and uncomplicated level, he chooses between staying in the community or going on to a residential training school.

In attempting to restore severe, chronic delinquent boys to a more normal life (normal in the sense of being non-delinquent), it seemed that those boys who had the poorest chance of being helped were those in whose family some catastrophe had occurred to enhance rejection. Those with a somewhat better chance of being helped were those who were rejected—unloved and unwanted children but without this catastrophic situation. Those for whom the picture was the brightest were those who were not actually rejected. One can not say they were accepted by their parents, but they were not actively rejected. There is a difference.

Through this project have passed 170 boys who were destined for training school, but who were spared such a commitment for a time at least. Eighty-six of these boys have stayed out of trouble and avoided commitment altogether, some for upward of two years. Our next steps are to find what this program can do for the two categories of boys who have had to be committed, for the key to working with the severe, chronic delinquent lies in the ability of the boy to relate.